Praise for *Integrating IFS (Internal Family Systems) into EMDR Therapy*

"With warmth and clinical precision, Dr. Fatter invites the reader into a model of trauma recovery that is at once structured and profoundly respectful of human complexity. This book will transform the way you think about integrating modalities—and about the people you serve."

—**Frank Anderson, MD,** author of *Transcending Trauma* and coauthor of *Internal Family Systems Skills Training Manual*

"Dr. Daphne Fatter illuminates the natural harmony between IFS and EMDR therapies. Her integrative model invites clinicians into a deeper relational presence where parts are honored, the nervous system is regulated, and healing unfolds organically. This book is both a guide and a gift—offering the field a framework rooted in compassion, wisdom, and respect for the sacredness of trauma recovery."

—**Stacy Ruse, LPC, E-RYT-500,** EMDR and IFS trainer and consultant

"Daphne Fatter's *Integrating IFS (Internal Family Systems) into EMDR Therapy* is an essential resource for trauma therapists seeking to enhance their practice and deepen their healing skills. This comprehensive guide skillfully bridges the gap between EMDR and IFS therapies, providing clear, practical strategies for integrating these powerful and complementary modalities. Fatter's insights into complex trauma recovery are invaluable, offering a nuanced understanding of the interplay between parts and the Self, which is crucial for effective treatment. The step-by-step approach, complete with therapist worksheets and scripts, makes it accessible for clinicians at all levels. Fatter's emphasis on consent-based interventions and the importance of attunement to clients' internal systems ensures that therapists can create a safe, supportive environment for healing. This book is a must-read for anyone committed to advancing their therapeutic skills in trauma recovery."

—**Dr. Gillian O'Shea Brown,** author of *Psyche's Awakening: A Path to Healing Through the Wisdom of Greek Myth*

"In this well-written book, Daphne Fatter solves the problem of how to integrate EMDR and IFS therapies thoroughly and elegantly. The former is typically viewed as one of the world's few gold-standard, highly researched treatments for PTSD, while the latter is an increasingly popular paradigm-shift model of therapy that is used for PTSD, among other diagnoses, and is growing a significant body of research with positive outcomes. Whether you're trained in one and want to add the other or you're trained in both and want to use them together, this book will be a great guide."

—**Martha Sweezy, PhD,** coauthor of *Internal Family Systems Skills Training Manual*

"This book is an important step in the unfolding history of parts work beginning with John G. Watkins through myriad contributors. It will be an important volume for those EMDR therapists with an IFS orientation in guiding the integration of those methods."

—**Sandra Paulsen, PhD,** author of *Looking Through the Eyes of Trauma and Dissociation* and *When There Are No Words*

"Dr. Daphne Fatter has written *the* book that trauma therapists have been waiting for. *Integrating IFS (Internal Family Systems) into EMDR Therapy* masterfully synthesizes two highly effective therapeutic modalities, offering clinicians a clear, practical roadmap for working with complex trauma. What makes this work exceptional is Dr. Fatter's ability to honor the integrity of both EMDR and IFS therapies while demonstrating how their integration creates something greater than the sum of its parts. She provides concrete protocols, session transcripts, and troubleshooting guidance that clinicians can implement immediately, addressing the critical challenges of working with dissociation, protective parts, and attachment wounds. This book is essential reading for any clinician committed to providing the most effective trauma care possible. Dr. Fatter has given us a practical, theoretically sound, and deeply humane approach to healing."

—**Jenna Riemersma, LPC,** certified IFS therapist, IFS clinical consultant, EMDR trained therapist, and bestselling author of *Altogether You* and *IFS Integration*

"*Finally*, we have the book that weaves EMDR and Internal Family Systems therapies into a nuanced, effective whole treatment model. Drawing on the strengths of both, Daphne provides us with handouts, worksheets, and scripts to help us turn theory into healing for our most complex clients. She includes lots of love for the therapists doing this challenging work too. Brilliant!"

—**Colleen West, LMFT,** IFS clinical consultant and author of *We All Have Parts* and *The IFS Flip Chart*

"This well-organized and insightful guide provides clinicians with a clear, step-by-step framework for integrating IFS therapy into EMDR practice—an essential resource for therapists seeking to deepen and broaden their clinical effectiveness."

—**Roy Kiessling, LISW,** founder of EMDR Consulting

"This book represents a timely and essential new contribution to the field of trauma therapy. Daphne has created something we have desperately needed: a clear, practical roadmap for combining two of the most sought-after and effective trauma treatments available today. As a therapist who uses both modalities extensively, I've seen firsthand how effective—and at times tricky—this integration can be. Daphne distills down the most important principles of each model, addressing the nuances and potential pitfalls of combining them. If you want to learn how to integrate IFS and EMDR therapies seamlessly and safely, this is the book for you. It's destined to become the go-to manual for trauma therapists committed to offering their clients the best that both approaches have to offer."

—**John Clarke, MA, EdS, LPCC,** trauma therapist and host of the *Going Inside* podcast

"*Integrating IFS (Internal Family Systems) into EMDR Therapy* is exactly what it promises to be. It's not a book to be summarized in one sentence, but, if I felt like trying, I'd say it's a book that answers the question 'I've learned these two powerful treatment models; how do I combine them?' Or perhaps the question 'I know EMDR, but sometimes it doesn't work—would IFS therapy help, and do I need that training too?' Yes, I'd say, but if you know something about it, or know something about working with parts, here's a book that can enhance your knowledge and help you use what you know to add dimensions to your use of EMDR! It is a book to be savored and to keep by your side in case you have a question about what to do when stubborn looping doesn't resolve with EMDR interweaves, when there are issues of neurodiversity and working with marginalized populations, when you as a therapist are stuck and experiencing countertransference, and more. I like books that provide clarity about options, and this one does this with illustrations, examples, and essential worksheets. It's an enriching time to be a therapist, when models that are wonderful in their own right can be used individually when that works and can be combined in ways that enhance the opportunity for our clients to heal more comprehensively and effectively."

—**Joanne Twombly, MSW, LICSW,** author of *Trauma and Dissociation Informed Internal Family Systems: How to Successfully Treat Complex PTSD and Dissociative Disorders*

The Step-by-Step Guide to Complex Trauma Recovery

Integrating IFS (INTERNAL FAMILY SYSTEMS) into EMDR Therapy

DAPHNE FATTER, PhD
EMDRIA Approved Consultant

Integrating IFS (Internal Family Systems) into EMDR Therapy
Copyright © 2026 by Daphne Fatter

Published by
PESI Publishing, Inc.
3839 White Ave
Eau Claire, WI 54703

Cover by Lisa Kerans
Interior by Abby Isackson
Editing by Rona Bernstein

ISBN 9781683738855 (print)
ISBN 9781683738862 (ePUB)
ISBN 9781683738879 (ePDF)

All rights reserved.
Printed in the United States of America.

Dedication

This book is dedicated to healing in all its forms.
To all those who pursue their own journey toward healing.
To all the therapists, healers, and helpers who are committed to making the world a better place.

Table of Contents

Introduction 1

1. **An Overview of EMDR and IFS Therapies: Shared Values and Distinct Differences** 11
   What Is Eye Movement Desensitization and Reprocessing Therapy? 11
   What Is Internal Family Systems Therapy? 13
   Limitations of EMDR and IFS Therapies as Single-Model Approaches 17
   Limitations to Integration 17
   Shared Values and Processes 18
   Memory Reconsolidation 21
   Differences of Each Model 22
   Five IFS Principles to Support Effective EMDR Trauma Reprocessing 24

2. **IFS-Informed Case Conceptualization and Integrative Treatment Planning During Phase 1** 27
   Phase 1 and History Taking in EMDR Therapy 27
   IFS-Informed Case Conceptualization 29
   Integrative Treatment Planning in Phase 1 33
   Considerations When Working with Specific Populations 40
   Therapist Worksheet: IFS-Informed Case Conceptualization and Integrative Treatment Planning 44

3. **Parts Mapping During Phase 1** 55
   Parts Mapping: Benefits and Functions 55
   How to Make a Parts Map 58
   Parts Mapping for Different Functions 59
   Therapist Script: Using Parts Mapping to Build Working Alliance and Support Stabilization 72
   Therapist Script: Using Parts Mapping to Identify Parts Connected to the Client's Presenting Issue 74
   Therapist Script: Using Parts Mapping to Track Sequences of the Client's System 76
   Therapist Script: Introducing Parts Mapping at the Beginning of the Session 78
   Therapist Script: Introducing Parts Mapping at the End of the Session 79
   Therapist Script: Using Parts Mapping to Create a Visualization for Reaching Therapy Goals and to Identify EMDR Targets 80

ix

4. **IFS Befriending Interventions for Protector Consent During Phase 2** 83
   - Why Befriend Parts Before Trauma Reprocessing in EMDR? 83
   - Befriending Benefits and Guidelines 85
   - Five Befriending Strategies to Use During Phase 2 88
   - Therapist Handout: The 6 F's 95
   - Therapist Handout: Using the 6 F's to Address Polarizations 99
   - Therapist Handout: Using the Conference Table Technique to Navigate Polarizations 101
   - Therapist Handout: Direct Access in Three Steps 106
   - Therapist Worksheet: The Therapist's Parts in Direct Access 109
   - Therapist Handout: Self Tapping for Attachment Readiness & Repair (STARR) 112
   - Contracting to Receive Consent from Protectors to Proceed to Phase 3 114
   - Therapist Handout: Phase 2 Road Map to Protectors' Consent 118

5. **IFS Interventions for Attuned Resource Development During Phase 2** 121
   - Integrating Culturally Based Strengths 121
   - Complex Trauma Tools for Resource Development 125
   - Therapist Handout: Sensory Befriending Phrases to Use with Young Parts 131
   - IFS-Informed EMDR Exercises for Resource Development 133
   - Therapist Worksheet: Integrative Approach to Stabilization and Resource Development .. 138
   - Therapist Worksheet: Client's Identified Resources for Stabilization and Resource Development 139
   - Therapist Handout: IFS-Informed Practices Outside of Session to Support Stabilization and Integration 140

6. **Assessment Options for Attuning to the Client's Internal System During Phase 3** 143
   - Common Scenarios for Accessing the Target 143
   - IFS-Informed Options to Ask Phase 3 Questions 148
   - Therapist Handout: IFS-Informed Options to Ask Phase 3 Questions 150
   - Identifying Legacy Burdens: Cultural and Intergenerational Trauma 153
   - Therapist Handout: Identifying Legacy Burdens 154

7. **IFS-Informed Desensitization During Phase 4** 159
   - Bringing an IFS Lens to Phase 4 Trauma Reprocessing 159
   - Phase 4 IFS Interventions 163
   - Therapist Handout: Phase 4 IFS Interventions 183
   - Other Options to Integrate IFS Interventions with EMDR's Phase 4 186

8. **IFS-Informed Installation and Body Scan During Phases 5 and 6** 187
   - Using IFS Interventions During Installing the Positive Cognition in Phase 5 187
   - Using IFS Interventions During the Body Scan in Phase 6 193

9. **IFS-Informed Closure and Reevaluation During Phases 7 and 8** 199
   - Using IFS Interventions During Phase 7: Closure 199
   - Therapist Handout: How to End an Incomplete Session 202
   - Therapist Handout: How to End a Complete Session 205
   - Using IFS Interventions During Phase 8: Reevaluation and Options for Future Targets 209
   - What Happens If There Is Backlash in the System? 210
   - Therapist Handout: How to Navigate Backlash 211

10. **Exploring Our Own Therapist Parts** 213
    - Therapist Worksheet: Our Own Parts That Show Up in Providing Therapy 214
    - Therapist Worksheet: Signs of Being Self-Led and Signs of Being Triggered 216
    - Therapist Worksheet: Get to Know Your Protector Parts 218
    - Therapist Worksheet: What Parts Emerge in Broaching Cultural Content? 221
    - Therapist Worksheet: Exploring What It Means to Have Needs 224
    - Therapist Worksheet: Exploring Legacy Burdens 227

Conclusion 229
Resources for Complex Trauma 230
References 232
Acknowledgments 238
About the Author 239

Introduction

Being a trauma therapist requires extensive knowledge about the complexities of trauma, along with specialized treatment skills. Even with a strong knowledge and skill base, though, challenges are inevitable. If you are working with clients with a history of trauma, you may feel confused, overwhelmed, or unsure of how to make clinical treatment decisions. You may sense that your clients need more support or skills but you don't know what interventions to use to support their stabilization. Or you may be well-versed in interventions but struggle with how to appropriately prepare your clients for trauma treatment.

If you are trained in Eye Movement Desensitization and Reprocessing (EMDR), you are aware that the standard EMDR protocol is not a one-size-fits-all approach. You may often wonder how to prepare your clients for trauma reprocessing, how to identify which trauma target to start with, or how to help clients if they get stuck in the process. You may be familiar with parts models, such as Internal Family Systems (IFS), but you may be confused about what to *actually do* with parts in therapy or what that looks like within the eight phases of EMDR treatment.

If you are familiar with and perhaps have received training in IFS therapy, you may conceptualize cases with a parts lens but lack clarity about the clinical goals of IFS interventions in the context of trauma treatment. If you're working with clients with more complex trauma histories, you may get overwhelmed by the clients' many parts and not know how to provide a trauma-informed structure across treatment that includes EMDR therapy for effective trauma reprocessing.

EMDR and IFS therapy are both effective modalities for treating trauma. However, when used as stand-alone approaches, or when aspects of one or the other model are interjected into treatment without clear guidelines, they may not adequately address clients' unique needs, particularly in cases of complex trauma. What's needed, therefore, is an integrated approach. This book is a step-by-step guide that will teach you how to integrate IFS and EMDR to achieve a stronger therapeutic outcome for your clients. You will learn numerous IFS tools to apply to the eight phases of EMDR therapy with a wide variety of clients, including those with complex trauma.

This book is for any therapist who works with trauma and who is interested in EMDR and IFS. However, if you have not yet completed basic training in EMDR, experiential training in IFS, or both, it is essential that you do so before attempting to use these approaches with your clients. Additional resources are located at the end of the book for continued learning in both IFS and EMDR.

What Is Complex Trauma?

Complex trauma—prolonged or repeated exposure to traumatic events—involves multiple and interconnected traumatic experiences, which can make clinical treatment more complicated (Herman, 1992a; Shapiro, 2018). While complex trauma can manifest in many different psychiatric diagnoses and comorbidities, including posttraumatic stress disorder (PTSD), major depressive disorder (MDD), and substance use disorders, many clinicians are not aware that the diagnosis of complex PTSD has distinct features over and above those of classic PTSD (Cloitre, 2020, 2021).

A complex PTSD (CPTSD) diagnosis includes, in addition to PTSD diagnostic criteria, pervasive problems in self-organization that occur across various contexts. These problems comprise three key aspects: (1) emotion dysregulation, (2) negative self-concept, and (3) relationship difficulties (Cloitre, 2020). While PTSD and CPTSD are both categorized in the *International Classification of Diseases* (11th revision; *ICD-11*; World Health Organization, 2019/2021) under the umbrella category of Disorders Specifically Related to Stress, CPTSD is currently not a diagnosis in the *Diagnostic and Statistical Manual of Mental Disorders* (5th ed., text revision; *DSM-5-TR*; APA, 2022). The *ICD-11* specifies that a person can be diagnosed with either PTSD or CPTSD, but not both. Given its distinct features, CPTSD treatment warrants adaptation to the EMDR standard protocol (Shapiro, 2018), specific trauma-informed considerations in IFS therapy (Twombly, 2022), and an individualized treatment plan (Cloitre, 2020, 2021).

Complex Trauma Treatment: Why Integrate IFS and EMDR?

Based on recent research, Cloitre (2020, 2021) recommends a multi-intervention and multimethod approach for complex trauma treatment. Yet there is little published literature on how to use EMDR and IFS together for complex trauma treatment for adults and children (see Fatter, 2023b for review). This book will walk you through how to apply IFS interventions in EMDR therapy.

Integrating IFS interventions into EMDR therapy enables you to create a flexible, adaptable individualized treatment plan that addresses potential ongoing stressors and attunes to the multiple parts within clients, particularly among clients with complex trauma histories. Clients with complex trauma may present with avoidance, dissociation, difficulties trusting the therapist, premature termination, or an increase in symptoms during EMDR therapy (Shapiro, 2018; Hensley, 2021). Including IFS interventions in the treatment plan will increase your ability to target these symptoms (Fatter, 2023b). The following table lists therapist and client factors indicating that an integrative approach would be beneficial.

Indicators That a Client Can Benefit from an IFS-Integrative Approach to EMDR Therapy

(Adapted from Fatter, 2023b)

Therapist Factors	Client Factors (Adapted from Gonzalez & Mosquera, 2012)
Uncertainty about client readiness for EMDR	Needs more stabilization before EMDR treatment
Difficulty choosing which target to start with due to current client stressors and ongoing triggers	Has complex symptomology or complex trauma history
Uncertainty about what to do next or how to proceed despite your clinical intuition saying to slow down	Has a diagnosis of complex PTSD; PTSD, dissociative subtype; PTSD and dissociative disorder; or PTSD and other comorbidity
Difficulty determining the client's integrative capacity or ability to be in their window of tolerance	Has difficulty with state change in EMDR or responds negatively to phase 2 coping skills or traditional relaxation-oriented or grounding practices
Awareness that the client experiences significant activation between sessions despite your attempts to employ traditional coping skills in therapy	Decompensates between sessions (an indicator of what IFS therapy calls "backlash")
Uncertainty about whether you have the complete clinical picture or there is unknown history of your client	Reports not remembering what they did last session (indicator of potential dissociation)

Not only can IFS interventions enhance EMDR therapy, but EMDR can also provide an effective trauma-reprocessing model to integrate into traditional IFS therapy (Fatter, 2023b). One of EMDR's strengths is its ability to provide rapid trauma reprocessing (Shapiro, 2018). In a review of randomized controlled trials of EMDR, 7 of 10 studies found EMDR therapy to be more effective and/or more rapid than trauma-focused cognitive behavioral therapy (Shapiro, 2014).

"Slower is faster" is a motto commonly used in trauma treatment (Kluft, 1993)—in IFS therapy, it means the therapist trusts the natural pacing of a client's system (Schwartz & Sweezy, 2020). However, clients with complex trauma may have difficulty maintaining access to Self (a key aim of IFS) during the IFS steps of trauma healing. In addition, it may not be realistic for a client with a history of multiple traumatic experiences to remain in therapy and befriend (get to know) vulnerable exiled parts one at a time using the traditional IFS protocol (Fatter, 2023b). Therefore, when working with clients with complex trauma, IFS therapy can be adapted to support these clients' stability, sense of control, safety, and choices across therapy (Fisher, 2017; Twombly, 2022). This book will help you identify what autonomic state parts are in—based on Porges's (1995) polyvagal theory—so that clients with more complex systems can learn a variety of coping and co-regulation skills to support an adaptive, regulated nervous system.

Before further discussing integration, let's review some IFS terms used in this book (Schwartz & Sweezy, 2020):

- **Self:** One's core nonjudgmental, loving essence that is undamaged by trauma and should be the leader of the internal system.

- **Parts:** These are subpersonalities in one's internal system that have natural gifts and positive intentions to help the system. Parts may be unburdened or burdened. When parts become burdened, they get stuck in specific roles in the system due to trauma, making it hard for them to share their natural gifts with the system. Through restorative connection with and understanding from Self, parts can unburden, change roles in the system, and share their innate gifts. Follow the client's lead in the language you use to describe any given part in their system (he/she/they/it/etc.).

- **Burdens:** These are trauma-related internalized beliefs about oneself, others, or the world (e.g., *I am unlovable*), trauma-related feelings (e.g., shame, terror), and trauma-related body sensations (e.g., tension in stomach).

- **Exiles:** These are burdened vulnerable parts that carry trauma-related beliefs, feelings, and body sensations from adversity and trauma. These parts are typically stuck in the past and are often what is focused on in EMDR reprocessing.

- **Protectors:** These are burdened parts whose job it is to protect an exile from overwhelming the system. There are two types of protector parts:

  - **Managers** try to prevent the exile from getting activated. They tend to be future-focused, help manage relationships, and keep a person functioning.

  - **Firefighters** reactively show up after the exile is triggered to help numb or distract the system until the pain of the exile is not felt.

- **(Un)blended:** A part is considered **blended** when it is not well differentiated from Self, making it hard to access Self. This shows up as the client fully experiencing a given part's perspective and feelings, speaking *as* that part (e.g., "I am angry"). When parts are **unblended**, there is enough internal space between the parts and Self for the client to access their Self. The client can speak *for* their parts with less reactivity (e.g., "A part of me is angry").

- **Backlash:** When an exile is accessed in the system without the consent of the protector parts, burdened firefighter parts reactively take over the system to try to self-soothe the system. This results in clinical decompensation (e.g., increased self-harm, suicidality, substance abuse, impulsive behavior).

- **Contracting:** This refers to a discussion with a part to receive consent regarding how to use the session (e.g., to get to know a specific part through befriending) and/or to come to a mutual agreement (e.g., that a protector part will watch an EMDR reprocessing session from the sidelines).

- **Befriending:** This IFS intervention involves the client getting to know a part and be with it from a place of curiosity and allyship.
- **Target part:** This is the part in the client's system that you and the client will focus on (e.g., during befriending or during EMDR reprocessing).

The following clinical scenarios are indicators that integrating EMDR into treatment would benefit a client receiving IFS therapy:

- The client has difficulty maintaining "enough" access to their Self to witness their parts in IFS therapy alone due to getting blended and overwhelmed by an exile.
- The client is befriending an exile that carries multiple burdens or a double bind (e.g., *I'm too much* and *I'm not enough* at the same time).
- There are multiple exiles of many ages that carry a shared burden (due to the client having prolonged and repeated trauma exposure over the course of their childhood or lifetime).
- A group of exiles gets activated in IFS therapy and the client has difficulty maintaining enough access to their Self for befriending them.
- A client struggles with recurrent depression and has difficulty unblending from parts that are emotionally numb or that shut down the system.
- Somatic parts—parts that express themselves through body sensations—have difficulty unblending from the system.
- The client has been in IFS therapy for some time and is moving through the healing steps of IFS, but the client's system or clinical symptoms are not changing. This may indicate Self-like parts or performative parts "doing therapy" or may indicate a lack of Self-to-part connection.
- Exiles unburden, but the burden keeps coming back or there seem to be "endless" layers to the burden that don't completely resolve through IFS.
- The body sensations or somatic reactivity in the client does not change despite IFS therapy.
- There is a lack of continuity between IFS sessions and no change in clinical symptomology despite IFS therapy.

Integrating IFS interventions into each of EMDR's eight phases of treatment benefits clients in the following ways:

- **Increases stabilization and emotion regulation during EMDR's phases 1 and 2:** During the process of history taking (phase 1) and preparation for EMDR (phase 2), IFS interventions can help (1) address emotion dysregulation and the difficulties in self-organization characteristic of complex trauma; (2) increase a client's capacity to tolerate and therapeutically benefit from

EMDR trauma reprocessing; and (3) provide a whole-system consent-based approach to trauma reprocessing (Fatter 2023b; Kolodny & Mazero, 2022; Krause & Gomez, 2013; O'Shea Brown, 2020; Twombly & Schwartz, 2008).

- **Helps clients access and release negative internalized beliefs, cognitions, and burdens during EMDR's phases 3 and 4:** The foundational principles of IFS align with EMDR's belief in the client's natural ability to heal trauma-related beliefs, feelings, and body sensations (Fatter, 2023b). Using IFS interventions to assist in accessing trauma targets (phase 3) and when a client is stuck or has blocked reprocessing in EMDR (phase 4) enables you to focus treatment on what the parts of the client's system need for healing. IFS interventions can also help clients feel more stable and equipped with resources at the end of an incomplete EMDR reprocessing session.

- **Enhances positive qualities and the positive cognition during EMDR's phase 5:** IFS interventions can support the client in working with parts that may block the positive cognition or that may have fears or concerns about feeling good, which may be very unfamiliar to clients with complex trauma histories.

- **Increases attunement to parts in the body during EMDR's phase 6:** Integrating IFS interventions into the body scan of phase 6 of EMDR can enable the client to more fully attune to and include any somatic parts or parts that hold pain or body sensations related to trauma.

- **Facilitates inclusive, integrative, and resourcing closure for parts during EMDR's phase 7:** Integrating IFS interventions into phase 7 of EMDR therapy can provide updating of the system's protector parts to make sure they are included during therapy. This helps support stabilization and integrating therapeutic gains within the internal system of the client.

- **Follows the client's system during EMDR's phase 8:** IFS interventions can help support the client in integrating shifts in their internal system throughout therapy and attending to ways the system has reorganized when reevaluating the target during phase 8 of EMDR therapy.

- **Focuses attention on relational triggers and attachment wounds:** Since IFS is a relational model, integrating it into EMDR therapy can help you attend to the client's parts that get activated in relationships. This includes making space for parts that carry wounds from attachment issues that arise in the client's life and can emerge in the therapeutic relationship.

How to Use This Book

This book includes the following features to help you integrate IFS interventions into EMDR treatment:

- **Therapist handouts, worksheets, and scripts:** Easy-to-use therapist handouts, worksheets, and scripts provide directions for how to use the interventions.

- **Case examples and vignettes:** Case examples and vignettes show you what the interventions look like in action.

- **Images and visual aids:** Graphics are included to make the concepts accessible across learning styles.

- **An opportunity to get to know your own system:** The final chapter, in particular, enables you to apply IFS interventions to your own system and get to know your own parts that can show up in your role as a mental health provider.

- **Resources for complex trauma:** At the end of this book you'll find a list of EMDR and IFS resources for complex trauma. I hope you will seek out some of these sources to further your knowledge of these approaches.

The chapters in this book will take you step by step through the process of integrating IFS into the eight stages of EMDR.

To begin, **chapter 1** provides an overview of EMDR and IFS therapies, including current research on each model. It also includes a comparison of IFS to other parts models to show what makes IFS unique. You will gain an understanding of the shared values and the role of memory reconsolidation in both IFS and EMDR and will learn key differences in each model's approach. This chapter provides a principle-based framework to help you navigate integrating these two models. You will learn practical tools to assess your client's access to Self and learn how to develop your own "parts detector" in your clinical practice. You will better understand how to recognize which type of part within your client's internal system is showing up in session. Finally, you will learn why parts get stuck and what they need to get unstuck.

Chapter 2 will teach you how to conceptualize a client's parts and apply an IFS lens to EMDR treatment planning to support stabilization. First you will learn what important information to gather during history taking in EMDR phase 1. You will then learn to use an integrative approach to case conceptualization, based on polyvagal theory, by considering what state of autonomic arousal a part may show up in. This chapter also provides an overall structure for how to integrate IFS into EMDR therapy using the evidence-based three-phase model of trauma recovery treatment for clients with complex trauma. We will address clinical considerations when working with specific populations, including neurodiverse clients, clients with marginalized identities, clients experiencing ongoing trauma, and clients experiencing traumatic grief.

Chapter 3 gives you all you need to know about parts mapping, an IFS tool to use during phase 1 after history taking. You will learn multiple ways to use parts mapping with your clients, including how to build a working alliance and provide structure and continuity across sessions; how to identify parts connected to the client's presenting issue; how to track sequences of the client's system; and how to create a visualization for reaching therapy goals and identifying EMDR targets.

Chapter 4 explains specific IFS techniques to befriend protector parts and to receive their consent during EMDR's phase 2. You will learn how to shift from talking about parts to guiding clients to *be with* their parts. You will learn five specific IFS befriending interventions to help you and your client become aware of the client's protector parts and ultimately receive consent to proceed with EMDR trauma reprocessing. This chapter will guide you to navigate complex systems, work with polarizations, and help the client connect to parts even when the client has little access to their Self.

Chapter 5 provides IFS interventions to use for resource development and preparation for trauma reprocessing during EMDR's phase 2. You will learn how to integrate culturally based strengths to enhance resourcing, which is particularly beneficial for clients embodying marginalized identities. You will also learn multiple complex trauma tools, including how to identify dissociative and numb parts, how to use IFS techniques when working with dissociative and numb parts, how to work with young parts, and how to work with parts that don't want the client to "go inside." You will learn how to integrate IFS with traditional coping skills and EMDR phase 2 resource development approaches so you can provide integrative approaches to stabilization and IFS-informed practices clients can utilize outside of sessions.

Chapter 6 lays out an IFS approach to EMDR's phase 3: assessment. This chapter describes common clinical scenarios you may encounter, each of which has choice points for multiple ways to access the traumatic memory network for EMDR trauma reprocessing. You'll learn IFS-informed options to ask phase 3 questions. This chapter also discusses befriending techniques and clinical signs to identify legacy burdens—the IFS term referring to intergenerational trauma—and provides tools to work with systemic and oppression-based traumas.

Chapter 7 features a comprehensive discussion of IFS interventions to use during EMDR's phase 4: desensitization. This chapter addresses signs of looping and blocked trauma reprocessing in EMDR from an IFS lens. It includes step-by-step guidance for which IFS interventions to use during phase 4 and when to use each intervention.

Chapter 8 gives you options for integrating IFS interventions during EMDR's phase 5—installing the positive cognition—and phase 6, which involves the body scan. You will learn IFS techniques to use when working with parts that may have blocking beliefs about experiencing positive feelings, as well as how to attune to somatic parts if they do not naturally come up in EMDR's traditional body scan. Finally, you will learn ways to integrate somatic approaches to befriend parts in the body as needed during phase 6.

Chapter 9 offers an IFS approach to the final two phases of EMDR: closure (phase 7) and reevaluation (phase 8). You will learn IFS interventions to use when closing an incomplete EMDR reprocessing session, as well as how to include protector parts once an EMDR target is complete, as the involvement of the protectors will deepen therapeutic gains. You will learn how to navigate backlash if it occurs in a client's system in response to EMDR reprocessing. This chapter will also give you a road map for how to return to the target using an IFS-integrative approach to phase 8.

Since you also have parts and a Self, **chapter 10** will help you identify signs that you have access to your Self as a therapist. The therapist worksheets in this chapter invite you to become familiar with your own parts (including your protector parts, parts that show up in providing therapy, and parts that may arise when you broach cultural content with clients), to explore what it means to have needs, and to learn more about legacy burdens you may have. Getting to know your own parts will help you better guide your clients in befriending theirs. If you find yourself stumped as you read the earlier chapters of this book, skip to this final chapter to complete a therapist worksheet first. Sometimes we therapists need to get to know our own parts first before the IFS lens makes sense, lands for us in our systems, and becomes familiar.

I hope this book will serve you in your clinical work to:

- Feel more confident in using IFS interventions and EMDR therapy with a wide variety of clients, including those with complex trauma histories or complex internal systems
- Apply practical IFS interventions for more integrative, flexible, and accessible EMDR therapy
- Identify when to integrate EMDR into IFS therapy for an individualized treatment plan
- Better attune to the needs of clients' parts and create a stronger working alliance by applying an IFS lens, using parts mapping interventions, and broaching cultural content
- Enhance your clinical competency and ability to serve your clients on their healing journeys

Now that you understand what you will learn in this book and why, let's dive in.

CHAPTER 1

An Overview of EMDR and IFS Therapies: Shared Values and Distinct Differences

You are about to embark on an exciting journey of learning how to integrate Eye Movement Desensitization and Reprocessing (EMDR) and Internal Family Systems (IFS) therapy. Before you begin, though, it's vital that you have a solid understanding of both approaches, along with their similarities and differences. Even if you are already familiar with both models, this chapter will serve as a refresher and offer some new facts and perspectives.

What Is Eye Movement Desensitization and Reprocessing Therapy?

EMDR therapy, developed by Francine Shapiro, PhD, is based on the premise that by activating a traumatic memory, it will naturally progress through the organic path in the brain until it is appropriately and adaptively resolved. When a traumatic memory is adaptively resolved, the client has less emotional and somatic reactivity to it. The meaning making the client ascribes to the traumatic memory also changes to include more adaptive information. For example, through EMDR therapy, the client develops more positive self-worth in relation to the traumatic memory (e.g., *I do the best I can*), and any negative beliefs related to the traumatic memory (e.g., *This is my fault*) dissipate (Shapiro, 2018).

EMDR involves a technique called bilateral stimulation (BLS)—stimulating each brain hemisphere in a rhythm, alternating left and right, activating the traumatic memory to be reprocessed and move through the natural path in the brain toward adaptive resolution (Shapiro, 2018). We do BLS naturally as we move through our day. For example, when we walk, jog, swim, or play the drums, we are stimulating each brain hemisphere in a left-right rhythm and thus performing BLS. In EMDR therapy, BLS is conducted through eye movements, self-tapping, holding on to a device that provides alternate vibrations in the hands, listening to alternating audible tones, or other activities.

EMDR consists of eight phases:

1. History taking and treatment planning
2. Preparation

3. Assessment
4. Desensitization
5. Installation
6. Body scan
7. Closure
8. Reevaluation

These eight phases are the foundational framework of EMDR therapy. You guide the client through these phases over multiple sessions. Each phase has specific goals, which will be discussed in this book. The structure of the eight phases enables you to have clarity regarding where the client is within EMDR therapy.

The Adaptive Information-Processing Model

Key to understanding how EMDR works is the adaptive information-processing (AIP) model, which assumes that the psyche is designed to self-heal from a trauma, just as the body is designed to self-heal from a physical injury. EMDR therapy is based on the notion that clinical symptoms, such as PTSD and complex PTSD (CPTSD), are indicators that the AIP system is blocked. In EMDR therapy, the client is guided to focus on the block: the disturbing images and maladaptive beliefs, feelings, and body sensations associated with the traumatic memory itself. While focusing on the block, the client receives BLS, which activates the AIP system. This, in turn, naturally helps the block become unstuck and move toward healing, resulting in the traumatic memory no longer being experienced as traumatic. In other words, by activating the AIP system in the brain through BLS during EMDR therapy, adaptive information will connect to the traumatic memory through the organic pathway in the brain, and the traumatic memory will no longer be experienced as threatening or overwhelming to the client (Shapiro, 2018).

Current Research

EMDR has been demonstrated in the research to be an effective treatment for PTSD (Maxfield, 2019; Novo Navarro et al., 2018), depression (Hofmann et al., 2022), CPTSD (Korn, 2009; Bongaerts et al., 2021), and other clinical symptomology (Shapiro, 2018). Over 80 percent of the clients in a recent study no longer met the diagnostic criteria of PTSD and CPTSD after completing EMDR treatment (Bongaerts et al., 2022). As shown in PET scans, clients who received EMDR therapy demonstrated clear clinical improvement in PTSD symptoms associated with metabolic and electrophysiological changes in limbic and associative cortex regions of the brain (Pagani et al., 2018).

What Is Internal Family Systems Therapy?

IFS therapy, developed by Richard Schwartz, PhD, is based on the belief that the psyche is naturally divided into subpersonalities, called parts. In addition, IFS therapy upholds the premise that everyone has a Self, an innate, compassionate, internal essence that is undamaged by trauma. Thus, according to IFS therapy, everyone—including us, as mental health providers, and our clients—has parts, and everyone has a Self. In IFS therapy, the client connects to their Self and moves into direct relationship with their parts for transformation and healing (Schwartz & Sweezy, 2020).

According to IFS therapy, when a traumatic or overwhelming experience happens, our parts and Self internally reorganize. Self goes offline and parts move into specific roles to protect us and help us survive. However, when the threat of the trauma is over, the parts remain stuck in these specific roles. This is just like what happens in families where each family member changes roles within the family system after a trauma occurs, moving into scapegoated roles, parentified or protective roles, and exiled roles. In an individual client, the system becomes parts-led as opposed to Self-led. This results in parts trying to be the leader of the system, causing imbalance and disharmony among parts of the system. A system of parts being stuck in rigid roles can lead to clinical symptoms. Through IFS therapy, parts can shift out of the rigid and extreme roles they have taken on due to trauma and share their natural gifts with the client's system, which can then become Self-led (Schwartz & Sweezy, 2020).

What Is Self?

IFS therapy is based on the notion that a client's system is optimally functioning when it is Self-led—that is, when Self is the leader and decision maker of the system, rather than the system being led by parts. So what, actually, is Self? Self is multidimensional and comprises characteristics known as the 8 C's and 5 P's (Schwartz & Sweezy, 2020), which are shown in the following table.

The 8 C's and 5 P's of Self

The 8 C's	The 5 P's
• Compassion • Curiosity • Clarity • Connectedness • Creativity • Calm • Courage • Confidence	• Presence • Perspective • Persistence • Playfulness • Patience

What Are the Three Types of Parts in IFS Therapy?

When a client experiences trauma or an overwhelming event, parts reorganize internally, moving into one of three roles in the client's internal system: exiles, managers, or firefighters. Regardless of their role, parts all have positive intentions for the system. They think they are helping the system in the way they know how, even if it isn't working or isn't beneficial to the client. Parts can show up visually, behaviorally, emotionally, or in specific thought patterns (e.g., ruminations, fantasies, or belief systems about oneself, others, and the world), inner dialogues, dreams, scenes, or memories. Parts can also show up spatially in a location around or in the client's body and can be expressed through body sensations and physical symptomology (Schwartz & Sweezy, 2020).

Let's examine the three roles more closely.

Exiles

Exiles are vulnerable parts that become isolated from the system to protect the client from the sheer pain of a traumatic event (Schwartz & Sweezy, 2020). Given that the human brain is designed to compartmentalize under stress, exiles move into the unconscious (implicit memory) so they don't overwhelm the system. Exiles are parts that carry trauma-related feelings, body sensations, and beliefs from the past. They can be any age; they are frozen in time at the age and developmental stage of the client at the time of the trauma. Exiles hold sensory fragments that form traumatic memory. In more complex systems, they can carry an array of pure body sensations connected to a given traumatic event (e.g., one exile showing up as a lip quiver, another exile showing up as pain in the jaw) while other exiles can carry trauma-related emotions (e.g., shame, horror, terror).

Protectors

Protector parts will keep using the strategy that originally worked to keep away the pain of an exile. There are two different types of protectors in IFS therapy: *managers* and *firefighters*. These parts protect the exiles in different ways.

- The job of **managers** is to proactively prevent exiles from getting activated. They are task oriented and work hard to help the client function and succeed in the future. In IFS therapy, manager parts respond well when they are respected for what they do for the system (Schwartz & Sweezy, 2020).

- The job of **firefighters** is to respond reactively when an exile gets triggered. They work hard to help the client not feel the emotional pain of the exile by anesthetizing, numbing out, or distracting the client. If one firefighter (e.g., an alcohol-abusing part) doesn't get rid of the exile's pain, then another firefighter (e.g., a suicidal part) will take over the system, and so on until the exile's pain is not experienced by the client. Firefighters are acutely attentive to the present moment and take over the system when an exile is triggered, no matter the consequences. In other words, a suicidal firefighter may think it's helping the system by giving the client suicidal thoughts to take away the emotional pain of an exile that got triggered (Schwartz & Sweezy, 2020).

You can learn to recognize how different parts tend to show up and what it looks like when a client has a Self-led system in any given moment, as described in the following table.

How to Recognize Parts and Develop Your Parts Detector

Protector Parts (Managers or Firefighters)	Exiles	Self-Led System
• Have "jobs" in the client's system • Parts that are overly responsible, rigid, minimizing, or critical (e.g., "I should . . ." or "You should . . .") are likely managers • Parts that are strongly reactive, are impulsive, have a strong urge, or shut down the system are likely firefighters • Firefighter parts tend to show up as behaviors that attempt to soothe, distract, or numb the system	• Vulnerable parts that hold trauma-related beliefs and feelings from the past • Often express themselves as emotional overwhelm, despair, shame, terror, sadness, and intense emotions • Often are stuck in traumatic memories or scenes from the past • Examples: A client may report being flooded with emotional pain or a visceral reaction, or a client may report seeing a younger version of themselves in a specific memory	• Demonstrates self-awareness of parts in the system and can hold space for their parts' experience • Can differentiate between their parts • Demonstrates some amount of the 8 C's and 5 P's • Can maintain an exploratory, nonreactive, and self-reflective presence • Can show equanimity, even during hardship • Relates to oneself with compassion • Example: A client is able to speak for their parts (e.g., "A part of me feels . . . and another part of me feels . . .") • The Self is not a part

Current Research

Although in its infancy in randomized controlled trial research, IFS has been found to be a promising treatment for generalized anxiety disorder (GAD) and PTSD in individual therapy (Hodgdon et al., 2022; Lucero et al., 2017), PTSD in group therapy (Ally et al., 2025; Comeau et al., 2024), physical health conditions and symptoms (Shadick et al., 2013), internet addiction (Mehrad Sadr et al., 2023), and depression (Haddock et al., 2017; Shadick et al., 2013). The bulk of IFS research has involved case studies, demonstrating the use of IFS treatment for sexual trauma (Jones et al., 2022; Miller et al., 2007; Wilkins, 2007), PTSD in a combat veteran (Lucero et al., 2017), suicidal ideation (Sweezy, 2011), dissociative identity disorder (Twombly, 2013), addiction recovery (Sykes, 2017; Sykes, et al., 2023), and an eating disorder (Catanzaro, 2017).

Research has demonstrated the effectiveness of IFS in combined treatment with EMDR (Bilbao Bourke et al., 2021). In addition, research on a pilot program combining art therapy or EMDR with IFS for complex trauma treatment showed decreased symptomology (de Boer et al., 2023). Several case studies also detail the benefits of using IFS interventions in EMDR therapy (Krause & Gomez, 2013; O'Shea Brown, 2020; Twombly & Schwartz, 2008) and in integrating art therapy with IFS within EMDR therapy (Kolodny & Mazero, 2022).

IFS Therapy Compared to Other Parts Models

"Parts models" are psychotherapy frameworks that conceptualize one's personality as having separate, identifiable parts. IFS is a unique parts model because it holds that not only does everyone have parts, but they also have a Self that can serve as the leader for the system. This is a revolutionary notion among parts models and gives clear direction within any IFS intervention to support the connection between a client's parts and their Self. The goal of IFS therapy is to liberate parts from being in exile, manager, or firefighter roles so they can share their natural, valuable gifts with the system, and the system can be Self-led for optimal functioning (Schwartz & Sweezy, 2020).

IFS differs from the two most commonly used parts models within trauma therapy: ego state therapy and the theory of structural dissociation of the personality. *Ego state therapy* is a brief psychodynamic-based model initially proposed by psychoanalyst Paul Federn that was further formally developed by John and Helen Watkins (Eitan & Torem, 2018). It intends to help ego states have internal harmony within the client's system (Lobenstine & Courtney, 2013). Unlike IFS, ego state therapy does not support the notion of a Self as the organizing leader of the system. Ego state interventions used during EMDR guide the client to have one ego state soothe an upset ego state—for example, asking a nurturing mother part of the client to soothe an overwhelmed younger part. One case study demonstrated that the use of ego state therapy during three weeks of intensive EMDR treatment for a client with comorbid PTSD, MDD, and GAD significantly decreased symptoms of each diagnosis (Lobenstine & Courtney, 2013).

The *theory of structural dissociation of the personality* (TSDP), developed by Onno van der Hart, Ellert Nijenhuis, and Kathy Steele (1993), posits that there are two types of parts within a traumatized client: apparently normal personality parts and emotional parts. The emotional parts of the personality are in "trauma time" and associated with traumatic memories. The apparently normal parts of the personality help the client avoid traumatic experiences and function in daily life. The goal of TSDP is integration into one coherent personality through steps of apparently normal personality parts and emotional parts meeting and working together toward a functional cooperative relationship (van der Hart et al., 1993). This differs from IFS, which holds that the internal system of parts can be Self-led and that parts can release burdens (traumatic memories) they are carrying and shift to sharing their gifts as parts in the system. Van der Hart and colleagues (2014) proposed that EMDR be integrated into TSDP to support the integration of traumatic memories.

In short, while IFS shares the notion with other parts models that the psyche is divided into subpersonalities, its distinction is the concept that in addition to parts, everyone has a Self, and that a Self-led internal system of parts is optimal. As discussed throughout this book, integrating IFS into EMDR helps support the client's system to be Self-led.

Limitations of EMDR and IFS Therapies as Single-Model Approaches

As discussed in the introduction, there are clear clinical indicators that clients would benefit from an IFS-integrative approach to EMDR therapy. This is bolstered by the fact that scholarship and research illuminate their limitations as single-model approaches, as demonstrated in the following table.

Limitations of EMDR and IFS

EMDR	IFS
Limitations of research (Wilson et al., 2018): • Limited follow-up data and limited evidence of long-term efficacy • Evidence is strong for EMDR treatment for adults with PTSD and less strong for treatment of adolescents and children with PTSD	Limitations of research: • Mainly case studies • Very limited published empirical studies using control groups • Quantitative research is primarily pilot studies • Abreactions: no research data yet • Side effects: no research data yet
Shapiro (2018) acknowledges the need for adaptations of the EMDR standard protocol with complex trauma	Adaptations to IFS with complex trauma have been recommended, particularly when clients have dissociative disorders (Twombly, 2022)

Limitations to Integration

Despite the benefits of integrating EMDR and IFS, the limitations to doing so must be noted. The guidelines of Evidence-Based Practice in Psychology (APA, 2021) states that treatment decisions need to consider the best available research, clinical expertise, and patient characteristics, culture, and preferences. Ethically, in order to use IFS interventions and EMDR, therapists must have competency in both methods and maintain fidelity to the eight phases of EMDR (Fatter, 2023b), given that treatment fidelity leads to positive treatment outcomes (Finley et al., 2017).

Shared Values and Processes

When integrating therapy approaches, it's crucial that their values and processes be compatible. EMDR and IFS share the following values and processes:

- Having trust in the client's innate drive and capacity toward healing
- Being trauma-informed models
- Reorganizing the client's system
- Eliciting memory reconsolidation
- Instilling hope in the client

Let's take a closer look at each of these shared values and processes.

Trust in the Client's Innate Drive and Capacity Toward Healing

EMDR and IFS are both based on the premise that humans are inherently driven, and able, to heal, and each model approaches this differently. As mentioned previously, EMDR's foundational premise is that everyone naturally has an adaptive information-processing system. The belief is that by activating the AIP system through EMDR processing, the brain will naturally move the traumatic memory toward resolution, including connecting it with relevant adaptive information. IFS's foundational premise is that everyone has Self, and that Self is undamaged by trauma. IFS posits that when parts are known and understood by Self, parts naturally will shift roles in the system and release the trauma-related feelings, beliefs, and burdens they are carrying (Fatter, 2023b).

Trauma-Informed Approaches

Both EMDR and IFS recognize the impact of trauma on individuals and theorize that the past drives the present. EMDR holds that past experiences influence current clinical symptomology, emphasizes treating every memory with respect, and believes in the client's capacity to transform. Similarly, IFS is a nonpathological approach that values parts' gifts in the client's internal system and welcomes all parts to be befriended and understood. IFS holds that exiles, the vulnerable parts carrying trauma-related burdens from the past, drive protector roles that show up as current clinical symptomology. IFS is also consent-based; it respects the client's protective system by asking permission from protector parts to work with exiles prior to trauma reprocessing.

Reorganization of the Client's System

EMDR therapy and IFS therapy both reorganize the client's system. In EMDR therapy, this reorganization happens through adaptive information connecting with maladaptively stored traumatic memory. In IFS therapy, this reorganization happens through exiles unburdening due to the reparative relational connection and leadership of Self.

In order to understand the process of reorganization of the client's system, it's critical to first understand why parts get stuck in burdened roles, preventing the client from being Self-led. The following figure illustrates the potential factors contributing to this scenario.

Why Do Parts Get Stuck in Burdened Roles?

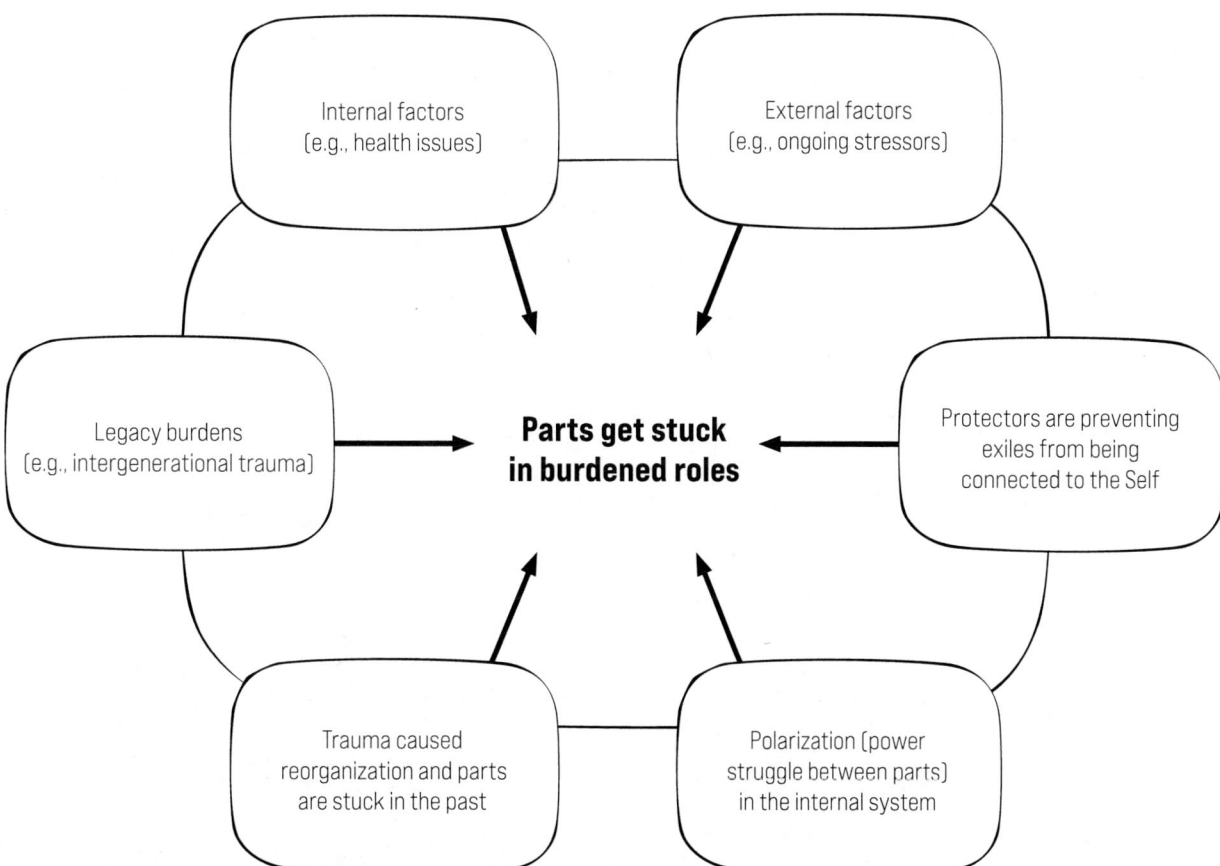

For reorganization to occur, according to IFS, parts need to heal and move out of their burdened roles. There are many paths to this transformation. While these interventions can occur in pure IFS, they are ideally suited to be integrated into the eight phases of EMDR therapy, as illustrated in the next figure.

What Do Parts Need to Get Unstuck?

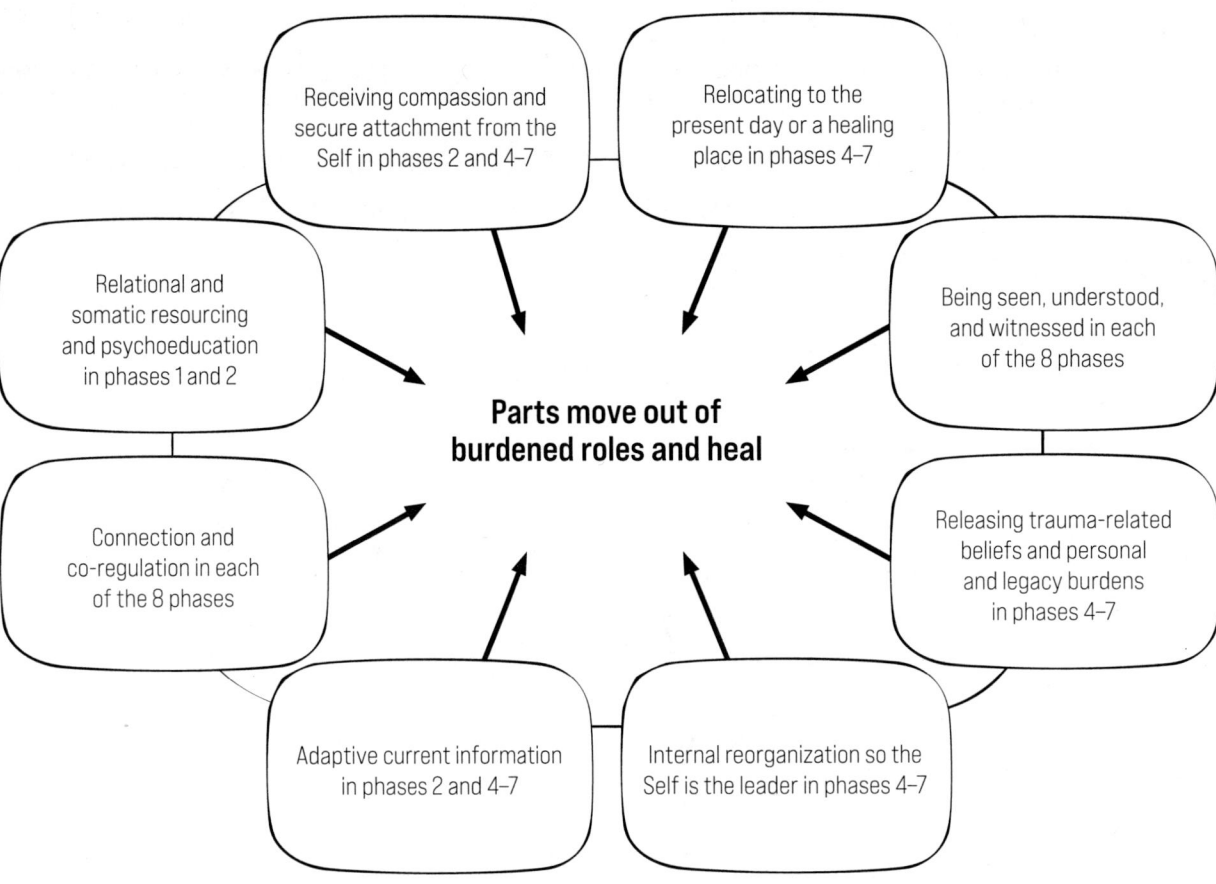

Memory Reconsolidation

Both EMDR and IFS therapies elicit the neurobiological process of memory reconsolidation, which naturally changes the meaning making and emotional learning in the traumatic memory itself. To initiate the memory reconsolidation process, an original memory is reactivated, then repeatedly met with a juxtaposed mismatch, which leads to the synapses becoming unstable. When the synapses become unstable, they can be edited and updated through new experiential learning in which the original emotional learning becomes annulled. This three-step process, termed the "empirically confirmed process of erasure" (ECPE; Ecker, 2018), has been proposed to occur in both EMDR and IFS therapies (Ecker et al., 2012; Ecker & Bridges, 2020; Ecker & Vaz, 2022; Fatter, 2023b; Fatter, 2024). The following table outlines how this process occurs in both approaches.

EMDR and IFS Steps That Align with Memory Reconsolidation

The 3 Steps of ECPE to Elicit Memory Reconsolidation (Adapted from Ecker et al., 2012; Ecker & Bridges, 2020; Ecker & Vaz, 2022)	EMDR (Ecker et al., 2012; adapted from Fatter, 2023b)	IFS (Ecker et al., 2012; Fatter, 2023b; Kredler, 2023; adapted from Anderson, 2021)
Intentional reactivation of target emotional learning: the client is emotionally, somatically, and cognitively experiencing the reactivation	Phase 3	Target exile is identified and accessed after getting permission from protector parts
The client experiences a concurrent mismatch to juxtapose the emotional learning, leading neural encoding to become unstable, initiating the reconsolidation process	Starting trauma reprocessing in phase 4, which continues through phase 6	Emotionally corrective Self-to-part relationship with exile: befriending, witnessing, do-over
Erasure occurs through the client continuing to have a mismatched experience, leading to rewiring and annulling the original emotional learning	Phases 4-6 through completion of a target in the standard EMDR therapy protocol	The exile is retrieved and unburdened; positive qualities are invited in; integration via protectors that were previously protecting the exile choosing new roles for themselves

Adapted with permission from "Integrating Internal Family Systems into EMDR Therapy's 8 Phases," by D. Fatter, 2024, *Go With That Magazine, 29*(2), p. 15. Copyright 2024 by EMDR International.

Instilling Hope

Finally, both IFS therapy and EMDR therapy use strategies to instill hope. In IFS, by eliciting the client's willingness to try something new and offering that any extreme feelings or distorted beliefs can change and be released, the therapist serves as a "hope merchant" (Schwartz & Sweezy, 2020, p. 199). In EMDR, the therapist can also instill a sense of hope through traditional phase 2 resource development to help set up effective EMDR trauma reprocessing (Hensley, 2021).

Differences of Each Model

In addition to their different methodologies (as explained earlier in this chapter), EMDR and IFS therapies differ in their conceptualization of clinical symptoms, their emotion regulation strategies, how they assess client readiness for trauma reprocessing, and how they identify targets (areas of focus) for trauma reprocessing.

Posttraumatic Stress Disorder Conceptualization

EMDR and IFS therapies conceptualize PTSD from vastly different theoretical orientations. EMDR views PTSD symptoms as the result of how the traumatic memory was encoded and inadequately stored in the brain (Shapiro, 2018). In contrast, IFS holds that PTSD symptoms are due to parts taking on extreme survival roles at the time of the trauma and getting stuck in those roles (Schwartz & Sweezy, 2020). These differences are shown in the following table.

EMDR (Shapiro, 2018)	IFS (Shapiro & Sweezy, 2020)
PTSD is a result of traumatic memories that are inadequately stored in the brain.	PTSD is a result of parts being stuck in extreme roles or states due to trauma.
Hyperarousal and hypoarousal symptoms are indicators of traumatic memories not yet connected to adaptive information.	Hyperarousal and hypoarousal symptoms are parts that have good intentions and try to help the system in the way they know how.

Emotion Regulation Strategies

EMDR and IFS therapies also differ in their approach to emotion regulation. In EMDR, the therapist reviews traditional coping strategies with the client during phase 2 and pairs BLS with positive resources (e.g., a healing/calm/safe place visualization, relational resources, positive memories and attributes). EMDR therapists encourage the client to practice coping skills, including grounding and self-care practices, to manage trauma triggers throughout treatment (Shapiro, 2018).

As a stand-alone model, IFS therapy posits that emotion regulation naturally occurs through the relationship between the client's Self and a given part. When trust is restored in Self from the part, it can trust Self's leadership, which naturally lends itself to emotion regulation. One way to gain trust is through the IFS process of "befriending," or getting to know, parts. As a trauma-informed approach, IFS involves befriending protectors first, before befriending exiles, to ensure that trauma reprocessing is consent-based. Contracting with exiles to not overwhelm the system is also the main IFS intervention to help clients regulate emotional intensity (Schwartz & Sweezy, 2020). Thus, an IFS approach relies on the client's ability to connect with their Self while the therapist guides them to contract with and befriend their parts to help support emotion regulation.

Assessing for Client Readiness

EMDR and IFS therapies also differ in how the therapist assesses a client's readiness for trauma reprocessing. In EMDR, practiced as a stand-alone model, after adequate screening for dissociative disorders and considering issues of stabilization, dual diagnoses, and the client's life conditions, the client is deemed ready to move forward with phases 3 and 4 for trauma reprocessing if they can state change and effectively practice coping skills to manage activation between sessions (Shapiro, 2018).

In IFS, practiced as a stand-alone model, client readiness for trauma reprocessing (which occurs through befriending an exile) is based on whether the client has enough access to Self. When enough Self is present, the client can befriend protectors and ask for their permission to befriend exiles. If the protectors give consent, then it is assumed the client is ready for befriending an exile. This initiates what are known as the healing steps in IFS (befriending, witnessing, do-over, retrieval, unburdening, and the invitation), which is trauma reprocessing (Schwartz & Sweezy, 2020).

Identifying Targets for Trauma Reprocessing

Both EMDR and IFS therapies trust the organic emergence of targets for trauma reprocessing. In EMDR therapy, the therapist keeps an ongoing log of potential targets. In IFS therapy, the therapist notes parts that naturally emerge in the system or that the client reports wanting to return to in the future. When integrating IFS into EMDR therapy, once exiles are revealed, they can become the target for phase 3 and phase 4 reprocessing in EMDR therapy, as we'll discuss in chapters 2 through 6. Both EMDR and IFS share the premise that the past impacts the present, but how they get to those memories from the past for healing is very different.

EMDR therapy traditionally organizes treatment plans using a symptom-based, three-pronged approach: targeting the past memories first, then the present triggers or events, and then future events or scenarios. Standard EMDR protocol recommends reprocessing the earliest memory connected to the presenting symptomology, then going to the worst experience, then moving to the most recent, and ultimately conducting a future template of how the client would like to respond emotionally and behaviorally in the future (Shapiro, 2018).

In contrast, IFS therapy traditionally follows the natural pace and sequence of parts that organically emerge in the client's system. Through befriending protector parts, exiles naturally reveal themselves. The client's Self befriends protectors first and gets permission to work with exiles for trauma reprocessing (Schwartz & Sweezy, 2020).

Five IFS Principles to Support Effective EMDR Trauma Reprocessing

Five IFS principles can help guide the integration of IFS interventions with EMDR. Throughout the rest of this book, you will learn how to use these five principles throughout the eight phases of EMDR. These principles will help guide you with direction and clinical decision-making throughout EMDR therapy so you can feel confident in applying IFS case conceptualization and interventions.

Principle 1: We All Have Self and Parts

IFS interventions provide the perspective that one part is not *all* of a client. This helps the traumatized client understand that they can have opposing and dialectal feelings and thoughts at the same time. This offers a nonpathological view of the client. This principle also provides an IFS perspective on case conceptualization to use throughout EMDR therapy by inviting you to continually hold the questions "How much access does the client have to their Self?" "What part might this be?" and "What is this part's job in the system?" Exploring parts' roles in a client's system by using IFS interventions within the eight phases of EMDR therapy can help identify and untangle polarized parts and double binds. Parts can be befriended to help them soften, becoming less rigid, less defensive, and more open to the system changing internally. When parts soften, they can give consent for EMDR reprocessing, and trauma-related beliefs and feelings that parts are carrying can change in EMDR reprocessing, helping support a Self-led system.

Principle 2: All Parts Are Welcome

From an IFS perspective, all parts have positive intentions for the system. This helps depathologize the client's mental health symptoms and creates a therapeutic relationship that is inclusive and welcoming of all the client's parts. This principle also reinforces that you are not trying to get rid of any given part, but offering parts an opportunity for transformation and releasing burdens they carry through EMDR reprocessing. If a part is emerging that prevents EMDR reprocessing, that is the system's way of letting you know which part needs to be addressed next. Thus, rather than being seen as a problem or impediment to treatment, parts are relationally welcomed and valued within EMDR therapy. In applying IFS interventions, you develop the skill to discern what type of part may be present and how much the client is functioning from a Self-led system.

Principle 3: Receive Consent from Protector Parts First

IFS interventions respect the client's protector parts. Before doing EMDR reprocessing or accessing the exile, you ask the client for consent from their protector parts. This provides consent-based trauma reprocessing. You must be attuned to the client's pace and trust the pace their system needs for healing. **IFS slows down the pace of trauma reprocessing. EMDR speeds up the pace of trauma reprocessing.**

Principle 4: The Self-to-Part Relationship Is Healing

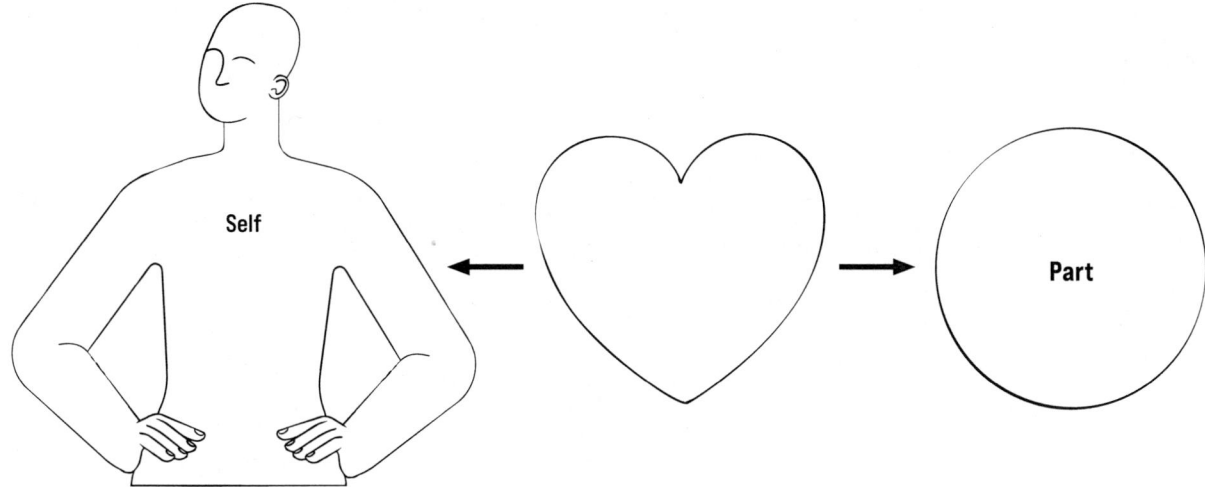

As the figure demonstrates, when a part receives connection to Self, it is innately healing. Throughout EMDR therapy, you are using IFS interventions to ultimately support a Self-to-part relationship. Self-energy can be provided to parts from the client's Self, the therapist's Self, Self experienced through any relational resources (e.g., human, animal, nature, or spiritual), or Self-energy from being in community. In traumatized systems, some parts initially may only be able to take in the presence of Self through an integrative coping skill for co-regulation. Integrating coping skills can help parts to receive Self and can be used to strengthen the Self-to-part relationship for co-regulation. Thus, early on in phases 1 and 2, IFS interventions help support the Self-to-part relationship. Phases 3 and 4 help strengthen the Self-to-part relationship through EMDR reprocessing. Throughout phases 4 through 8, IFS interventions offer an opportunity for Self-to-part relationship as needed in EMDR therapy.

Principle 5: If Parts Feel Understood, They Will Soften

Parts get stuck in burdened roles (manager, firefighter, or exile) in the system due to trauma, legacy burdens (intergenerational trauma), and internal and external constraints. Parts can get stuck in the past, stuck in protecting vulnerable parts, or stuck due to a polarization (power struggle) in the internal system.

Any IFS intervention is a relational invitation for parts to be understood. When parts feel safe, seen, soothed, and secure, this fosters secure attachment between Self and parts (Siegel, 2010). In any IFS intervention, you guide the client not to get rid of or change their parts, but to understand their parts from a place of curiosity and nonjudgment. Resourcing parts through integrative coping skills and relational, cognitive, and somatic resources, in addition to restoring trust in Self-leadership, helps parts receive co-regulation and attachment repair with Self.

When parts feel understood, they will soften. Parts can be relocated to the present day or a healing place, and parts can receive adaptive current information through the relationship with Self and through EMDR reprocessing. When their stories are witnessed through EMDR reprocessing or IFS interventions, they will ultimately release trauma-related beliefs, personal and legacy burdens including trauma-related feelings, and physical reactivity in the body. This reorganizes the internal system of parts so that Self is the leader of the system.

Now that you have an understanding of EMDR and IFS therapies, the values and processes they share, and the IFS principles that support its integration with EMDR, you are prepared to learn how to conduct IFS-informed case conceptualization and integrative treatment planning during phase 1 of EMDR.

CHAPTER 2

IFS-Informed Case Conceptualization and Integrative Treatment Planning During Phase 1

This chapter will focus on integrating IFS into EMDR phase 1 in case conceptualization and treatment planning. We will start with a brief review of phase 1 and history taking during the intake process. Then you will learn how to apply an IFS case conceptualization based on the information received in the client's intake. You'll learn how to incorporate polyvagal theory to identify and attune to parts' autonomic states. This will enable you to develop an integrative treatment plan to support arousal regulation and help identify what the client may need to develop in order to prepare for EMDR reprocessing. We'll also cover considerations for a variety of clients—including autistic or neurodiverse clients, marginalized populations, clients with ongoing trauma exposure, and clients with traumatic grief—with regard to case conceptualization and treatment planning. A therapist worksheet is included that guides you through the process of IFS-informed case conceptualization and integrative treatment planning. At the end of this chapter, I will demonstrate an IFS-informed case conceptualization and integrative treatment plan with a case example that we will revisit throughout the book.

Phase 1 and History Taking in EMDR Therapy

Phase 1 of EMDR involves obtaining the client's history; providing psychoeducation about therapy, including what to expect during EMDR reprocessing; receiving informed consent for treatment; screening for dissociative disorders; and determining the client's stability, distress tolerance, timing of treatment, and readiness and capacity for the accelerated trauma reprocessing of EMDR (Shapiro, 2018). Through history taking during the intake process, you gather information to form your IFS-informed case conceptualization, which helps guide IFS-informed integrative treatment planning.

The AIP model in EMDR is based on the notion that past unprocessed trauma is the reason for the client's current symptoms, coping behaviors, and triggers. So it is important to ask about both past traumatic experiences and present-day symptomology to help ultimately identify unprocessed trauma from the past that is causing the client's current symptoms. This information is then used to guide the rest of treatment in terms of which traumas from the past to target in EMDR reprocessing to resolve the client's current symptoms (Shapiro, 2018).

In history taking, you want to find out about the client's traumatic experiences, including life-altering or life-threatening events (e.g., prolonged abuse, death of a loved one, or exposure to violence), challenging experiences that are indicative of developmental trauma, and relational and attachment trauma (e.g., microaggressions, emotional abuse, being bullied, moving frequently, being separated from a parent). Oppression-based traumas and present-day experiences of discrimination also need to be identified. Having an overall timeline of these traumatic events helps you identify potential targets for EMDR reprocessing.

You then identify potential EMDR targets that are current triggers or anticipated future scenarios. You also identify current coping behaviors to find out what resources the client may need to develop for safety, stability, and emotion regulation before EMDR reprocessing. This involves gathering information about the client's current symptoms, current triggers, intrusive symptoms (e.g., flashbacks, nightmares, intrusive memories), current coping behaviors, and any current negative beliefs. Specifically, you are assessing for the client's negative beliefs related to their sense of safety, sense of responsibility, self-worth, sense of control, and sense of connection and value (Shapiro, 2018).

To further assess potential positive resources to strengthen in preparation for EMDR reprocessing, you identify the client's resilience factors. This includes the client's strengths, positive attachment figures from the past and present, positive life experiences, and current positive aspects of the client's life (e.g., supportive personal relationships, joyful experiences, meaningful career). You also ask about future desired states (how the client wants to feel, what positive beliefs they want to develop about themself, etc.), which also help inform treatment goals (Shapiro, 2018).

In this process, you help make the client more aware of how past traumas impact their current symptoms as you provide psychoeducation about the impact of trauma. You organize the information from history taking into three categories: past traumas, present triggers/stressors, and future scenarios (any anticipated future events). You use this information to conceptualize the case using EMDR's three-pronged approach: past trauma informs present symptoms and future anticipated scenarios. (You can see this three-pronged approach during phase 1 in the table "Categorizing Clients' Intake Information to Inform Treatment Planning" on page 36.)

With the information you gather during history taking in the intake process, you can begin to form an IFS-informed case conceptualization. EMDR and IFS are both transdiagnostic modalities, meaning that the format you use to develop your case conceptualization is applicable to any client and can be utilized across clinical diagnoses.

IFS-Informed Case Conceptualization

The key to applying an IFS case conceptualization to any client is to remember that mental health symptoms are parts of the client that have positive intentions for the system (Schwartz & Sweezy, 2020). This brings a nonpathological perspective to the client's symptoms. IFS-informed case conceptualization in EMDR phase 1 has three purposes: (1) identifying parts connected to the client's presenting symptoms, (2) assessing the client's current constraints, and (3) identifying the client's window of tolerance (how much stress they can tolerate). Using an IFS-informed case conceptualization honors the uniqueness of each client and provides a client-centered approach to understanding the parts in the client's system that contribute to the client's symptoms. IFS-informed case conceptualization is a dynamic, ongoing process that initially occurs through history taking and parts mapping, then continues to be informed by guiding the client to get to know their parts using the IFS intervention called *befriending* in phase 2. The information gathered using IFS befriending interventions helps identify what coping skills and resources are needed to further support stabilization, prepare for EMDR reprocessing, and determine the client's readiness to proceed with EMDR reprocessing in phases 3 through 8.

Identifying Parts in IFS Case Conceptualization

After identifying the client's current symptoms and conceptualizing those symptoms as parts, the next step is to identify which of the three burdened roles each of these parts is in (manager, firefighter, or exile) due to the client's traumatic experiences. Recall that, like EMDR's AIP model, IFS holds that past traumas lead to the client's current symptoms. According to IFS, it is parts getting stuck in burdened roles in the system due to past traumas that cause current clinical symptoms.

Using the therapist worksheet "IFS-Informed Case Conceptualization and Integrative Treatment Planning" (included on page 44), you can consider what manager parts (the parts that help the client "keep it together" and manage daily functioning and relationships) may be showing up as specific current symptoms (thoughts, feelings, body sensations, or behaviors). To identify firefighter parts (the parts that reactively take over when there is a trauma trigger or intense internal stress), consider what coping behavior the client is using. What does the client do that helps them numb their feelings, self-soothe, or distract themself?

To identify exiles, consider the client's current invasive symptoms (e.g., flashbacks, nightmares, intrusive memories) that were identified during the intake. Since you conducted a trauma history during the intake, you can hypothesize that the client potentially has exiles at each age that they experienced a traumatic event. From history taking, you also will consider that the client's negative core cognitions are likely exile parts. For example, if a client shares a core belief of "I am not good enough," "I am powerless," "It's my fault," or "I don't belong," you can hypothesize that the client experienced past traumas that led to those negative cognitions. From an IFS lens, exiles experience those negative cognitions as true because they carry unprocessed trauma.

These are what IFS calls *burdens*. Exiles typically are what is targeted in EMDR reprocessing; in other words, the unprocessed traumatic memories resulting in the client's current symptoms are targeted.

The following table lists the functions of the three roles: managers, exiles, and firefighters.

Roles of Manager, Exile, and Firefighter Parts

(Sykes, 2017; Schwartz & Sweezy, 2020)

Managers	Exiles	Firefighters
• Try to prevent the client's exiles from getting triggered (i.e., try to prevent the client from experiencing vulnerability). • Help the client function daily. • Focus on the future.	• Carry intense emotions from any age in the past. • Express themselves through traumatic nightmares or flashbacks (emotional, somatic, visual, or visceral). • Managers and firefighters are driven to protect them.	• React after a client is triggered. • Help the client numb, distract, soothe, and escape from the pain of the exile. • Focus on reducing distress in the here and now. • Are not concerned about the impact of how they help the system.

From the client's intake process, you initially hypothesize that parts are creating the client's presenting symptoms. Then you and the client collaboratively identify parts in their system through an IFS process called *parts mapping*. You use parts mapping interventions to help make parts conscious, initiating the client's awareness of the connection between their symptoms and parts, and the parts' connection to specific past traumas. Through parts mapping, you gather more information to help you clinically assess the client's stability, capacity (e.g., How well does the client manage stress?), and response to the interpersonal process of disclosing information about their internal system with you (e.g., Are any firefighter parts that show up due to parts mapping feeling too vulnerable for the client?). Parts mapping will be further described in chapter 3.

Assessing Constraints

Another aspect of an IFS-informed case conceptualization involves assessing constraints—in other words, internal or external factors that might hinder the client's ability to do EMDR reprocessing. Assessing constraints helps you determine whether the client is a good candidate for EMDR reprocessing and whether it's the right time in the client's life to do EMDR reprocessing. During phase 1 of EMDR, you and the client can collaboratively and transparently identify any internal and external constraints through the history-taking process as well as in parts mapping. Internal constraints may include chronic health conditions, acute grief due to a recent loss, or mental health symptoms that require more of a focus on stabilization, such as life-threatening substance abuse, recent suicide attempts, or active psychotic episodes. External constraints include relational, social, and environmental factors such as chronic instability at home or work, a limited support system, ongoing exposure to violence, ongoing systemic oppression (e.g., microaggressions, discrimination), or involvement in a legal battle, marital separation, or divorce.

IFS case conceptualization during phase 1 focuses on identifying, through parts mapping, what parts show up in response to these constraints. Talking about how these constraints impact the client's parts helps the client better understand themself and elicits more self-compassion. Later, in phase 2, you can guide the client to befriend these parts to help strengthen coping skills and further support the client's stabilization and resources.

Assessing the Client's Window of Tolerance Through an IFS Lens

The third essential feature of an IFS-informed case conceptualization is assessing the client's window of tolerance. This term, coined by Dr. Dan Siegel (2012), is commonly used in trauma treatment to refer to the client's capacity to experience an optimal regulated arousal state in which the client can tolerate both distress and positive feelings. Assessing the client's window of tolerance in phase 1 helps you determine how much resourcing and IFS befriending the client may need in phase 2 before proceeding to EMDR reprocessing in phases 3 through 8.

The first step of assessing the client's window of tolerance from an IFS lens is to determine what autonomic state a part is stuck in during phase 1. This is done through the intake process and the parts mapping process. Then, in phase 2, you further assess the client's window of tolerance by seeing how well their parts respond to coping skills and to co-regulation through the use of befriending interventions. Providing resources and connection to parts in phase 2 widens the client's window of tolerance, helping the client develop more emotion regulation skills, which further informs their readiness for moving to phases 3 through 8 for EMDR reprocessing.

So, let's first talk about how to identify what autonomic state a client's part may be stuck in. Parts can show up in a particular trauma-related autonomic state. Polyvagal theory (Porges, 1995) provides a framework to help you identify which autonomic state—hyperarousal, hypoarousal, freeze or fawn, or ventral vagal—a given part may be stuck in. Integrating polyvagal theory into IFS case conceptualization is especially important when working with clients with complex trauma histories. When a client has experienced many traumatic events or has been exposed to traumatic stress over the course of their life, they are more likely to have unprocessed traumatic memories. The more unprocessed traumatic memories the client has, the more likely their parts are to be in extreme burdened roles and stuck in these autonomic states. When the client experiences more arousal (due to ongoing trauma triggers, dealing with everyday stress, or the accumulative nature of stress, for example), their parts can more easily blend and potentially take over the client's system, manifesting in clinical mental health symptoms.

Through an IFS lens, in a burdened system, parts can show up in specific states of arousal due to trauma. For example, parts can be stuck in:

- **Hyperarousal** due to activation of the sympathetic nervous system (e.g., hypervigilant or anxious parts)
- **Hypoarousal** due to activation of the dorsal vagal lower branch of the parasympathetic nervous system (e.g., dissociative parts or parts that emotionally numb)
- **Freeze or fawn responses**, which polyvagal theory proposes are due to both the sympathetic fight-or-flight response and the dorsal vagal immobilization response being activated at the same time (Porges, 2011; e.g., parts that are in shock or parts that help the client go through the motions while experiencing disconnection)

During phase 1, as part of your case conceptualization, consider the client's symptomology as parts potentially stuck in specific autonomic responses. You can use the therapist worksheet "IFS-Informed Case Conceptualization and Integrative Treatment Planning" (on page 44) to begin to make an ongoing record of what autonomic states different managers, firefighters, and exiles are in. To help you identify the autonomic states of the client's parts, you can explore the following as a follow-up after history taking and in parts mapping:

- When the client has a trauma trigger or something stressful or upsetting happens, how does their body respond?
- When the client gets triggered in relationships, how does their body respond?
- What is the client's experience, in their body, of social connection?

Complex trauma recovery includes supporting the client's nervous system to be adaptive, which means that the parts are not stuck in hyperarousal, hypoarousal, freeze, or fawn but rather are able to access a ventral vagal state. A Self-led system leads to a client's nervous system adaptively moving through autonomic states and returning to a regulated ventral vagal state after a threat or stressor is over.

When clients can receive support in positive relational connection, they can experience a ventral vagal state, which occurs when the upper branch of the parasympathetic nervous system is activated (Porges, 2011). When a client can access their own Self-energy or receive co-regulation through Self, through you, or through other beings (e.g., a person, an animal, nature, a spiritual relational resource, or a community), arousal will decrease in their nervous system and they will naturally move to a regulated ventral vagal state.

The following figure depicts these states of autonomic arousal through an IFS lens.

States of Autonomic Arousal and How Parts Respond

(Adapted from Dana, 2018; Porges, 1995, 2011; Rothman, 2023)

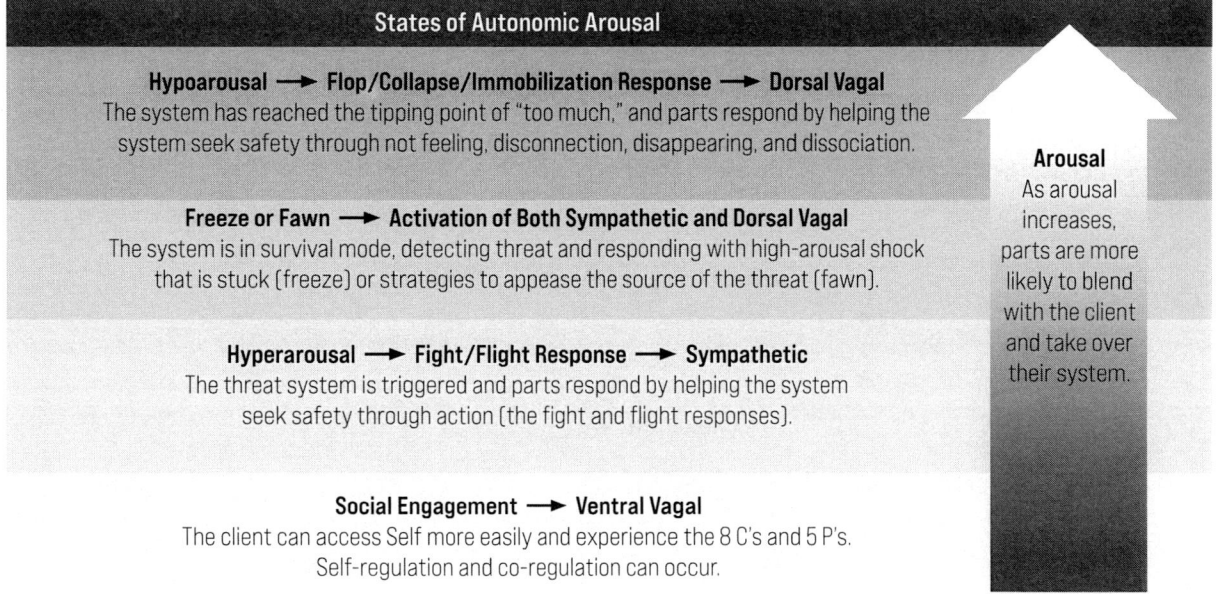

Once you've developed your case conceptualization, taking into consideration the client's autonomic state of arousal, you then develop a treatment plan in coordination with the client. Treatment planning begins in phase 1 and continues in phase 2 as you determine which EMDR target to start reprocessing first based on the client's treatment goals, their capacity, their window of tolerance, the timing in the client's life, and how prepared the client is for EMDR reprocessing.

Integrative Treatment Planning in Phase 1

In addressing treatment planning, let's start by laying out the big-picture framework for complex trauma treatment. The evidence-based three-phase model of trauma recovery is the gold standard for creating treatment plans for complex trauma recovery (Courtois & Ford, 2016). As shown in the following table, EMDR's eight-phase model, along with specific IFS interventions, naturally fits within this framework for an integrative approach to complex trauma treatment. IFS interventions support attunement to the client's system and slow the pace down, whereas EMDR is designed for accelerated trauma reprocessing. IFS interventions provide gradual scaffolding of emotional intensity in treatment, attunement to the client's system, support for stabilization and emotion regulation, insight, and integration of therapeutic gains at the speed most beneficial for the client's system.

EMDR's Eight Phases and IFS Interventions within the Trauma Recovery Model

Three Phases for Trauma Recovery (Courtois & Ford, 2016; adapted from Herman, 1992b)	EMDR's Eight Phases (Shapiro, 2018)	IFS Interventions to Use Within EMDR Phases

• **First Phase: Stabilization**
  ○ Skill building
  ○ Building rapport
  ○ Increasing the client's window of tolerance
  ○ Developing a strong working alliance and trust in the therapeutic relationship
	• **Phase 1:** History Taking and Treatment Planning
	• **Phase 2:** Resource Development
	  ○ For complex trauma, phase 2 resources are integrated early in phase 1 as needed for stabilization
		• In phase 1:
		  ○ IFS-informed case conceptualization
		  ○ Parts mapping
		• In phase 2:
		  ○ Get consent to befriend the client's parts connected to their presenting symptoms
		  ○ Befriending supports stabilization; ask parts what coping skills they like
		  ○ Befriending protectors will reveal potential EMDR targets; ask protectors for permission to proceed with EMDR reprocessing

• **Second Phase: Trauma Reprocessing and Grieving**
  ○ Decreasing emotional and sensorimotor reactivity to traumatic memories
  ○ Changing the meaning of traumatic events to a more adaptive perspective
	• **Phase 3:** Assessment
	• **Phase 4:** Desensitization
	• **Phase 5:** Installing the Positive Cognition
	• **Phase 6:** Body Scan
	• **Phase 8:** Reevaluation
		• **Phase 3:** Target what protectors gave consent to process (e.g., the touchstone, worst, or most recent incident)
		• **Phase 4:** The 6 F's for blocking beliefs or when the subjective units of distress (SUDs) rating is not decreasing
		• Self Tapping for Attachment Readiness & Repair (STARR®)
		• If looping: witnessing, updating, do-over, retrieval, unburdening
		• **Phase 5:** The 6 F's if validity of cognition (VOC) is not increasing
		• **Phase 6:** Ask for parts scared of feeling good in the body and use somatic interventions if the body scan does not clear
		• **Phase 8:** Ask for protectors' consent when returning to a phase 4 target during reevaluation

• Third Phase: Life in the Present Day
   ◦ Integrating therapeutic gains
   ◦ Preparing for termination if the treatment goals have been met
	• Phase 7: Closure
	   ◦ Consider proceeding with additional EMDR reprocessing on present triggers and future template
		• In phase 7:
		   ◦ Invite protectors to change roles as needed
		   ◦ Integration toward a Self-led system

Supporting stabilization, providing interventions in bite-sized pieces to limit overwhelm, developing coping skills, and fostering a strong therapeutic relationship are key prior to the client doing trauma reprocessing.

Let's delve into the various components of the integrative treatment plan. First, I'll explain how the IFS concept of exiles represents the EMDR concept of touchstone memories. Then, I'll describe an IFS-informed approach to EMDR target sequencing. Finally, I'll present an overview of IFS-informed treatment planning across the eight phases of EMDR.

Touchstone Memories from an IFS Lens

During phase 1, you try to identify the past trauma that is most related to the client's current symptoms. From an IFS lens, this means you are trying to identify potential exiles (vulnerable parts holding unprocessed traumatic memories that you will target in EMDR reprocessing) and protector parts (managers and firefighters) connected to the client's presenting issue and clinical symptoms.

What EMDR calls a *touchstone memory* is the core memory that leads to the client's current triggers and anticipated future scenarios. The touchstone memory is the first memory that formed the maladaptively encoded memory network causing the negative belief and subsequent mental health symptoms. From an IFS lens, the touchstone memory may be held in one core exile or several exiles holding fragments and visceral aspects connected to that touchstone memory (e.g., one exile holding specific trauma-related body sensations, another exile holding the emotional terror, and a third exile holding feelings of shame). The most recent trigger and the client's thinking about future anticipated scenarios may be the trigger that the core exile or the group of exiles connected to the touchstone memory.

You identify exiles by asking the client about the touchstone memory (the first memory in which the client experienced the negative cognition, or similar emotions or body sensations as the current symptoms); present triggers for the negative cognition, emotions, or body sensations; and future anticipated events or scenarios where the negative cognition, emotions, or body sensations could be triggered.

IFS-Informed Treatment Planning for EMDR Target Sequencing

EMDR's three-pronged approach (i.e., looking at how past memories impact the present and beliefs about the future) helps you decide which target to process first in EMDR reprocessing, then which potential targets to process across the course of EMDR therapy after the first memory resolves in phases 3 through 8 (Shapiro, 2018). This is called *target sequencing* in EMDR.

The following table demonstrates how to categorize information you obtain from the client's intake during phase 1 to inform treatment planning, including specific questions to ask the client during the intake process to identify potential EMDR targets (adapted from Hensley, 2021). The therapist worksheet "IFS-Informed Case Conceptualization and Integrative Treatment Planning" (page 44) will further guide you through this process.

Categorizing Clients' Intake Information to Inform Treatment Planning

EMDR Targets Connected to the Presenting Symptoms/Issue	How to Ask the Client This During the Intake Process
The most recent trigger/incident	"Tell me a specific recent experience or trigger that occurred when you experienced anything related to the presenting issue."
Identifying the negative cognition and related emotions and body sensations (burdens)	"When this recent trigger happened, what words best describe any negative belief you had about yourself? What feelings and body sensations did you experience?"
The touchstone memory	"What is the first time you had this negative belief or had similar feelings or body sensations?"
The worst memory	"What is the worst incident where you had this negative belief or had similar feelings or body sensations?"
Other related past experiences	"Can you think of any other times or events where you believed the same negative belief, felt the same way, or had the same body sensations?"
Anticipated future scenarios	"Tell me about any anticipated scenarios or events where you are concerned that this presenting issue may get triggered."

Traditional EMDR treatment planning would focus on preparing the client in phase 2 to process the touchstone memory in EMDR reprocessing in phases 3 through 6. Then, after the touchstone memory resolves, the client's present or most recent triggers would be targeted in EMDR reprocessing until resolution, followed by future anticipated scenarios the client could encounter that might trigger the original belief or feeling. Resolving the touchstone memory has a generalizing effect on how the memory network is stored. So when you start EMDR reprocessing by targeting the touchstone memory, resolving that target has the greatest potential impact on changing the client's response to current and future triggers (Shapiro, 2018).

Thus, a standard EMDR treatment plan focuses on resolving past traumas first in EMDR reprocessing, then addressing present triggers and the impact of current stressors, and, subsequently, addressing future anticipated scenarios. However, following this order is not always clear or most beneficial for clients with complex trauma histories, depending on their capacity, their treatment goals (e.g., symptom reduction vs. comprehensive treatment), and the timing of doing EMDR reprocessing in the client's life. This is why using the IFS interventions of parts mapping and befriending are key to trusting the client's system to identify which target to start with in EMDR.

The figure on the next page describes options for EMDR target sequencing and IFS interventions used to identify parts connected to the presenting issue.

Target Sequencing Chart for EMDR Reprocessing

PTSD (Shapiro, 2018)	Complex Trauma (Shapiro, 2018)	IFS Interventions for Any Client
• First target: 　○ Touchstone (the first time the burden/negative cognition was experienced by the client) *or* 　○ The traumatic memory most linked to the current symptoms • Upon resolution, **second** target: 　○ Client's flashbacks • Upon resolution, **third** target: 　○ Client's nightmares • Upon resolution, **fourth** target: 　○ Current triggers (internal and external) • Upon resolution: 　○ Desired future functioning; future template	• First target: 　○ Recent trigger *or* 　○ Most recent adult-onset trauma • Upon resolution, **second** target: 　○ Current triggers (internal and external) *or* 　○ Client's flashbacks *or* 　○ Client's nightmares (whichever is currently most invasive) • Resource development installation is interwoven throughout treatment to strengthen therapeutic gains and support skills needed for adaptive and desired functioning in the future. • IFS can be used to support stabilization and a Self-led system. • Depending on the client's system's integrative capacity and therapeutic gains, the client eventually can move toward the touchstone memory associated with the present symptomology, other traumas from the past connected to the present symptomology, and then the future template.	• To identify parts: 　○ Make a parts map connected to the agreed-upon first target. • Guide the client to befriend these parts. Stabilization occurs through co-regulation with the Self. • In complex trauma systems, parts may need coping skills that align with their autonomic state (hyper/hypoarousal) first before they can receive co-regulation through the Self. • Integrate coping skills that help parts feel connected to support secure attachment and trust with the Self. • EMDR targets emerge naturally through befriending parts that show up as presenting symptoms: 　○ Start with the 6 F's (Schwartz & Sweezy, 2020) 　○ Ask the parts: 　　– "What fears and concerns do you have?" 　　– "What is your job?" 　　– "What are you afraid would happen if you didn't do your job?" (This can reveal the exile and targets for EMDR.) • Get permission from these protector parts prior to transitioning to EMDR reprocessing.

IFS-Informed Treatment Planning Across the Eight Phases of EMDR

In this section, I'll provide a brief overview of an IFS-informed treatment plan spanning the eight phases of EMDR, including how the five IFS principles inform these phases. In phase 1, you are introducing the notion of parts, helping the client access more Self-energy through parts mapping. You are modeling Self and relating to the client's system with compassion. Parts mapping helps scaffold trauma-related emotional intensity by first talking about parts in the client's system to support stabilization and emotion regulation. Parts mapping gives the client a structured, step-by-step approach to help widen their capacity and window of tolerance and supports the client's naming of and discovery process about their own parts. Thus, in phase 1, you are employing the IFS principles "We all have Self and parts" and "All parts are welcome."

In phase 2, you are guiding the client to befriend the parts on the parts map connected to their current symptoms, since those parts are ultimately connected to the touchstone memory. You are identifying relevant coping skills and resources to support a more adaptive nervous system (i.e., more access to Self). You are continuing to support the client's stabilization, building a trusting, nonpathologizing therapeutic relationship, and preparing the client for EMDR reprocessing. In phase 2, you are guiding the process of befriending and employing the IFS principles "Receive consent from protectors first," "The Self-to-part relationship is healing," and "If parts feel understood, they will soften."

In phases 3 through 8, you guide the client to proceed with EMDR reprocessing until resolution of the target. You use IFS interventions as described in the later chapters of this book to help support the client's system in not getting stuck during EMDR reprocessing, and to fully integrate therapeutic gains as the client's system becomes more Self-led as EMDR targets resolve.

Phases 3 through 8 are considered the trauma reprocessing phases of EMDR therapy. In terms of the complex trauma framework, this is where unprocessed memories change to adaptive resolution, which leads to the client's meaning about the targeted trauma changing to be more adaptive. So the client's cognitions, emotions, and body sensations change—the client's exiles unburden—leading to a change in the client's system of parts. The IFS principles "The Self-to-part relationship is healing" and "If parts feel understood, they will soften" are used to navigate the client's system through these phases. As EMDR targets resolve, the client's system naturally becomes more Self-led.

IFS provides a deepening of therapeutic gains achieved in EMDR reprocessing. Throughout the process of EMDR reprocessing and once targets are resolved, the client can return to protectors that were initially befriended as needed, inviting them to change out of those stuck protector roles. This is called the *integration* intervention in IFS. Per the complex trauma treatment framework, once treatment goals are achieved in EMDR, it is important to highlight and support the client in integrating therapeutic gains from EMDR reprocessing into their daily life. The focus of treatment changes to supporting the client's Self-led system in navigating present-day life and preparing for termination.

Considerations When Working with Specific Populations

Now that we have discussed IFS-informed case conceptualization and integrative treatment planning across the eight EMDR phases, we are going to discuss relevant factors in working with neurodiverse populations, marginalized populations, clients with ongoing trauma exposure, and clients with traumatic grief. I will discuss each of these populations and specific considerations in case conceptualization and treatment planning.

Neurodiverse Populations

Neurodiversity shows up as natural traits of a client, not parts or burdens (Christiansen & Martinez-Dettamanti, 2023). Clients who are neurodiverse—whether they have attention-deficit/hyperactivity disorder (ADHD), autism spectrum disorder (ASD), sensory reprocessing issues, or learning differences—can especially benefit from IFS interventions to help elicit self-compassion and foster insight.

During history taking, you want to specifically ask about bullying experiences, rejection, not feeling understood by others, social isolation, and any experiences of being stigmatized, all of which are more commonly experienced by neurodiverse populations (Darker-Smith & Clarke, 2024). You would want to consider these experiences as potential targets for EMDR reprocessing.

An IFS-informed case conceptualization offers a nonpathological view of neurodiversity and would consider neurodiversity a natural aspect of the client's "hardware" (i.e., how the brain is wired) and their internal parts as the "software" (Christiansen & Martinez-Dettamanti, 2023, p. 345). Collaboratively you identify and explore with neurodiverse clients what environmental factors contribute to sensory sensitivities, which can then elicit protector parts that may shut down the client's system. For example, in history taking and in phase 1, you can help the client identify specific things in their life and even in your office (e.g., noise level, lights, smells) that may elicit sensory overwhelm (Christiansen & Martinez-Dettamanti, 2023).

With neurodiverse populations, you will bring in resources traditionally from phase 2 early in phase 1. For example, after you identify anything in your therapeutic setting that may contribute to sensory overwhelm or distraction, you then encourage the client to self-soothe, including utilizing stimming behavior (self-soothing movements common among clients with ASD) and any needed sensory input (e.g., dimming the lights, using a weighted blanket, rocking back and forth) to help establish a sense of safety with you and in your therapeutic setting (Christiansen & Martinez-Dettamanti, 2023).

You and the client can collaboratively map out parts that show up in response to the client's neurodiversity. This can help the client differentiate between traits of their neurodiversity and their parts (Christiansen & Martinez-Dettamanti, 2023). For example, the client may identify:

- Parts with negative self-talk, shame, inner criticism, or negative feelings about a particular diagnosis or how it impacts their life

- Parts that show up when the client is overwhelmed (e.g., irritated or agitated parts that show up when the client is overstimulated; parts that feel ashamed when the client struggles to focus)
- Parts that have pride or feel good about the gifts of their own neurodiverse system

In treatment planning for clients on the autism spectrum, research indicates that flexibility and coping skills to increase cognitive flexibility and decrease rumination are especially important in preparing for EMDR (Fisher et al., 2023). Other recommendations include (Christiansen & Martinez-Dettamanti, 2023; Darker-Smith & Clarke, 2024):

- Finding ways to support autistic clients' window of tolerance, including providing a sense of safety with you and in your office setting using resource development prior to EMDR
- Befriending the parts that show up when a client becomes overstimulated or overwhelmed with sensory input, to help the client understand themself better and elicit self-compassion
- Starting EMDR reprocessing with present-day triggers or future anticipated scenarios (rather than past traumas) to decrease symptoms first, enabling the client to achieve therapeutic gains prior to addressing past traumas

Marginalized Populations and Clients with Ongoing Trauma Exposure

It is important to assess any client for trauma exposure due to discrimination based on any aspect of the client's identity (e.g., race, sexual orientation, gender identity, socioeconomic class, faith, cultural identity, immigration status). This can be done during the intake process using measures such as the Trauma Symptoms of Discrimination Scale (Williams, Osman, et al., 2023). This will help you better understand the client's current trauma exposure; identify current, ongoing stressors; and determine resources to be strengthened prior to EMDR reprocessing. You also want to specifically ask about any coping strategies and coping behaviors the client is using in response to ongoing trauma exposure (i.e., what helps them and what doesn't).

In IFS-informed case conceptualization, you want to consider how ongoing stressors are impacting the client's parts and clinical symptomology. It's important to conceptualize that it is adaptive and a healthy coping mechanism to have protector parts in a state of hypervigilance, as those parts are accurately detecting threat. Thus, in considering the autonomic state parts may be in, when a client has ongoing threats to their safety, dignity, or well-being, you can conceptualize that these protector parts may not be "stuck" in a state (like they can be stuck in an autonomic state from a past trauma), but that protector parts being in a hyperaroused state, for example, is adaptive.

In the parts mapping process in phase 1, you want to ask how the client is coping with these ongoing stressors, and you can map out parts that show up in response to ongoing traumatic stress. While IFS trusts the organic nature of parts that emerge in the client's system in parts mapping, you want to directly acknowledge the client's lived experience of marginalization and coping with ongoing traumatic stress exposure. You may need to overtly ask what parts help them navigate these ongoing stressors, and normalize and affirm any protector parts that emerge for doing their job of helping the client survive, adapt, and cope. This helps strengthen the therapeutic relationship.

In IFS-informed integrative treatment planning, you need to consider regularly assessing the client's safety and include relevant safety plans as needed. If the client is not clinically stable, treatment goals need to include supporting the client's system in maintaining an adaptive nervous system and stabilization. This is done through providing tailored coping skills given the client's unique intersectional factors, helping the client access and strengthen communal support, and providing relevant communal resources. Integrating additional client-centered, culturally based strengths during phase 2 will be discussed further in chapter 5, and additional tools to work with intergenerational trauma and systemic and oppression-based traumas will be discussed further in chapter 6.

When a client has ongoing traumatic exposure, whether it be from ongoing experiences of discrimination or acute threats to their safety, these are considered external constraints that naturally impact the client's parts that are trying to survive and adapt to ongoing trauma exposure. These external constraints may impact the client's capacity (how much stress they can tolerate), whether they are a good candidate for EMDR reprocessing, the appropriate timing of EMDR reprocessing, and which target to start with in EMDR reprocessing.

The clinical goal of befriending parts in phase 2 when a client has ongoing trauma exposure—including when working with marginalized populations coping with anything from microaggressions to targeted violence to systemic barriers—is to help parts be understood and restore trust in Self-leadership. Even if the client is in an unsafe situation or external environment, parts can still restore trust in Self-leadership by the client asking their parts: "What do you need from me right now?"

It is common for clients with complex trauma to view hope as dangerous or to experience specific parts getting activated in response to hope. These frequently show up as blocking beliefs in phase 4 EMDR reprocessing. When these parts show up in therapy, you can use IFS interventions to befriend and witness the part's authentic experience. You can directly ask: "Are there any parts that have fears about having hope?" If parts emerge, guide the client to ask the part: "What does this part want you to know about these fears about having hope?" and "What does this part want to show you or tell you about what it's like to be them?" This can allow space for the client's parts to be witnessed and their truth honored. This will help these parts feel understood and help prepare the client for EMDR reprocessing.

Clients with Traumatic Grief

Grief feelings naturally emerge during trauma reprocessing. For clients who are focusing on a traumatic loss, the grief process can include feelings about what happened during the event, feelings related to the loss of a loved one, and feelings about what did *not* happen (e.g., who did not show up, developmental needs that were not met, and the reality of secondary losses). Treatment planning needs to consider that the client's mental health symptoms will naturally escalate around anniversary death dates and birthdays of the deceased loved one as well as any other times of year that serve as a trauma reminder of the loss. So plan for the client needing more resources during these specific anniversary dates or triggering times of year.

In IFS-informed case conceptualization, when a client is experiencing acute grief, the client's system reorganizes toward adapting to and accepting the loss of the loved one. Oscillations normally occur between the cluster of parts that are feeling the acute pain from the loss and the cluster of parts that are trying to help the client move forward in their life (Scott, 2017). It is also normal for there to be parts in the grieving client that have fears of feeling good or living a full life without their loved one.

Parts mapping may only be minimally helpful for a client who is actively grieving, as their system is actively adapting to the loss. So parts that may show up in a given session are more likely to change from session to session. This is natural and you can normalize this for clients who are grieving. You can conceptualize this as the client's parts not getting stuck in burdened roles but simply feeling the pain and adapting to the reality of the loss.

If a client has prolonged grief disorder or PTSD due to a loss, or has extreme difficulty adapting to the loss, parts mapping can still be therapeutic and normalizing for the client as a first IFS intervention in phase 1. These parts can be befriended and understood using IFS interventions, prior to focusing on the loss in EMDR reprocessing.

Let's now look at a therapist worksheet to guide you through the process of making an IFS-informed case conceptualization and integrative treatment plan. Following the worksheet, you will see a case example of what process this looks like in action. Note that this worksheet includes content about parts mapping, which we will be covering in depth in the next chapter.

Therapist Worksheet

IFS-Informed Case Conceptualization and Integrative Treatment Planning

This worksheet is a comprehensive, hands-on tool to use with clients in phase 1 to form an IFS-informed case conceptualization and integrative treatment plan. Answering the questions will help you apply EMDR's three-pronged approach of identifying potential EMDR targets, the presenting issue, present triggers, and future desired outcomes, along with parts of the client connected to the presenting issue. This worksheet will also help you determine whether this client is a good candidate for EMDR reprocessing, the appropriate timing of doing EMDR reprocessing in treatment, any constraints, and what resources the client will need prior to EMDR reprocessing. Lastly, as you consider all this information, you will identify which target to address first in EMDR reprocessing.

Presenting Symptoms

What are the client's presenting symptoms? (These are parts.)

_____
_____
_____

Identifying Parts

Identify protector parts (managers and firefighters) that will need to be befriended during phase 2 before moving to phases 3 and 4.

Manager Parts

Identify manager parts: Clients tend to overidentify with these parts of themselves. To identify manager parts, consider what the client does to try to keep it together, get through the day, and prevent getting triggered. This can show up as specific thoughts, feelings, or behaviors.

_____
_____
_____

What autonomic state (e.g., hyperarousal, hypoarousal) do managers show up in? (This information comes from the intake and parts mapping and informs what resources will need to be developed in phase 2.)

_____

_____

_____

Future template: Prompt the client: "Tell me about any anticipated future scenarios or events that you are concerned may trigger this presenting issue." Manager parts tend to be the parts worried about the future. This information may reveal a manager part carrying a specific fear about the future. This information can be used when doing a future template in EMDR reprocessing.

_____

_____

_____

Firefighter Parts

Identify firefighter parts: To identify firefighter parts, consider what happens when the client gets triggered. What do they do that helps soothe, distract, or numb them? This can show up as specific thoughts, feelings, or behaviors. Firefighters tend to show up reactively, impulsively, and compulsively. What is the client's impulsive, compulsive, or reactive behavior?

_____

_____

_____

What autonomic state (e.g., hyperarousal, hypoarousal) do firefighters show up in? (This information comes from the intake and parts mapping and informs what resources will need to be developed in phase 2.)

_____

_____

_____

Exiles

Identify exiles: These are potential targets for EMDR reprocessing. During the intake, you identify exiles by directly asking about the most recent trigger of the client's presenting issue; the negative cognitions, feelings, and body sensations that occurred during the most recent trigger (what IFS calls burdens); other past traumas in which the client felt the same way; the first time the client felt this way (the touchstone memory); and the worst incident in which the client felt this way. Consider the following questions: When the client is triggered, what do they feel or think? How does their body respond? What are the most invasive thoughts, feelings, body sensations, or memories for the client? What is the content of the client's flashbacks or nightmares?

_____
_____
_____

Most recent trigger: What is the most recent time/event the presenting issue showed up for the client? Say to the client: "Tell me a specific recent time or event when you experienced anything related to [*name the client's presenting issue*]." This can become the target called "the most recent event" in EMDR reprocessing.

_____
_____
_____

Negative cognition: Ask the client: "When this happened, what words best describe any negative belief you had about yourself? What does that mean about you? What feelings and body sensations showed up when this recent incident happened?" This is identifying negative cognitions/beliefs, feelings, and body sensations (the burdens) of the exile(s) activated in the recent trigger.

_____
_____
_____

Potential past contributing traumas: What experiences from the past are most connected to the client's current experience of the presenting issue (i.e., involved similar negative cognitions/beliefs, feelings, or body sensations)? Ask the client: "Can you think of any other times or events where you had the same beliefs, feelings, or sensations?" This is identifying other memories that may be on the same memory network. This could be the same exile or a group of exiles that carry the same burden/negative cognition/belief. These may organically emerge in EMDR or can become specific EMDR targets.

_____
_____
_____

Touchstone memory: What is the first time the client experienced this negative cognition/belief, feeling, or body sensation? Ask the client: "What is the first time you believed/felt/experienced [*repeat the* *negative cognition/belief, feeling, or body sensation]?"* This can be used as the touchstone memory in EMDR reprocessing.

_____
_____
_____

Worst memory: What is the worst incident in which the client experienced this negative cognition/belief, feeling, or body sensation? Ask the client: "What is the worst time when you believed/felt/experienced [*repeat the negative cognition/belief, feeling, or body sensation*]?" This can be used as the worst memory in EMDR reprocessing.

_____
_____
_____

Exiles can also be identified by the ages the client was when specific traumatic events occurred. Exiles get frozen in time at the age and developmental stage of the client at the time of traumatic events. These specific exiles may or may not be connected to the client's presenting issue. **These are also potential targets for EMDR reprocessing if treatment goals are beyond symptom reduction and if these traumas are connected to the presenting issue.** Write the ages the client was when specific traumatic events occurred.

_____
_____
_____

What autonomic state (e.g., hyperarousal, hypoarousal) do exiles show up in? (This information comes from the intake and parts mapping and informs what resources will need to be developed in phase 2.)

_____
_____
_____

Treatment Goals

What are the client's treatment goals? These are developed collaboratively and mutually agreed upon. Factors that impact treatment goals and treatment planning include whether the client wants symptom reduction or more comprehensive treatment and how long and how frequently the client can be seen in treatment with you.

_____
_____
_____

Future desired outcomes: Ask the client: "How would you like to see yourself handling [*name the presenting issue*] in the future? What would you like to believe? How would you like to feel? How would you like to feel in your body?" **This helps identify positive cognitions. Resources can be developed in phase 2 to support strengthening the positive cognition. This also can be used in a future template in EMDR reprocessing.**

_____
_____
_____

Assessing the Client's Capacity and Constraints

Assess the client's capacity and stability during the intake and parts mapping process.

How stable is the client? Are there any other mental health concerns that need to be addressed before EMDR reprocessing?

_____
_____
_____

How well does the client's system manage stress? How well can they regulate their emotions? Do they have destructive coping behaviors?

_____
_____
_____

Are there any external factors or stressors that make it an unfavorable time to do EMDR?

_____
_____
_____

Factors to assess the client's capacity using parts mapping:

How well can the client differentiate parts of themselves?

_____
_____
_____

How well can the client unblend from a part that is captured on the parts map?

_____
_____
_____

How well can the client access Self? Do they demonstrate any of the 8 C's (curiosity, compassion, calmness, clarity, courage, creativity, confidence, connectedness)?

_____
_____
_____

How well does the client return to Self after being activated or blended with a part? How easily can the client change states and access perspective?

_____
_____
_____

How well does the client stay present in the process of parts mapping? (Do they dissociate or check out? Do they have difficulty maintaining focus during the process?)

_____
_____
_____

How well does the client disclose and describe their internal experiences to you?

_____
_____
_____

Are there any protector parts that show up with concerns about anything disclosed during the intake process or revealed in the parts map? Are there any firefighter parts that react to the process of parts mapping, whether it be about being seen and understood or disclosing about parts on the parts map?

___

What internal constraints does the client have? (These may include medical conditions, comorbidity, etc.)

___

What external constraints does the client have? (These may include ongoing trauma exposure, specific current stressors, environmental stressors, systemic stressors, etc.)

___

What parts show up in response to these constraints? (These parts can initially be identified in a parts map in phase 1, then can be befriended in phase 2.)

___

Based on this information thus far, what resources need to be developed or strengthened in phase 2 before the client will be ready for EMDR trauma reprocessing?

___

Consider what autonomic state parts are in during the intake and parts mapping. What specific resources can help the client if they experience hyperarousal? (These resources will be further explored in phase 2).

_____
_____
_____

What specific resources can help the client if they experience hypoarousal?

_____
_____
_____

Which target will you start with for EMDR reprocessing?

Based on the client's treatment goals, which target would be most beneficial to start with in EMDR reprocessing (e.g., the touchstone memory, the worst memory, the most recent trigger/incident)? If the client has a more complex trauma history, consider starting with the most recent trigger or trauma related to the most invasive clinical symptoms.

_____
_____
_____

CASE EXAMPLE

IFS-Informed Case Conceptualization and Integrative Treatment Planning

Meet Noah

Noah is a 32-year-old Mexican American, heterosexual, cisgender man who is married and has two young children. He was recently diagnosed with PTSD following multiple deployments during his military service. We will be revisiting Noah throughout the book to show you how to apply IFS interventions through integrative EMDR therapy.

Noah's main symptoms are chronic anxiety, flashbacks, nightmares, and suicidal thoughts. His treatment goals are to reduce his PTSD symptoms, decrease his suicidal thoughts, and increase his coping skills to manage PTSD triggers. He is seen for therapy in a time-limited therapy setting. When discussing his trauma history, Noah reveals a history of multiple traumatic events and situations, including ongoing physical abuse as a child and being bullied during adolescence. In terms of constraints, he expresses current financial stress and strained relationships with his family of origin. His future desired states are to feel more at ease when triggered and more confident in navigating stress.

Given that Noah has suicidal thoughts, the therapist does a risk assessment and obtains a history of his suicidal behavior, including what led to his first suicidal thought. This can be added to the potential EMDR target list. Noah has suicidal thoughts, yet no plan or intent to self-harm. He agrees to use a crisis hotline as needed should he have a plan or intent to self-harm between sessions. The therapist then gives Noah a dissociative screener and conducts a full clinical intake. Noah's dissociative screener indicates normative dissociative experiences; therefore, a formal assessment for a dissociative disorder is not warranted.

Given Noah's ethnicity, the therapist also conducts a racial trauma assessment. Noah reports that English is his second language and that some of the bullying he experienced during adolescence was due to having an accent.

Noah reports that the most invasive symptoms are his flashbacks and nightmares. The therapist asks briefly about the content of these flashbacks and nightmares, and Noah shares that they are memories related to his military deployments. Thus, the therapist conceptualizes that the parts most relevant to Noah's PTSD symptoms are related to traumas experienced during his military deployments (i.e., adult traumas). Given this, the therapist determines that Noah's first EMDR target needs to be focused on his traumatic experiences during his deployments.

The therapists asks Noah what words best describe any negative belief about himself based on his most recent trigger to determine what Noah believes this means about him. Noah shares that "I'm bad" was the negative belief he most believed during his recent trigger. The therapist also explores what emotions and body sensations Noah experienced when he was most recently triggered. Noah describes having felt suddenly anxious, ashamed, and "jumpy" and that his heart was "pounding" in his body. This helps the therapist identify the autonomic states of Noah's exiles so that specific coping skills can be identified to help him move out of a specific autonomic state. The therapist conceptualizes that Noah's exiles may be stuck in hyperarousal based on his anxiety and body sensations and given that his most common symptom is anxiety.

To identify potential targets for EMDR reprocessing, the therapist asks about the first time Noah experienced "I'm bad" (i.e., the touchstone memory, which may or may not be during his military deployments). Noah discloses a memory from childhood of being beaten by his father when he was five. The therapist also asks him to identify the worst memory in which he felt "I'm bad," other past traumatic experiences in which he felt this way, and other present triggers. The bulk of what Noah shares are traumatic memories from his deployments.

Next the therapist provides psychoeducation about PTSD and the nervous system, including that anxiety can be indicative of a fight-or-flight response of the sympathetic nervous system. Noah reports that he finds this information helpful. The therapist discusses general coping skills to help with acute anxiety and hyperarousal symptoms and explains that before beginning EMDR reprocessing, they will identify more coping skills and build resources to help him better manage his symptoms.

The therapist uses parts language and explains that parts that help protect us during a trauma can be stuck in a protector mode, even after the trauma is over. The therapist also provides psychoeducation on EMDR, including side effects, benefits, and what to expect in treatment. Last, the therapist and Noah discuss the treatment plan, and the therapist explains that the timing of when they start EMDR reprocessing may change as the therapist gets to know Noah better.

Applying an IFS-Informed Case Conceptualization

In applying an IFS lens to Noah's case, there is a system of parts trying to keep his traumatic experiences related to deployment from being felt in the system. The therapist hypothesizes that Noah has an anxious part, a part expressing itself through flashbacks, a part expressing itself through nightmares, and a part that is giving him suicidal thoughts.

In clients with PTSD, exiles tend to express themselves through traumatic memories, either through flashbacks when the client is awake or through nightmares when the client is asleep. Noah's therapist hypothesizes that these parts in Noah's system are exiles and that the anxious part and suicidal part are protector parts. Based on his trauma history, the therapist considers Noah a client with a complex trauma history and chooses an IFS-integrative approach to support further stabilization, resourcing, and learning more about Noah's system of parts before proceeding with EMDR reprocessing.

Noah's IFS-Informed Integrative Treatment Plan

The therapist and Noah discuss and agree upon the treatment plan, which includes doing parts mapping in the next session to learn about parts of Noah that are connected to his current symptoms. Then, with Noah's consent, the therapist can guide him to befriend these parts. The befriending process will further help support his stabilization and symptom reduction and help Noah practice resources and coping skills to ultimately prepare him for EMDR reprocessing on traumas from his deployments. Once Noah has coping skills, and with the consent of his protector parts, he will then proceed with phases 3 through 8 of EMDR reprocessing.

Noah's First EMDR Target

Because (1) Noah's most invasive symptoms are flashbacks and nightmares related to his military deployment, (2) his main treatment goal is PTSD symptom reduction, and (3) he is being seen for time-limited treatment, the therapist and Noah agree to focus on his military trauma in EMDR reprocessing. This choice aligns with the "Target Sequencing Chart for EMDR Reprocessing" (page 38), which indicates that for a client with a complex trauma history, like Noah, EMDR reprocessing can start with either the most recent trigger or the most recent adult trauma (which in Noah's case were traumas during his military deployments). In other words, instead of focusing on the touchstone memory of the negative cognition "I'm bad," which Noah associated with childhood traumatic memories, the therapist and Noah can decide to focus on the worst traumatic memory of his military trauma. The therapist can confirm this decision as they get closer to beginning EMDR (based on the consent of his protectors and whether this results in the highest SUDs rating during phase 3). The therapist can then check in with Noah to see how this information is landing for him and if he has any questions.

CHAPTER 3

Parts Mapping During Phase 1

Now that you have an understanding of IFS-informed case conceptualization and an IFS-integrative approach to EMDR treatment planning, we'll begin to delve into the first IFS intervention to use with clients: parts mapping. I'll provide you with several types of parts maps and explain their purpose. I'll also give you some case examples of what different parts maps can look like and therapist scripts to help you create parts maps with your own clients.

Parts Mapping: Benefits and Functions

Parts mapping is an IFS intervention that involves the creation of any visual, external representation of one or more parts'—or a system of parts'—relationship with each other in the client's internal system. This key intervention has many benefits, including making parts conscious, helping clients access Self, and facilitating the IFS interventions of contracting and befriending.

When integrated into EMDR therapy, parts mapping in phase 1 facilitates the process of IFS and EMDR therapy in numerous ways. Specifically, parts mapping:

- Offers a simple way to make the notion of parts tangible to the client
- Builds working alliance so the client can experience feeling heard and understood by you
- Helps the client unblend from their parts (i.e., not be overpowered by them) so they can gain more access to Self
- Titrates arousal dysregulation early in therapy
- Identifies and clarifies which parts to befriend (see chapter 4 for IFS befriending techniques)
- Provides a visual anchor for consistency between sessions
- Can be used at the beginning of a session to identify parts to befriend or at the end of the session to help summarize and organize what emerged in the session
- Serves to help the client transition from talking about parts to *being with* their parts in phase 2
- Reveals potential targets for EMDR trauma reprocessing

Benefits of Parts Mapping in Phase 1

In phase 1, you invite clients to talk about parts on the parts map, which helps the client become more aware of their parts and limits how much activation (arousal of their nervous system) may happen in session. Talking about parts on the parts map gives the client more internal distance from their parts to help them access Self from their own system. You and the client are collaboratively creating a parts map, which helps strengthen the therapeutic relationship by you attuning to the client and the client feeling understood. You are modeling how to approach the parts map with curiosity and nonjudgment from a place of wanting to understand the client's parts—that is, you are leading this process from your own Self-led system.

In addition to both you and the client learning more about the client's parts on the parts map, you also get the opportunity to see how their internal system reacts or responds to different parts being identified on the parts map. The parts identified on the parts map may not be conscious for the client. So clients may discover parts for the first time, which may make them feel vulnerable.

In clients with complex trauma histories, there may be parts that have adaptively been self-sufficient in trying to "keep it together" and "look okay" to others even though internally they may not be feeling okay. The more trauma a client has experienced, the more parts in the system are likely to be in burdened roles trying to help the client survive in the way they know how. There may be protector parts that have a strong reaction to what is disclosed in therapy. Particularly if clients have trauma histories in which they had to keep family secrets or there was a rule to keep their abuse or trauma a secret, disclosing parts out loud to you in therapy may feel scary or threatening to some parts in the client's system that have worked hard to keep things hidden from others. Talking about parts on the parts map helps the client gradually identify parts in their internal system with less chance of the process being overwhelming or leading to backlash.

You are trying to support the client to talk about their parts in a way that helps them stay present in the process. From a brain perspective, you are trying to keep their prefrontal cortex online by talking about parts first before moving to the IFS befriending intervention of the client relationally *being with* their parts in phase 2. This helps the client maintain awareness of what they are learning about their system in therapy and integrate it in their life.

Benefits of Parts Mapping Within the Integrative Treatment Plan

Used in phase 1, parts mapping gives you clinical information to help you determine whether a client is a good candidate for EMDR and their readiness for EMDR reprocessing—critical elements of the treatment plan. Through the parts mapping process, you can learn about the client's capacity and stability, the level of complexity of their internal system, and the client's ability to share with you about their internal experience. These are all important determinants of whether the client can therapeutically benefit from EMDR, and if so, parts mapping helps identify what inner work may need to happen first in phase 2 to prepare the client for EMDR reprocessing in phases 3 through 8.

Parts mapping can be used for any type of client with any clinical presentation. It helps you gather clinical information about the client's capacity to tolerate internal stress, take in new information, use new information learned in therapy, and stay present in the process, all of which inform treatment planning. You are learning how much a client can unblend (not be merged with a part), which helps you determine how well they can change states and what state change looks like for them (e.g., can they access a ventral vagal state?). As we discussed in chapter 2, parts may show up with various levels of autonomic nervous system arousal. Learning how much distance a client can have from the parts on the parts map in order to talk about them (rather than the client *being* the part) will let you know the client's capability to access more Self. With this clinical information, you can then better identify resources that may need further development in phase 2 before beginning EMDR reprocessing (in phases 3 through 8). All of this information helps you determine the client's readiness for EMDR and the timing of EMDR reprocessing that will best serve the client.

Through parts mapping, you also are learning about the client's stability. When a client discloses their trauma history, they may feel vulnerable, which may inadvertently activate an exile connected to a specific trauma. This can cause a ripple effect in the internal system, resulting in a backlash. When a backlash happens, a firefighter part or group of firefighter parts reactively and protectively take over the system, which can lead to potential clinical decompensation. If a client experiences any backlash in their system in the parts mapping process, you will observe how well they can self-regulate and what resources they use to self-soothe. You can also identify what additional resources are needed to support the client's ability to regulate their emotions and stabilize, which you then focus on in phase 2. By shedding light on the client's capacity and how stable they are, the process of parts mapping helps you better determine whether they are a good candidate for EMDR and how ready they are for trauma reprocessing.

If a client begins therapy with low capacity for stress or with instability, parts mapping can support client stabilization by helping increase the client's understanding of what is happening internally in their system. By talking with the client about parts once the parts map is created, you are providing a structure for the client that helps them orient to their internal world, gain perspective, and titrate emotional intensity, which supports stabilization. In other words, talking about a system of parts or one part at a time first during phase 1 can provide the client with a dose of introspection and self-reflection with less chance of it overwhelming the client. If medication is needed for stability, note that according to IFS theory, medication is seen as supporting protector parts so they do not have to work so hard and bolstering the client's capacity to access their own Self-energy (Anderson, 2021). You will also include in the treatment plan a focus on coping skills and resource development early in therapy to support stabilization, as we'll discuss in chapter 5.

Parts mapping also enables you to clinically assess whether the client can share with you what is happening internally in their system. Relationally, this may feel vulnerable to clients who have relational trauma histories or significant attachment trauma. This is important to learn about the client because, for EMDR to be beneficial, the client needs to be able to give you accurate feedback about their internal experience when they do EMDR reprocessing.

Finally, the shared task of creating and fine-tuning the parts map can feel very validating for clients and help them feel seen and understood by you. If the client has difficulty doing this shared task or describing their internal experience, more clinical work may need to be done first to develop trust in the therapeutic relationship and support the client in self-reflection and introspection (e.g., Can they identify what emotions their parts are feeling using a feelings wheel or a group of images of faces? Can they make a parts map privately?).

How to Make a Parts Map

Parts maps can be made using a variety of methods and media. They can include a visual of several parts, the relationship between the parts, or the sequence in which parts emerge. They can be drawn on paper or a whiteboard (either in the office or on a telehealth platform), and they also can be made using a sand tray, art materials, or other objects in the therapy room or the client's home that represent different parts of them. These latter options are particularly helpful to clients that may need some tactical or sensory input to help them stay present in the process.

The simplest way to introduce a parts map is to explain to the client that you are going to draw a visual diagram of what parts of the client you are hearing the client describe. This can be done within the first few sessions or as the therapeutic relationship is forming over the course of phase 1, after the client shares about their experience since their last appointment. You are using your "parts detector" to help the client differentiate parts within their own internal system, and then drawing them on the map. You then ask the client if the parts in the parts map resonate for the client or if the parts map needs to be altered to best reflect their experience. This collaborative process enables you to make sure that the parts map accurately mirrors the client's experience. The following instructions can help guide you in making a parts map with a client.

Parts Mapping Process

- **Say:** "I'm going to draw out what you are sharing with me so that we can talk more about it."
- After the client shares, draw out a visual representation to reflect back parts you heard. Show the client the parts map.
- **Say:** "These are the parts of you that I heard you describe." (Use the language the client used to describe the parts displayed on the parts map.)
- **Ask:** "Does this resonate for you? Does it feel like I'm getting it? Give me some feedback so I know if what I wrote is accurately capturing these parts of you. Let me know if anything needs to be added or changed about this."
- Adjust the parts map accordingly as the client gives you feedback. You can also ask the client if they would like to take over the parts map process to give them a choice about who is making the parts map.
- **Ask:** "Would you like to draw or add anything more about these parts of you?"

Once the parts map has been created, you then describe how it can be used in the client's therapy. You will see in the next section how to do this with different types of parts maps.

Parts Mapping for Different Functions

Parts mapping has different uses and functions. You have the choice about which parts map to use throughout phase 1. You may want to use several different types of maps with the same client, given that each map has a different purpose, or you may find that one type of map is best for a particular client, while another type is useful for another client. Different parts maps may elicit different levels of arousal in the client's nervous system due to parts becoming more conscious. The table "Impact of Parts Mapping on the Client's Arousal and Activation" (which appears later in this chapter, on page 71) can help you decide which parts map is the best fit for a given client.

There are five main functions of parts mapping:

1. To build working alliance and support stabilization
2. To identify parts connected to the presenting issue
3. To track sequences of the client's system
4. To open or close a session
5. To create a visualization statement

For each function, I'll describe the parts mapping process and—for all but one function—present a case example that includes a parts map. At the end of the chapter you'll find therapist scripts for using each type of parts map.

Note that with the exception of the last function (to create a visualization statement), you are the one initially creating a visual of the parts map. At any point, this can be handed over to the client to draw or add to the parts map. Many clients with complex trauma histories are blended, making it challenging for them to access their own Self-energy and differentiate their parts from one another. Thus, initially offering a visual parts map can serve as a first step in helping both you and the client to differentiate one part from another in the client's system and then collaboratively work together on making sure the parts map mirrors the client's experience.

1. Using Parts Mapping to Build Working Alliance and Support Stabilization

A parts map for building working alliance is used early in phase 1, ideally at the end of the intake session or during the second session.

Begin by asking the client two questions: "Do you have any fears and concerns about starting therapy? Do you have any fears or concerns about anything you shared during the intake process?" Then draw any parts with concerns on the parts map. Providing a visual diagram of what the client said lets them know you hear their concerns. Relationally, this communicates that you are present and that the client's experience, including their fears, matters. This process helps set up a therapeutic relationship affirming that the client is welcome to voice any concerns and that you will attend to any concerns. It helps builds working alliance by communicating that the client's concerns matter, whether they be about starting therapy or something they disclosed during the intake process.

Including on the parts map the client's concerns about starting therapy helps the client gain more perspective by seeing an external representation of their parts. This helps them become more aware of and less blended with their parts. Additionally, it enables you to therapeutically respond to any of their concerns and to normalize and validate the client's fears about starting therapy. This gives you an opportunity to provide any needed psychoeducation about the therapy process or what to expect.

Asking the client if any parts of them have fears or concerns about anything they shared during the intake process helps them become conscious of any protector parts in their system. By reflecting these parts on a parts map, the client can further explore and talk about any fears around what was disclosed during the intake process, or how that information will be used in therapy. This gives you the opportunity to respond to these concerns and provide psychoeducation about how information from the intake process will be therapeutically used throughout treatment. This also helps support stabilization by preventing backlash in the client's system. Protector parts that may be activated from the intake process itself can be acknowledged and their fears discussed, minimizing the need for them to take over the system due to their feeling bypassed in the intake process.

CASE EXAMPLE

Using Parts Mapping to Build Working Alliance and Support Stabilization

Let's revisit Noah, our case example from chapter 2. Remember that Noah has been diagnosed with PTSD related to his military deployments and that he disclosed suicidal ideation during his intake. Using this parts map, Noah's therapist asks him if he has any fears or concerns about starting therapy or about anything he disclosed during the intake process. Noah reports that he has no concerns about starting therapy but that he has some embarrassment and shame about having suicidal thoughts. Noah's therapist shares that having an external representation of these parts on a parts map can be helpful for Noah to gain perspective and learn more about his internal experience.

Noah's parts map simply depicts the part that has some embarrassment and shame in response to the part of him that has suicidal thoughts. Noah's therapist draws an arrow to reflect that the shame and embarrassment occur internally in response to suicidal thoughts. Because it can also be helpful to draw a symbol to represent the client's Self, the therapist draws a heart to introduce the notion that these parts aren't all of Noah; they are just parts of him.

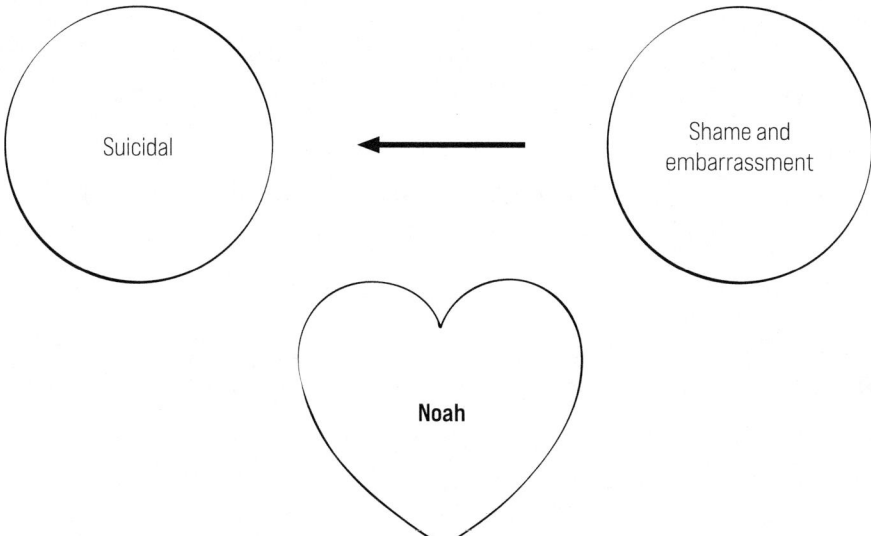

Once Noah confirms that this parts map resonates for him, Noah's therapist asks about any other times he notices the shame and embarrassment. The therapist normalizes Noah's experience and asks more about what it means to him that he is having suicidal thoughts. The therapist then reaffirms the importance of sharing these parts in therapy so that Noah knows he is not alone in trying to cope with suicidal thoughts and the feelings of shame and embarrassment. The therapist introduces coping skills for when he has these thoughts or feelings.

It is common for complex trauma clients to become dysregulated during the history-taking process of therapy. Using this type of parts map can help decrease arousal in the client's system and help the client gain space from their parts so they can have more access to Self. If you sense your client is getting overwhelmed or starts dissociating during the history-taking process, you can use this parts map to titrate history taking. For example, you can say: "I am aware that you have been sharing some important personal details about your history. I just want to pause and check in. It is normal for parts of you to show up when sharing your personal history. Check inside and see: Are there any parts of you that are having a reaction to anything that you have shared so far?"

You can draw circles and label each part per the client's description and provide support to the client before returning to history taking.

2. Using Parts Mapping to Identify Parts Connected to the Client's Presenting Issue

An important function of parts mapping, early in therapy, is to help the client gain insight into what is bringing them to therapy, using an IFS lens. As you reflect to the client their presenting problem, you draw the parts map and ask the client if it resonates for them (this will be described in more detail in the therapist script on page 74).

This relational attunement to the client's parts that are connected to their presenting problem aligns with the affirming IFS principle "All parts are welcome," which can strengthen the therapeutic relationship by not pathologizing any part in the client's system. You model that you are not trying to get rid of any parts by making this parts map, but are trying to understand them. This helps the client gain perspective that what is bringing them to therapy is connected to a part or parts of them, but is not all of them. This can help minimize shame and instill hope in the client that their presenting issue can be addressed in therapy.

After you make this parts map, you can then transition to further adjust the treatment plan (e.g., the timing of EMDR reprocessing based on the client's stability), explain how you will be integrating an IFS approach into EMDR therapy, set up a mutual agreement that in therapy you will be returning to these parts to get to know them better (i.e., befriending), and identify potential EMDR targets for therapy.

CASE EXAMPLE

Using Parts Mapping to Identify Parts Connected to the Client's Presenting Issue

Let's now see what this form of parts mapping looks like with Noah. Given that Noah's treatment goals are focused on symptom reduction, this map would most efficiently help identify and acknowledge parts connected to his current symptoms in order to then move to preparing him for EMDR reprocessing in phase 2.

Noah's therapist draws a circle for each symptom to represent a part. Similar to the first parts map, Noah's therapist draws a heart symbol to represent the client's Self, to continue to affirm that these parts aren't all of Noah, just parts of him. The therapist includes the parts identified in the previous parts map (shame and embarrassment, in response to the suicidal part), and adds parts to reflect Noah's presenting problems, which he describes as anxiety, flashbacks, and nightmares. The therapist shares this parts map with Noah and asks for his feedback to attune to his internal experience. Once Noah confirms that the parts map accurately acknowledges the parts connected to his symptoms, Noah's therapist and Noah talk more about each part, finding out more clinical information as to present-day triggers, when they show up, and how Noah tries to cope with his symptoms. The therapist then adds information about Noah's current triggers to the EMDR target list that was started during the intake process.

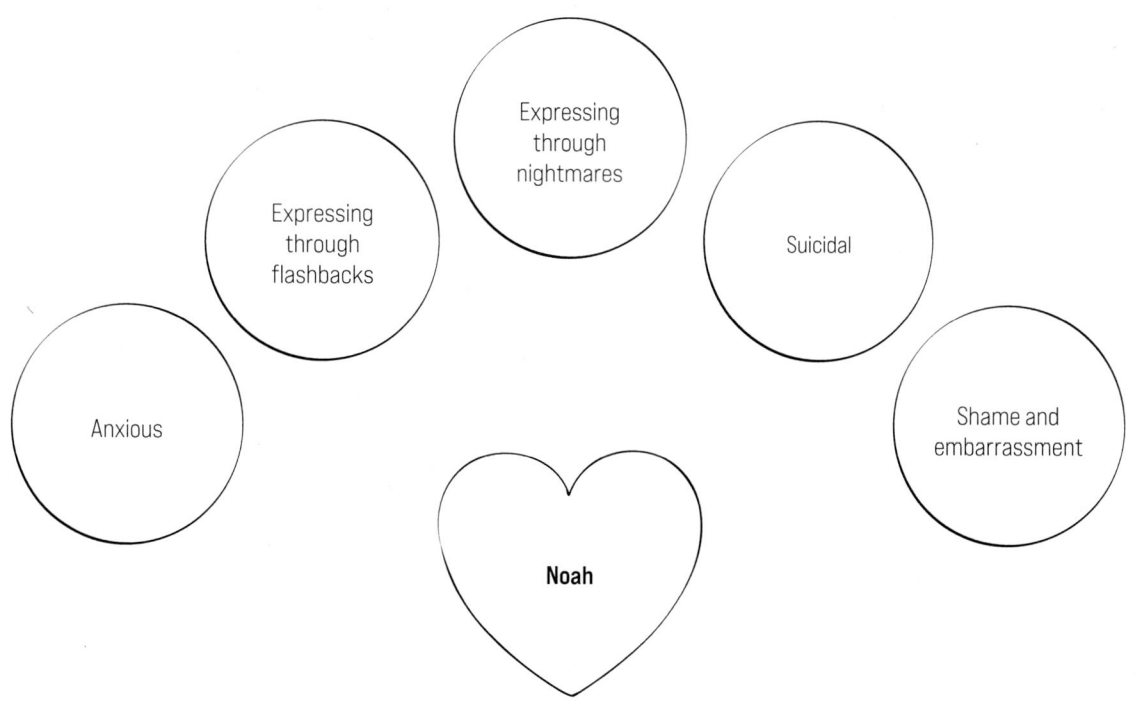

3. Using Parts Mapping to Track Sequences of the Client's System

Parts mapping can also be used to track sequences of the client's emotional, cognitive, somatic, and behavioral responses. This can validate the client's internal experience and help both you and the client notice patterns of the same parts showing up repeatedly. This is particularly helpful for clients who may have less awareness of their internal system, may have low insight, or may be unable to notice their own patterns of thoughts, feelings, body sensations, or behaviors. Potential EMDR targets can be revealed through this process and added to the client's potential EMDR target list.

Using parts mapping for this purpose helps you identify the specific order in which parts show up. For clients with complex trauma histories, it can be particularly useful to identify the sequence of parts that show up when there is a trauma trigger, including the sequence of parts that attempt to help the client cope when triggered (i.e., firefighter parts). After a client discloses in a session that they were triggered, you can make this parts map with the client to identify and track the sequences of parts that were activated by the trigger. To start making this parts map, you can simply say: "Talk me through what you experienced when you were last triggered. I am going to draw this out so that we can talk about it." As the client speaks, you draw parts for each response that happened after a trigger.

Using parts mapping to track sequences of parts can be particularly helpful in working with clients with active addictions, self-harm, or suicidality. From an IFS lens, these behaviors and thoughts are firefighter parts trying to help the client self-soothe through numbing, distracting, or ceasing to feel the pain. Hierarchies are common in firefighter systems (Schwartz & Sweezy, 2020). This means that if one firefighter part does not soothe the system, another firefighter part will step in, and so on until the client isn't feeling emotional pain in their system. This parts map can help the client gain more awareness about their firefighters' efforts to self-soothe. Clinically, gathering this information is helpful to better determine any necessary stabilization resources the client needs in relationship to their firefighter parts and the client's readiness and timing of EMDR reprocessing in their treatment (as the client needs stability first, before moving to EMDR reprocessing).

If you feel confused about where the client is in the therapy process as a whole or are asking yourself "What do I do?" with a client, parts mapping for sequencing is a helpful, collaborative therapy task that can reestablish "what are we doing" and "where are we going." After making this parts map, you can revisit the treatment plan and discuss how you can use this parts map in therapy as an anchor for giving you direction in therapy. By talking about these parts first, you can invite the client to begin to notice how these parts show up in their daily life or when they are triggered. Clinically, you are able to see how well the client can integrate what they are learning about their internal system through parts mapping outside of therapy. This further helps you determine whether they are a good candidate for EMDR and their readiness for EMDR reprocessing.

Relationally, you are demonstrating curiosity about the relationship between the parts (being Self-led in your own system when you do this with a client). You are not telling the client what their parts are or what the relationships between them are, but you are offering this visual representation to try to mirror what is happening internally for the client and are open to their feedback if it needs to be changed.

> **CASE EXAMPLE**
>
> # Using Parts Mapping to Track Sequences of the Client's System
>
> To explore this type of parts map, let's turn to a new case example.
>
> ## Meet Ava
>
> Ava is a 55-year-old African American, heterosexual, cisgender woman who has been diagnosed with complex PTSD and MDD, which stem from childhood sexual abuse from her father that occurred frequently from age 5 through age 12. Ava has been in a 25-year marriage and describes feeling "flat" and disconnected in her marriage. She reports that both of her parents were emotionally abusive throughout her life. She physically cared for her father when he aged until his death two years ago. In addition to CPTSD and MDD symptoms, she reports frequent emotional dysregulation, low self-esteem, and frequent relational triggers. When these relational triggers occur, she consistently has multiple reactions including physical pain, anger, and feeling flat. Additionally, Ava reports that she has been gaining weight and does not understand why.
>
> Ava expresses that her desired outcomes are to resolve her CPTSD and to feel empowered to be herself, use her voice, and navigate any triggers with ease. Her treatment goals are to decrease her CPTSD symptoms, improve her communication and sense of connection in her marriage, and increase her emotion regulation coping skills. Ava communicates during the intake that she is interested in comprehensive trauma treatment (i.e., not solely symptom reduction, but resolution of CPTSD) and commits to long-term therapy.
>
> Due to her complex trauma history, Ava's therapist decides to use an integrative IFS and EMDR treatment approach. In developing the treatment plan, Ava's therapist consults the "Target Sequencing Chart for EMDR Reprocessing" (see page 38) and considers that the first EMDR targets can be current triggers given Ava's lifetime of emotional abuse, her prolonged childhood sexual abuse, her long-term caretaker role of her father (who was also her perpetrator), and multiple relational current triggers.
>
> The therapist has various options for making Ava's parts map, including those described next. For the purpose of this case example, I'll demonstrate each option as if the therapist has chosen that method.
>
> ## Option 1: The therapist draws parts on a whiteboard.
>
> Due to Ava's symptom complexity, Ava's therapist chooses this type of parts map to begin to identify parts that show up regularly for Ava. In her first parts map, the therapist asks Ava to describe her response to a recent conflict with her spouse. Ava describes that after a conflict, she noticed she was feeling sad. The therapist initially draws a circle on the whiteboard to represent a sad part.
>
> After seeing this visual representation of her sad part, Ava reports feeling frustrated when she feels sad. The therapist draws a circle to represent a frustrated part. The therapist then asks Ava what it is like to see these parts on the whiteboard and if the parts map resonates for her or if anything needs to be changed. After Ava confirms that the parts map is accurate, the therapist adds a zigzag arrow, a family genogram symbol, to show that the frustrated part is in conflict with the sad part, explaining what this symbol means and asking for feedback about whether Ava experiences this. The therapist and Ava talk about when and where she

notices this pattern of parts showing up and how they impact her life and clinical symptoms. Based on their discussion, the therapist adds specific triggers to the potential EMDR target list.

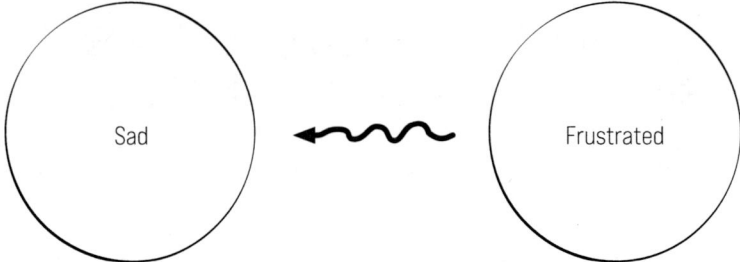

Parts maps can be added to as the client gains more insight about familiar patterns of their thoughts, feelings, and behavior. Let's see how Ava's therapist uses this parts map over time in phase 1.

As Ava's window of tolerance widens, as trust is built in the therapeutic relationship, and as she becomes used to the structure of parts mapping to increase her awareness, Ava becomes better able to identify and notice her own internal experience. She shares how familiar the feelings of frustration and sadness are to her. She becomes more aware of what she feels and what she behaviorally does when she has relational triggers with her husband between sessions. Importantly, she notices more parts between her experience of sadness and frustration. Ava and her therapist draw a parts map to identify these parts:

Ava's therapist provides positive feedback that Ava is becoming more aware of her internal system of parts that show up as regularly as a pattern of parts when she is relationally triggered. Ava and her therapist discuss what it was like to share this parts map with the therapist and to discover this pattern of parts. These process-oriented inquiries support Ava's staying present during the therapeutic process and integrate the insight, therapeutic gains, and what she is learning about her internal system.

Option 2: The client uses crayons or markers to draw parts.

Ava's therapist felt that this approach would be especially helpful to Ava because she had initial difficulty verbalizing her internal experience of the recent conflict with her husband. Ava draws a frustrated part in red (at the bottom of the image) and a sad part in blue (at the top). Ava's therapist uses the parts map to further explore with Ava when she notices these parts showing up (e.g., particular times of day, settings, or relational triggers). The therapist then adds specific triggers to the potential EMDR target list.

Option 3: The client uses objects around the room to represent parts.

Ava's therapist feels that having some tactical or sensory input will help Ava stay present in the process of making a parts map, so the therapist invites Ava to use objects around the room that represent her parts. Ava chooses a lion stuffed animal to represent her frustrated part, which Ava describes can come out aggressively like a lion. Ava then chooses a vase of stones to represent her sad part, which feels stuck and heavy.

This case illustrates how Ava's therapist can choose which medium to use to best serve Ava as she identifies parts and their relationships with each other. As you can see, each option mirrors and externalizes Ava's parts to help track sequences in her system.

4. Using Parts Mapping to Open or Close a Session

Using parts mapping at the beginning of the session can help you and the client focus on whatever occurred since the last session. It can also be very helpful for clients who may repetitively share stories or just talk, as it gives direction and structure to the rest of the session and an opportunity for deeper introspection and identifying more information about the parts on the parts map. Introducing parts mapping at the beginning of the session gives you the option of then transitioning to using the parts map to identify parts connected to the presenting issue or to track sequences of the client. As you and the client collaboratively identify parts in the client's system through parts mapping, you also have the opportunity to provide psychoeducation about the impact of trauma on the nervous system—if you have not already done so—to help normalize the client's internal experience.

Using parts mapping at the end of the session can support integration by providing a summary of what parts emerged. You can then discuss returning to the parts map in the next session to further learn about the parts that emerged. This helps with continuity between sessions, which is particularly beneficial for clients with complex trauma histories. This also provides a structured focus for reviewing what happened in the session and gives the client an opportunity to self-reflect on insights gained. Using a parts map at the end of the session is particularly helpful for clients who may be scattered or unfocused or who may oscillate between being blended with different parts. This can help the client end the session in a more stable state, as naming the parts on the parts map that emerged during the session helps the client unblend from them and access more Self.

5. Using Parts Mapping to Create a Visualization Statement

The final use of parts mapping is to guide the client to make a visualization statement. You can think of the visualization statement as what the client wants the future version of themselves to look like by the end of therapy. You can also use this to identify the client's desired future outcomes, as discussed on the therapist worksheet "IFS-Informed Case Conceptualization and Integrative Treatment Planning" (page 44). A visualization statement also helps you and the client identify protector parts and potential EMDR targets.

Making a parts map for this purpose is excellent for clients who may have a difficult time trusting therapy and who benefit from feeling in control of the parts mapping process. It can also be helpful for clients who tend to overthink things, be easily distracted, have low insight, or have difficulty putting their internal experience into words. Keep in mind that this type of parts map may elicit the most arousal in the client's nervous system due to parts that are likely initially unconscious to the client becoming conscious and represented in whatever way they want to be represented on the page.

CASE EXAMPLE

Using Parts Mapping to Create a Visualization Statement

Meet Zoe

Zoe is a 20-year-old, White, cisgender, bisexual single woman who has been diagnosed with GAD and ADHD. Zoe works part-time and is a full-time college student. She sought therapy to help her decrease the anxiety she experiences from relational triggers at work and decrease her emotional overwhelm in trying to get her schoolwork done. Zoe has experienced single-incident trauma from being sexually assaulted when she was 15 years old. Zoe reported that her anxiety started after her sexual assault.

Using parts mapping to create a visualization statement is a good fit for Zoe due to her tendency to be easily distracted as a result of her ADHD. For this type of parts map, Zoe will be in control of the process, which will help her stay present and engaged. Zoe's therapist explains what a visualization statement is and invites Zoe to create one. Zoe shares that her visualization statement is "I can feel and move through my feelings without getting overwhelmed. I can handle my feelings."

Zoe's therapist then guides her through using this parts map by asking Zoe to repeat her visualization statement aloud. The therapist asks her to notice if there are any parts with fears or concerns about this vision coming true, then to internally ask the part how it would want to be represented on the page. Zoe draws what she calls a "judge" part that is self-critical, then another part that she notices is scared of her feelings. Lastly, Zoe's therapist asks her, "If there were one vulnerable part that, if it got help in therapy, would have the biggest positive impact on helping this vision come true, what part would that be?" Zoe identifies a vulnerable part that she senses is overwhelmed by her many feelings. She draws that part on the page as well.

From this parts map, Zoe and her therapist become aware of parts connected to her visualization statement, giving them direction for which parts to talk more about in phase 1 and then befriend in phase 2. Zoe's therapist conceptualizes that the judge part and the part that's scared of her feelings are protectors and the vulnerable part is an exile. The therapist notes that the exile's sense of overwhelm can be a potential target for EMDR reprocessing.

Vision statement: I can feel and move through my feelings without getting overwhelmed. I can handle my feelings.

Which Parts Mapping Function to Choose?

As you've seen, you can use parts maps for different therapeutic purposes. Parts mapping as an initial IFS intervention helps both you and the client get to know parts within the client's system. The more complex the client's trauma history is or the more difficulty the client has in accessing Self, the more helpful it is to start using parts maps early in therapy. This will enable you to build a working alliance, foster trust in the therapeutic relationship, support the client in accessing Self, and observe how the client's system responds to parts being acknowledged. This can also help you determine whether the client is a good candidate for EMDR and how ready they are for EMDR reprocessing. Keep in mind that the more access the client has to their own Self-energy, the more autonomic arousal their system can tolerate, and the more likely the client will be a good candidate and more ready for EMDR reprocessing.

The following table describes how each function of parts mapping impacts the client's arousal and activation. This will help you choose which might be most beneficial with a given client or in light of where the client is in the therapeutic process.

On the next several pages are therapist scripts to guide you in using parts maps for the various functions we've discussed throughout this chapter.

Impact of Parts Mapping on the Client's Arousal and Activation

Potential arousal (stress) ← (decreasing from top to bottom)

Parts Mapping Function	Level of Potential Arousal and Activation
• To create a visualization statement for reaching therapy goals and to identify EMDR targets	By guiding the client to ask the part directly, "How do you want to be represented on the page?" more unconscious material is made conscious. While this may be stabilizing for some systems, it can potentially activate exiles. When exiles are activated without enough Self-energy, the client may feel emotionally overwhelmed and experience increased activation of their sympathetic or dorsal vagal system, which can lead to clinical destabilization due to reactive firefighter parts getting triggered.
• To track sequences of the client's system for complex trauma and to identify potential EMDR targets	This use of parts mapping involves talking with your client about sequences and gathering more information about the client's reactions and trauma triggers, which can be incorporated into a list of potential targets for EMDR reprocessing. This may initially elicit more arousal in the client's nervous system as parts that may have been unconscious become identified. However, externalizing parts on the parts map can offer a means to decrease emotional or somatic arousal.
• To ask about fears and concerns about starting therapy or what was disclosed during the intake process • To identify and talk about parts connected to the presenting problem • To begin a session • To close a session	These four uses of parts maps involve initially talking about parts. Clinically, this helps you gather information about the client's capacity, stability, susceptibility to backlash, and ability to describe their internal experience to you. This helps you determine whether they are a good candidate for EMDR and their readiness for EMDR. While this may initially activate parts of the client, this use of parts mapping has the least amount of risk of emotionally overwhelming or activating the client.

Therapist Script

Using Parts Mapping to Build Working Alliance and Support Stabilization

This script guides you in asking the client about fears or concerns they may have about starting therapy and about what was disclosed during the intake process, and incorporating this into a visual parts map. This parts map can help you build working alliance by supporting the client in communicating any concerns and by giving you a chance to respond to their concerns so they do not contribute to early termination or become a barrier in treatment. If you do not have time to do this parts map during the first session after the client has shared their history, then you can do this during the second session.

- "I'm aware we are just starting to work together, and you shared a lot of really important personal information with me during the intake. I would like to just pause for a moment and check in to ask what fears or concerns you may have about starting therapy."

- *Wait for the client to respond with any fears or concerns.*

- "I am going to make what is called a parts map to make sure that I'm hearing your concerns accurately. So, I am going to draw a diagram to try to acknowledge the parts of you that you just described."

- *Make a parts map, then name the parts reflected on the parts map using the language the client used.*

- "So there is a part of you that has a fear of [*name the fear*] and a part that has a fear of [*name the fear*]. Am I getting that right? Are there any changes that need to be made on the parts map to really acknowledge the parts of you that have fears about starting therapy?"

- *Once the client confirms the parts map is accurate, you can provide psychoeducation and respond to the client's concerns about starting therapy. You can also normalize that sometimes concerns arise from the intake process itself. Then proceed to ask about any parts with fears or concerns about anything shared in the intake process.*

- "I'm so glad that you shared these concerns with me. It is important that we can talk about any concerns you have throughout the therapy process and you can ask any questions at any time that may come up about your treatment. Sometimes after disclosing a lot of personal information, people can feel vulnerable or may notice parts of themselves react to what they shared. Do any parts of you have any fears or concerns about what you shared during the intake process?"

- *Wait for the client to respond with any fears or concerns.*

- "I am going to add to our parts map just to really acknowledge these parts also."

- *Draw any parts the client mentions.*

- "Does this parts map accurately acknowledge these parts? Give me some feedback to let me know if this is accurate or if there is anything we need to change or add to the parts map."
- *Wait for the client to give feedback and adjust the parts map as needed.*
- *Once the client confirms that the parts map is accurate, you can talk with the client about their fears about anything they disclosed and provide psychoeducation about how the information they shared will be used to inform their treatment plan, including what they may focus on in EMDR reprocessing. If you are concerned about the client's stability based on parts identified during the parts mapping (e.g., if a suicidal part emerges), then you can do a risk assessment, provide coping skills to support stabilization, and provide additional resources (e.g., a crisis hotline) for the client to access between sessions.*

Therapist Script

Using Parts Mapping to Identify Parts Connected to the Client's Presenting Issue

The purpose of this script is to guide you to make a parts map to identify parts connected to the client's presenting clinical concern. This type of parts map can be used with any client early in therapy to introduce the notion that parts of the client are showing up as mental health concerns. This can help the client develop self-compassion and gain perspective. It gives you the opportunity to gather more information about the parts of them connected to their presenting problem and to then describe how the parts map can be used going forward in therapy.

- "You started therapy to decrease your [*name a presenting symptom*]. Is this still what you want to focus on?"
- *Wait for the client to confirm or update their desired point of focus.*
- "I am going to draw what is called a parts map to help us get to know what parts of you may be connected to [*name the symptom*]. Would it be okay if we focus on this part of you that feels [*name the symptom*]?"
- *Then ask questions such as:*
  - "How does that show up for you?"
  - "What is your experience of that?"
  - "What does that look like?"
  - "What does that feel like?"
- *After the client shares, draw a parts map to reflect what they are sharing, even if initially only one part is showing up.*
- "Okay, so there is a part that [*name a part that is expressing a presenting problem using the client's language for that part*] and another part that [*name another part using the client's language*]. Am I getting this right?"
- *If the client says no, adjust the parts map to attune to the client. Once the client resonates with the parts map, you can talk with the client to find out more about present-day triggers, when these parts show up and when the client notices them, and how the client copes with these symptoms. You can add information about current triggers to the client's EMDR target list that was started during the intake process. You then can tie the parts map to steps within the overall treatment plan.*

- "Now that we have identified these parts in your system connected to what brought you into therapy and learned more about them, I'm going to share more information about how we can work collaboratively with these parts to help you reach your treatment goals of [*name the client's treatment goals*]."
- "One of the ways I work is to guide clients to be with their parts and get to know them better. This can help you gain insight and understanding as to why these parts are here. I use interventions in EMDR therapy from Internal Family Systems, which is an evidenced-based relational modality. To support your treatment goals, we can plan to return to this parts map in your therapy to get to know these parts, how they developed, and what coping skills would feel supportive to these parts. In terms of preparing you for EMDR reprocessing, we also can return to this parts map to help us identify potential EMDR targets and to get consent from these parts to proceed with EMDR. How does that sound?"
- *You can then ask the client if they have any questions and provide resources (e.g., books, podcasts) as needed on IFS and using an integrative treatment approach in EMDR.*

Therapist Script

Using Parts Mapping to Track Sequences of the Client's System

This script will guide you through the process of making a parts map to help you and the client identify the order of parts that show up regularly for the client. This is helpful to use for any client to gain insight into what is happening internally for them, which can elicit self-compassion. This helps identify patterns (cognitive, emotional, somatic, or behavioral), which can be used to gather more information, such as what triggers these parts and what additional coping skills may need to be developed for stabilization and to prepare the client for EMDR reprocessing. You can add any triggers that are identified to the EMDR target list.

- "Let's talk through what you experienced when [*refer to a recent trigger, conflict, substance abuse episode, or event that activated the client*]. I am going to draw what is called a parts map so that we can find out what parts of you showed up and try to understand what happened."

- *As the client shares, draw the parts map, noting which part showed up first, then second, then third, and so on. Then ask the client if the parts map is accurate or if anything needs to be changed. You can also invite the client to add to the parts map themselves if they prefer.*

- *Once the client confirms the parts map is accurate, guide the client to share more information about these parts.*

- "Okay, let's talk about what you already know about these parts."

- *Ask questions such as:*

    - "Does this sequence of parts that showed up seem familiar to you? What is familiar about it? When have you noticed this reaction before?"

    - "What triggers these parts? Are there any specific people, behaviors people do, or situations in which you notice these parts getting activated?"

    - "Are there specific places or locations where these parts get activated?"

    - "Are there any specific times of day, weather, or seasons that make it worse?"

    - "Is there anything internally that you experience that elicits these parts, such as body sensations, physical pain, feeling hot, or your heartbeat increasing?"

    - "When did you first notice having these responses?" [*This may lead to a touchstone memory that can be added to the target list for EMDR reprocessing.*]

- *With your client, collaboratively create a trigger list based on this data, which can be used for identifying EMDR targets. Then move to more process-oriented questions to help support the client's stabilization and integration of the new information identified through the parts map, and to continue to attune to the therapeutic relationship. You can normalize whatever the client's experience was of making the map or sharing the process with you, including any vulnerability about discovering parts. Particularly when clients talk about parts involved in an addiction cycle or disclose any suicidal parts, they may feel ashamed or stigmatized. Asking process-oriented questions gives you a chance to therapeutically respond to anything the client shared.*
- *Ask process-oriented questions such as:*
    - *"Now that we have gathered more information about these parts, what is it like for you to see this parts map?"*
    - *"What have you learned from making this parts map?"*
    - *"What do you feel you are leaving today's session with?"*
    - *"How is it to identify these parts with me?"*
- *You can then invite the client to begin to notice if any of the parts identified show up between sessions. You can suggest that they continue to gather information about when these parts show up, which may be added to the EMDR target list.*

Therapist Script

Introducing Parts Mapping at the Beginning of the Session

Using parts mapping toward the beginning of a session, during rapport building in phase 1, helps you and the client identify parts and potential EMDR targets and visually captures and acknowledges the client's experience since the last therapy session. As the client "checks in," you can provide a parts map as a means of reflection. This script can help you to collaboratively make a parts map with your client to be used as an anchor point for subsequent IFS interventions.

- "So as you are talking, I'm going to draw a visual of what I am hearing."
- *You can draw circles and label each part, per the client's description. Do this in view of the client, such as on a whiteboard either in person or on a telehealth platform.*
- "I'm hearing [*name the parts using the client's language for each part*]. Am I getting this right?"
- *If the client says no, you can ask any of the following:*
  - "Okay, what do I need to change here?"
  - "Okay, what do I need to change so it fits with your system? Are there any other parts that we need to include?"
  - "Would you like to draw what feels true for you?"
- *Once the client confirms that the parts map is resonant, you can ask:*
  - "What is it like to see this map of your parts?"
  - "What else do you know about each of the parts?" [*Name the parts and go one by one to gather more information.*]
  - "How do each of these parts show up? Do they show up more as a body sensation, a specific emotion, a specific negative belief, or a specific behavior?"
- *If parts on the parts map show up in specific autonomic states (e.g., hyperarousal or hypoarousal), then you can provide psychoeducation on the impact of trauma on the nervous system to help normalize parts getting stuck in specific states, as discussed in chapter 2. You can also use the parts map to support stabilization by discussing specific coping skills that may help the parts.*
- *You can then use the therapist scripts "Using Parts Mapping to Identify Parts Connected to the Client's Presenting Issue" (page 74) and "Using Parts Mapping to Track Sequences of the Client's System" (page 76) to obtain more information for the parts map.*

Therapist Script

Introducing Parts Mapping at the End of the Session

Parts mapping can be a helpful way to conclude a session to visually capture and acknowledge what parts were identified, discussed, or named through the clinical history taking. Offering a parts map at the end of the session can provide the client with a summary of what parts emerged during the session. This can help clients with complex trauma further integrate therapeutic gains from the session. You can then agree to return to the parts map next session for continuity between sessions. This gives the client a sense of structure, helps them end the session with self-reflection on insights gained, and helps them know what to expect in the next session. This is particularly helpful for sessions that may be scattered or unfocused, or in which the client may oscillate between being blended with different parts.

- "So, knowing that we have about 10 minutes left today, I would like to draw a visual of what we discussed today before we end our session."
- *You can draw circles and label each part per the client's description, draw sequences that the client identified in session, or draw relationships between parts.*
- "Okay, so some parts that you named and that we got to know today are [*name the parts using the client's language for each part*]. Am I getting this right?"
- *If the client says no, you can ask:* "Okay, what do I need to change here or what parts feel missing?"
- *Once the client confirms that the parts map is resonant for them for what came up in the session, then you can do any of the following:*
    - ***Choice to integrate coping skills:*** *Transition into discussing self-care between sessions. You and the client can review self-care and coping skills options to support client stabilization.*
    - ***Shift into a process-oriented closure:*** *Some clients might benefit from talking with you for closure of the session. This can help the client shift from being in therapy to interacting with the world outside of the therapy session.*
        - *For example,* "What is it like to see this visual map of these parts of you?"
    - ***Attune to the treatment plan:*** *Reiterate or make adaptations to the treatment plan or list of EMDR targets based on the parts map.*
    - ***Contract to return to the parts map next session:*** *You and the client can collaboratively decide to return to this parts map at the beginning of the next session to have continuity between sessions.*
        - *For example,* "We can return to this parts map at the beginning of our next session. It can give us a place to start and get to know your parts better. How does that sound?"

Therapist Script

Using Parts Mapping to Create a Visualization for Reaching Therapy Goals and to Identify EMDR Targets

(Adapted from Schwartz, 2018)

This script is intended to help you utilize parts mapping with your client to establish a visualization statement, which can then be used to help identify protector parts and potential EMDR targets. From an EMDR lens, a visualization statement is like a positive cognition self-statement for a future template. This helps the client access parts that they may not have been conscious of before. Thus, this process can elicit arousal in the client's system, foster insight, and give structure to future sessions using IFS interventions.

This script is best used for the entirety of one session to identify parts that can subsequently be befriended in future sessions. You can integrate coping skills, process-oriented exploration (e.g., "What is this like for you?"), or both to help decrease arousal as needed during the session.

- *Ask each of these questions to help the client create an "I am" statement. Have the client write down their answer to each of these questions:*
    - *"What would it look like if you met your treatment goals in therapy?"*
    - *"How would you know you'd met your goals? What would shift for you? What would happen?"*
    - *"What would that mean about you? Can you put that into an 'I am' statement? For example, fill in the blank: 'If I meet my treatment goals, I am _____.'"*
- *You can also draw upon the client's future desired outcomes identified in the therapist worksheet "IFS-Informed Case Conceptualization and Integrative Treatment Planning" (page 44).*
- *Once the client has their visualization statement in the form of an "I am" statement, have them write it down (e.g., "I am able to feel and tolerate my feelings without getting overwhelmed").*
- *Ask the client to read their "I am" visualization statement aloud.*
- *Then ask the following questions to help identify the client's protector parts (managers and firefighters):*
    - *"What parts do you notice?"*
    - *"What fears or concerns do parts have about this statement?"*
    - *"How do these parts want to be represented on the page?"*

- *Invite the client to draw the parts using any writing or art utensils available. Having parts represented on the page helps the client externalize their parts and have more access to Self. Go through this process until all parts with fears and concerns about the statement are represented on the page.*
- *Then ask the following questions in order to identify exiles, which can be EMDR reprocessing targets:*
    - "Now that parts with fears and concerns are represented on the page, if one vulnerable part could get our help that would have the biggest impact toward realizing this visualization, what part would that be?"
    - "How does this part want to be represented on the page?"
- *Pause until the client has drawn this part. Then ask the client if this map feels complete for now and if there are any other parts that they are noticing react to the statement.*
- "You now have a parts map."
- *You can move to process-oriented inquiry to decrease arousal as needed.*
- "What is it like to see this map? Are there any surprises? Next session, we can start to get to know the parts with fears and concerns using IFS interventions. How does that sound to you?"
- *This is contracting and being transparent about the options for the treatment plan. At the end of the session, you can discuss attending to the vulnerable part using EMDR therapy once protector parts on the map give consent.*

CHAPTER 4

IFS Befriending Interventions for Protector Consent During Phase 2

Now that we have discussed the elements of IFS-informed phase 1, let's dive into phase 2. Traditional phase 2 in EMDR is focused on preparation for trauma reprocessing through resource development (Shapiro, 2018). In IFS-informed phase 2, resource development happens relationally between parts and Self. In essence, you are shifting from talking *about* parts with a client to guiding the client to *be with* their parts through the use of befriending interventions (Fatter, 2023b). *Befriending* is an IFS term that means getting to know a part from a place of curiosity and openheartedness. This chapter will provide five specific befriending techniques to use during phase 2, with therapist handouts and case examples to help guide you through this process

Why Befriend Parts Before Trauma Reprocessing in EMDR?

According to IFS, when a trauma occurs, the client's internal system reorganizes. Parts move into roles in the system for survival, as discussed in chapter 2. When this reorganization happens, a client's system shifts to be parts-led. However, parts that moved into roles for survival can get stuck in these roles even after the immediate threat or experience of the trauma is over. Exiles, the vulnerable parts holding trauma-related beliefs and burdens, drive the protector parts' roles. Thus, after trauma has occurred, the client's system becomes organized around protecting the client from reexperiencing the pain of the trauma. In other words, protectors protect the exiles carrying trauma-related beliefs and burdens (Schwartz & Sweezy, 2020). Protectors try to help the system in the way they know how for survival. Protector parts, which all have positive intentions, try to protect the client from feeling the exiles' pain.

IFS interventions, including befriending, are designed to support the system to reorganize so that the client's Self is the leader of the system, rather than parts. In IFS's approach to healing, when the exiles release the pain from trauma that they are carrying, protector parts can move out of being in protective roles, and the client's system becomes flexible so parts can fully share their gifts (Schwartz & Sweezy, 2020). In its traditional protocol, EMDR reprocessing typically targets the exile's experience of trauma, including images of the traumatic memory, negative cognitions, feelings, and body sensations.

A Client's Parts-Led System

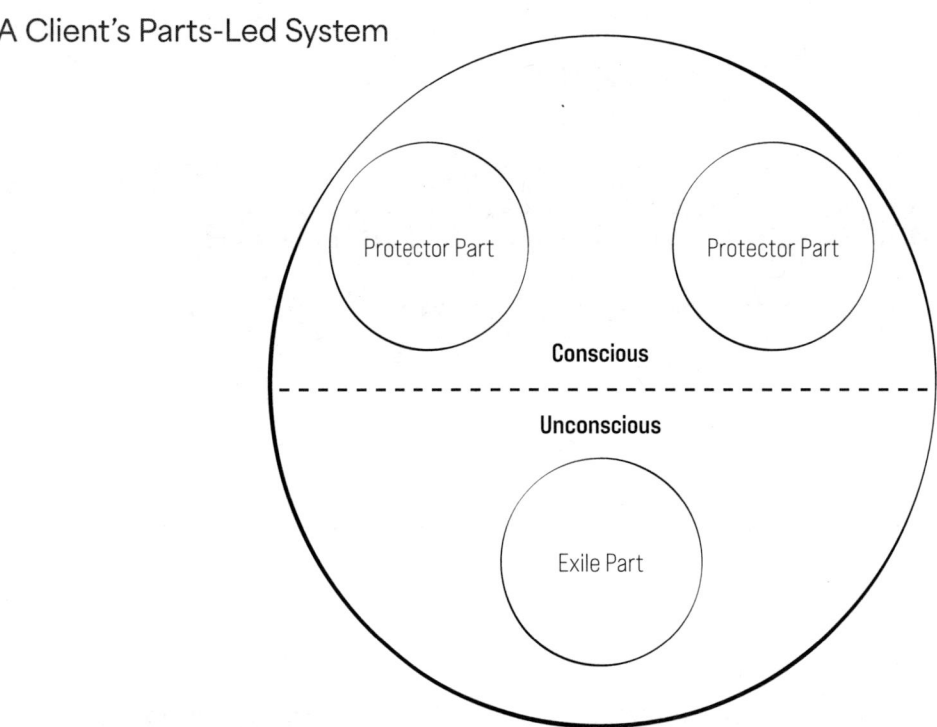

Contracting and Identifying Which Part to Befriend First

Before we discuss befriending, it's important to understand how IFS approaches contracting and how to determine which parts to befriend first. *Contracting* refers to the process between you and the client to mutually agree what you are going to focus on in a given session and in the overall treatment plan. In transitioning from parts mapping, you contract to shift the task at hand in therapy to befriending the parts on the parts map and agree on which part to befriend first. I provide a case example of shifting from parts mapping to befriending later in this chapter, on page 116.

In transitioning from talking about parts on the parts map to befriending, you simply ask the client if it's okay if, together, you get to know the parts better and hear more from them about their fears or concerns. You then ask for the client's input on what part to get to know first.

The following are some of the many ways you can contract to move to befriending:

- "Since there are parts on the parts map with fears or concerns about EMDR, let's take some time to really get to know what their fears and concerns are. Would it be okay to focus on these parts of you? Which one would you like to focus on first? Which part has the most energy or charge?"

- "Would it be okay for us to get to know these parts better? Turn your attention inward—which part needs our attention first? Which part has the most energy or charge?"

- "Now that we have talked about these parts on your parts map, let's get to know them better so we can find ways to support them in preparing you for EMDR reprocessing. How does that sound? Which part would you like to get to know first?"

If a client has a strong reaction to your using the word "parts" when you make a parts map, you can adjust your language to whatever language the client is using to refer to their parts when you shift to befriending (Schwartz & Sweezy, 2020). For example:

- "I hear you are concerned about becoming suicidal if we do EMDR. Would it be okay if we explore more about that fear of becoming suicidal?"
- "You have a fear about triggering a depressive episode if we do EMDR; am I getting that right? Would it be okay if we explored that more?"
- "I hear that you are worried about having more panic attacks if we begin EMDR. Let's explore that fear more—would that be okay?"

When you ask the client if there are any parts with fears or concerns about doing EMDR, you are eliciting protector parts in the client's system.

After contracting to get to know the parts with fears and concerns, you'll proceed with IFS befriending strategies.

Through befriending, you guide the client to *relationally be with* their parts, during which the client may initially experience more arousal in their nervous system. This is different from *talking about* parts on the parts map during phase 1 to gather more clinical information (e.g., What do you know about these parts? When do you notice them? How do they show up?). After there is Self-to-part connection and parts feel understood by the client, parts will soften and activation will diminish.

Next, we'll go over some general information to know about befriending before you utilize this intervention, after which we'll get into the specific strategies.

Befriending Benefits and Guidelines

In befriending, you guide the client to get to know their parts from a relational approach that is Self-led—that is, inviting, nonjudgmental, and with the intention to really understand the part's perspective and fears. You simply help guide the process of the client asking questions to their parts with curiosity, and parts organically respond with information (Schwartz & Sweezy, 2020).

As a general rule, you first want to befriend protector parts of the client's system: the managers with fears or concerns or the firefighters that show up to numb or distract the client from their emotional pain. Befriending protectors and developing a Self-to-part relationship ultimately helps stabilize the client's system. This is because when protectors feel better understood, they soften, there is more Self-leadership in the client's system, and the client's mental health symptoms decrease.

Befriending techniques during phase 2 guide the client to receive conscious consent from protector parts before directly activating exiles in phases 3 and 4 for EMDR trauma reprocessing. From an IFS lens, this can help:

- Support the trauma-informed nature of EMDR trauma reprocessing rather than potentially bypassing protectors with standard EMDR protocol (Fatter, 2023b)
- Contribute to working alliance by relationally attuning to the client's system
- Support a decrease in clinical symptoms and stabilization (Fatter, 2023b)
- Minimize blocked trauma reprocessing in phase 4, as parts with "blocking beliefs" can be befriended prior to phase 4 (Fatter, 2023b)
- Decrease the risk of what IFS calls a "backlash" in the client's system

A backlash occurs when an exile is activated, accessed, or witnessed without the consent of protector parts, resulting in protector parts feeling bypassed. This can lead to protector parts reactively taking over the system, which results in increased mental health symptoms, high-risk behavior (e.g., increased substance use, self-harm behavior, or suicidality), and potential client decompensation—all of which is less likely to occur if protectors are befriended first (Fatter, 2023b; Kolodny & Mazero, 2022; Krause & Gomez, 2013; O'Shea Brown, 2020; Schwartz & Sweezy, 2020; Twombly & Schwartz, 2008).

When applying any IFS intervention, including befriending, it's important to assess how much access the client has to their own Self-energy. As discussed in chapter 2, by applying an IFS-informed case conceptualization, you continue to hold curiosity about the client's access to their own Self throughout the entirety of therapy. To assess this, ask: "How do you feel toward this part?" (Schwartz & Sweezy, 2020, p. 132). You are listening for expressions of the client's Self through either the 8 C's (curiosity, compassion, calmness, creativity, connectedness, courage, clarity, confidence) or the 5 P's (presence, playfulness, persistence, perspective, patience) of Self. If the client has access to any amount of even one of these qualities, you can proceed with befriending (Schwartz & Sweezy, 2020).

If the client does not demonstrate any amount of Self, or responds with "I don't like that part," you can use a befriending technique called "addressing polarizations," which we'll discuss shortly.

How Much Self Does the Client Have Access To?

(Adapted from Schwartz & Sweezy, 2020)

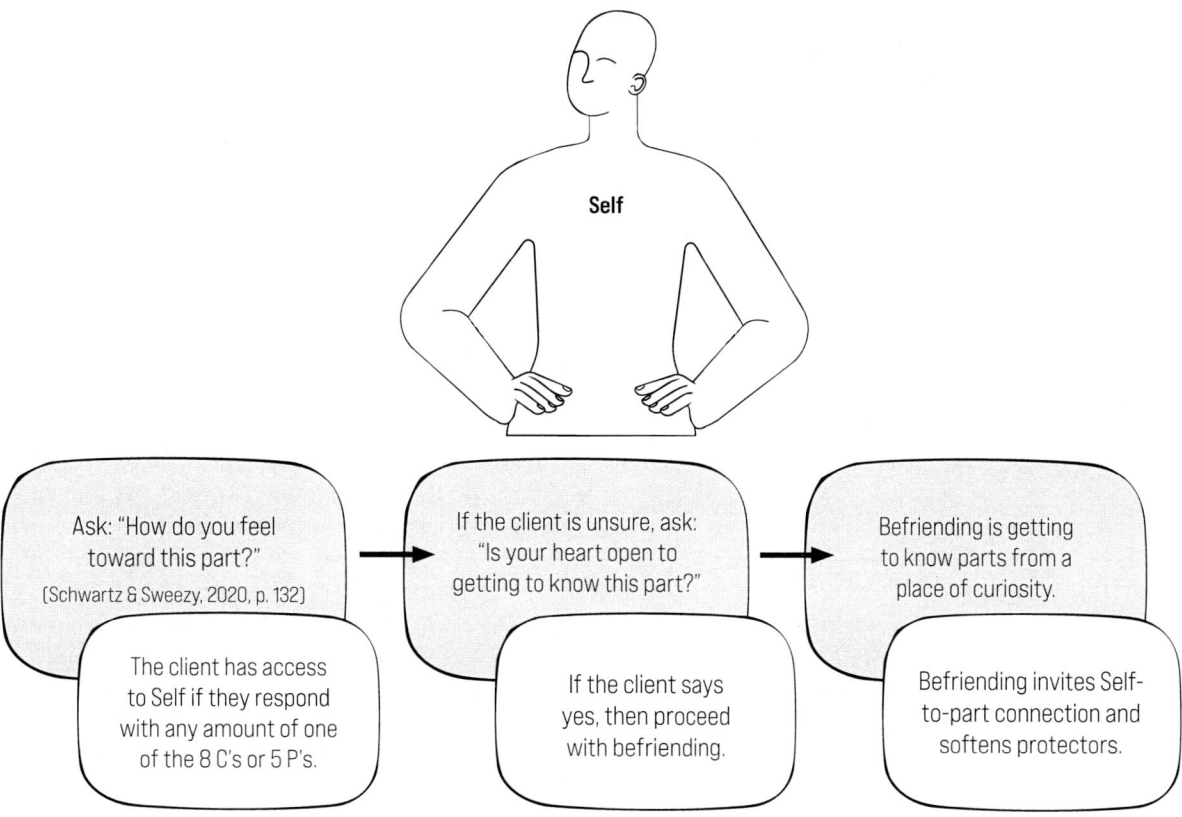

As discussed in chapter 1, keep in mind the five IFS principles when applying befriending:

1. We all have Self and parts.
2. All parts are welcome.
3. Receive consent from protector parts first. (This is what we are doing during phase 2).
4. The Self-to-part relationship is healing.
5. If parts feel understood, they will soften.

Five Befriending Strategies to Use During Phase 2

There are five befriending strategies to use during EMDR phase 2, each of which can be applied at different times and for different purposes.

Five Befriending Strategies to Use During Phase 2

(Adapted from Fatter, 2023b)

Technique	When to Use It
Befriending Protector Parts: 1. The 6 F's 2. Addressing Polarizations with the 6 F's 3. Addressing Polarizations with the Conference Table Technique	• Use the 6 F's to befriend protectors (managers and firefighters) in the client's system. • When parts are polarized, use the 6 F's first with each part of the polarization. • Use the conference table technique if the 6 F's technique doesn't work, if multiple parts are present, or if multiple parts are in a polarization.
4. Direct Access	Use direct access when there is not enough Self-energy present in the client and the client is blended with a part.
5. Self Tapping for Attachment Readiness & Repair (STARR)	Use STARR when a part is identified but not able to take in Self's presence. You can also use this as an alternative to direct access when the client is blended with a part.

Use the therapist handout "Phase 2 Road Map to Protectors' Consent," located later in this chapter (page 118), to guide you in implementing these five befriending techniques. As you use the road map and specific befriending interventions, you are relationally guiding the process of parts being understood by the client. Regardless of the befriending technique you are using, consider the following:

- What does this part need to experience being understood by the client?
- What can help elicit the client's awareness that a part is present, that this part is not *all* of them, and that the part has choice?

Befriending Technique 1: Using the 6 F's

The "6 F's" in IFS therapy are questions you ask the client once you have contracted and identified which part to befriend first. For most IFS interventions, including befriending, the client typically has their eyes closed, but this is optional. You can say: "Now that we've identified which part to get to know first, feel free to close your eyes if you like."

Then proceed with the 6 F's questions, pausing after each question to allow the client to respond (Schwartz & Sweezy, 2020):

1. **Find:** "Where do you notice this part in or around your body?"
2. **Focus:** "Bring your attention to this part."
3. **Flesh it out:** "How are you experiencing it right now?" (Is this an image, a felt sense?)
4. **Feel toward:** "How do you feel toward this part?" (This question checks for the client's access to Self-energy.)
5. **Befriend:** "How is this part trying to help you? What is this part hoping to accomplish? What is its job?"
6. **Fears:** "What are this part's fears and concerns?"

As the client shares with you what the part has shared, guide the bidirectional communication between the client's Self and the target part (the part the client is befriending in that moment). For example, as the part is sharing with the client information about its fears and concerns regarding doing EMDR, ask the client questions such as "Does that make sense to you?" If the client confirms that it makes sense, you can say: "Then let it know that you are getting that. See how this part is responding to feeling understood by you." At any time, you can also check for the client's Self-energy and harness that for connection with the part. For example, you can ask: "How do you feel toward this part right now as it's sharing this fear with you? Can you share that compassion with the part? How is it responding to feeling understood by you?"

Neither you nor the client should try to change or get rid of the part. Befriending engenders parts' feeling understood exactly as they are. When they feel understood, they will naturally soften and give the client more internal space. Additional EMDR targets can be revealed that can be added to the target list for EMDR reprocessing. Asking the question, "What is the part scared would happen if it didn't do its job?" typically reveals the exile the protector parts are protecting. The therapist handout "The 6 F's" (on page 95) provides further guidance on using this befriending technique. Before we get to that, though, we'll discuss some common fears that protector parts have and how to address them, after which I'll provide a case example to demonstrate the use of the 6 F's in session.

Addressing Common Protector Fears

In response to the last question of the 6 F's, "fears," it is normal for protector parts to express fears that arise in therapy, including in EMDR therapy. Here are some common protector fears (Anderson, 2021; Schwartz & Sweezy, 2020):

- Concern that the client will be overwhelmed by grief or other feelings (e.g., any change will destabilize the client and the client will feel immense grief)
- Concern that the client and/or therapist is trying to get rid of the part
- Concern that another part (e.g., a self-harm part) will take over the system

- Concern about consequences if the trauma is fully revealed in therapy (e.g., not being liked by the client or therapist, losing relationships/community, external loss, or loss of sense of identity)
- Fear that the therapist "can't handle it" or will have a negative reaction to the client (e.g., judgment, disgust, wanting to abandon the client, or becoming punitive)
- Fear that it's not safe enough or that something bad could happen (e.g., the client will be unprepared for future harm if the protector gives the client space)

Clients may also express specific fears about doing EMDR itself, including the following (Shapiro, 2018):

- Fear of going crazy
- Fear of not being able to tolerate EMDR
- Fear, anxiety, or embarrassment about sharing the memory or negative belief (the negative cognition) associated with the target memory

Providing psychoeducation about what to expect in EMDR and in therapy may help to assuage the client's fears (Shapiro, 2018). In addition, with any of these fears, you can:

1. Validate the part's concern and reassure the part
2. Give the part an alternate option by offering a choice (Anderson, 2021; Schwartz & Sweezy, 2020)

The following table provides examples of therapist responses to protector parts' fears, using these two methods.

Clinical Examples of Befriending Common Fears in Action

(Adapted from Anderson, 2021; Schwartz & Sweezy, 2020)

Protector Part's Fear	Example of Therapist Response	
	Validate and Reassure	*Offer a Choice*
Fear that the client will become overwhelmed	I hear that you are really scared about getting overwhelmed. That makes sense given all that you have been through.	EMDR can offer a different way of being with the overwhelm. Let this part know that it can watch on the sidelines while we do EMDR, and if it seems too overwhelming, or has other fears come up, it can let us know and we will stop EMDR to address its concern. How is this part responding to hearing that?

Fear that the client, the therapist, or the therapy itself is trying to get rid of it	I hear that it's concerned we are trying to get rid of it. Let the part know that we are not trying to get rid of it or take anything away from it.	Let the part know that it is a valued part of your system, and if EMDR is effective, then this part will be free to do something else in your system instead of this job. Would it be interested in that?
Fear of sharing a traumatic memory or negative belief in EMDR	I really hear that this part has a fear of sharing the traumatic memory or beliefs that come up. This is a common fear in doing EMDR.	You have choices in EMDR with how much you disclose to me about the details of what you went through. Also let the part know that our intention in EMDR is to help your system feel less emotional pain and shame about this trauma. Your feelings and beliefs about this trauma can change with EMDR. How does that sound to this part?

CASE EXAMPLE

The 6 F's in Action

Let's return to Ava, whom we met in chapter 3. Remember that Ava is a 55-year-old woman who has been diagnosed with CPTSD and MDD, stemming from childhood sexual abuse. Let's see how Ava's therapist is preparing Ava in phase 2 for EMDR reprocessing.

Contracting

THERAPIST: Thank you for sharing some of your fears and concerns. I want to make sure we have full consent from your system before we begin trauma reprocessing in EMDR. Would it be okay if we get to know the parts of you with these fears and concerns?

AVA: Sure.

Identifying Which Part to Befriend First

THERAPIST: Which fear has the biggest charge for you right now?

AVA: My biggest fear is of getting depressed again if we do EMDR.

THERAPIST: Okay, so there is a part that is scared of you getting depressed again; am I getting that right?

AVA: Yes.

The 6 F's "Find" Question

THERAPIST: Okay, so feel free to turn your attention inward. You can invite in curiosity about this part as you breathe. You can close your eyes if you like or just notice. Where are you noticing this part in and around your body?

AVA: It's on my right side near the front.

Eliciting Self-to-Part Awareness and Using the 6 F's "Focus" Question

THERAPIST: Okay, great awareness. Just bring your attention to this part. Invite the part to take in your presence in whatever way it can. How is it responding to you even acknowledging it this way?

AVA: It feels a little relieved. It's surprised that I'm noticing it.

The 6 F's "Flesh It Out" Question

THERAPIST: Good, and how are you experiencing this part right now?

AVA: It is just a feeling.

The 6 F's "Feel Toward" Question

THERAPIST: Okay, how do you feel toward this part?

AVA: I get it. I understand why it's concerned.

The 6 F's "Feel Toward" Question to Confirm There Is Self Present

THERAPIST: Okay. Is your heart open to getting to know this part more?

AVA: Yes.

The 6 F's "Befriend" Questions to Support Self-to-Part Connection

THERAPIST: Great—let the part know that you are right here with it and want to get to know it more. See how it is responding to you being here with it.

AVA: The part is really surprised that I'm here and is glad I'm here.

The 6 F's "Fear" Question

THERAPIST: Ask it about its fear of you getting depressed again. What is it scared will happen?

AVA: It's scared that I won't be able to work again if I get depressed.

Facilitating the Part Being Understood by the Client's Self

THERAPIST: Does that make sense to you?

AVA: Yes, it does.

THERAPIST: Let it know that you get that.

AVA: Okay.

THERAPIST: How is it responding to you really getting that?

AVA: It feels better. It likes that I'm listening.

THERAPIST: Great. Ask it if there is anything else it has fears about.

AVA: Okay... That is its only concern.

THERAPIST: All right. Ask this part what it needs from you right now.

AVA: It just wants me to take it seriously.

THERAPIST: Okay. Anything you want to say to this part in response to its fear?

AVA: Yes, I'm letting it know that I also don't want to be depressed again and that's why I'm here in therapy.

THERAPIST: How is the part responding to knowing you also don't want to get depressed again?

AVA: It's glad I'm here and that it's not the only one concerned about my depression.

Identifying EMDR Targets

THERAPIST: Ask the part: What is it scared would happen if it did not do its job?

AVA: It's worried about the overwhelming sadness I feel when I get depressed. It remembers how hard that was for me the last time I got depressed.

THERAPIST: Does that make sense to you?

AVA: Yes, it does.

THERAPIST: Let this part know that you get that and see how it's responding to being understood by you.

AVA: It's feeling better that I am understanding it.

THERAPIST: Great. Let it know that we are going to add the overwhelming sadness to our EMDR target list and that EMDR can help your system feel less overwhelmed by the sadness.

AVA: It's glad that we're going to focus on that. That's a relief to hear.

THERAPIST: So knowing that we are planning on doing EMDR, ask if it has any other concerns or fears about doing EMDR.

AVA: No, it doesn't.

Asking for Permission

THERAPIST: Do we have its permission to do proceed with EMDR?

AVA: Yes, it's saying we have its permission.

As you can see, Ava's therapist initially uses contracting in order to get consent to befriend the part with a fear or concern about EMDR. Then Ava's therapist facilitates connection, using the 6 F's, to help the part feel understood by Ava and foster Self-leadership. This enables the part to know it's not alone, as Ava does not want to be depressed again either. Ava's therapist then asks about any fears the part has if it does not do its job. This typically reveals the exile (the unprocessed traumatic memory network) that it is protecting. In this case, the target part is worried about the overwhelming sadness, which Ava's therapist then adds to the EMDR target list to address in EMDR reprocessing. Then Ava's therapist gets permission to proceed with EMDR. If Ava's part needed more from Ava, her therapist could have had Ava ask the part more about its fear and also could have brought in coping skills and resources to help regulate the part as needed. Resource development options and parts-specific coping skills will be further discussed in chapter 5.

You can use the following therapist handout to guide you through using the 6 F's.

Therapist Handout

The 6 F's

(Schwartz & Sweezy, 2020)

Goals of Befriending Protectors

In phase 2 of EMDR, the therapist and client can get to know the client's protective system. This includes addressing any fears or concerns parts have experientially to ultimately get internal consent to work with exiles. Through the process of befriending protector parts using the 6 F's, the client's window of tolerance naturally widens through the Self-to-part relationship. Befriending protectors during phase 2 also helps minimizes blocking beliefs in phase 4 and helps prevent system backlash (Fatter, 2023; Kolodny & Mazero, 2022; Krauze & Gomez, 2013; O'Shea Brown, 2020; Schwartz & Sweezy, 2020; Twombly & Schwartz, 2008).

1. **Find:** "Where do you notice this part in or around your body?"

2. **Focus:** "Bring your attention to this part."

3. **Flesh it out:** "How are you experiencing it right now?" (Is this an image, a felt sense, etc.?)

4. **Feel toward:** "How do you feel toward this part?" (Schwartz & Sweezy, 2020, p. 132; this question checks for client's access to Self-energy.)

5. **Befriend:** "How is this part trying to help you? What is this part hoping to accomplish? What is its job?"

6. **Fears:** "What are this part's fears and concerns?"

What This Looks Like in Action

(Adapted from Schwartz & Sweezy, 2020)

During the 6 F's, the therapist is guiding the client to ask these questions to a target protector part.	After the client verbally shares what the part said, the therapist guides the bidirectional relationship between the client's Self and the target part.
1. Find: "Where do you notice this part in or around your body?"	Invite the client to shift their attention inward. They can close their eyes if they choose. This initiates in-sight IFS (the client relationally and experientially being with their parts from their Self-energy).
2. Focus: "Bring your attention to this part."	Once the part starts sharing information, the therapist guides the client to validate it.
3. Flesh it out: "How are you experiencing it right now?" (Is this an image, a felt sense, etc.?)	"How is it responding to you acknowledging it in this way? Can you let it know you can see it? Can you make eye contact with it? How is it responding to being seen by you?"
4. Feel toward: "How do you feel toward this part?" (p. 132; checking for Self-energy)	If the client has some amount of one of the 8 C qualities of Self-energy, the therapist asks the client to share that with the part to foster the Self-to-part relationship: "Share your compassion with the part. Invite the part to take that in from you. How is it responding to receiving your compassion?"
5. Befriend: "How is this part trying to help you?" • "What is this part hoping to accomplish? What is its job?" • "What is the part scared would happen if it didn't do its job?" (The exile may be organically revealed, which can be the target for EMDR processing.) • "How old does this part think you are right now?"	"Does that make sense to you? Let it know you get that. How is it responding to you really getting it? Can it hear you understanding it right now? How is it responding to being heard by you?"
6. Fears: "What are this part's fears and concerns?" • "Does it have any fears or concerns about doing EMDR?"	"Is it okay with the part for you to just be with it? How is the part responding to you being with it right now as it shares its fears?"

Befriending Technique 2: Addressing Polarizations with the 6 F's

Polarizations occur when parts have opposing strategies despite sharing the same overall goal of helping the system. This can show up as conflicts between two parts or among several parts.

As illustrated in the following figure, polarization exists on a continuum. Parts are more cooperative, less rigid, and less in need of individual attention when they are less polarized. When parts are more polarized, they need more individual attention to soften through the befriending process (Schwartz & Sweezy, 2020).

Polarization Continuum

Less polarized systems	More polarized systems
• More cooperative	• More in need of befriending
• Less rigid and more flexible	• More rigid and extreme
• In need of less individual attention	• In need of more individual attention

Polarized systems are very common in clients with complex trauma or complex systems. When working with polarized systems, it is important to remember the IFS principles "All parts are welcome" and "When parts feel understood, they will soften."

How to Identify a Polarization

Sometimes polarizations are obvious and the client may be aware of having conflicting or opposing feelings or an internal struggle about an issue. In clients with complex trauma, it may be less obvious which specific parts are polarized with each other; this may be revealed when you initially befriend one part.

Polarizations are often identified when you ask the client: "How do you feel toward this part?" (Schwartz & Sweezy, p. 132), and the client responds with reactivity or a negative feeling (e.g., "I don't like that part"). Once a polarization is identified, guide the client to use the 6 F's with each part when there are two parts in a polarization. For example, as shown in the following figure, you would use the 6 F's first with the reactive part (the part that said "I don't like that part") and then with the original part, inviting each part to hear the other one with the client's Self neutrally and nonjudgmentally mediating. This will enable the client to better understand their parts' fears and also to identify shared concerns, including that they likely protect the same exile(s).

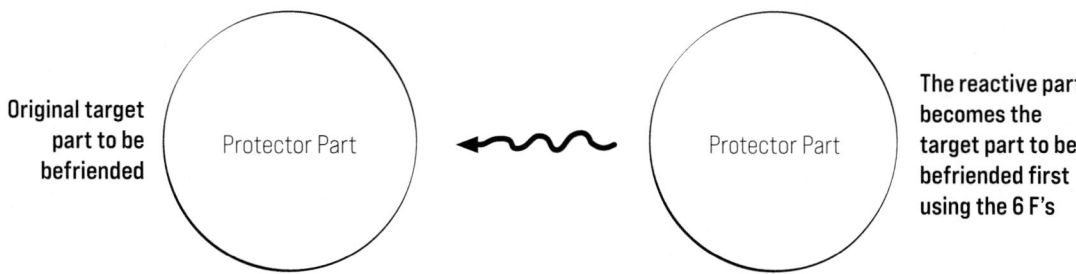

> **CASE EXAMPLE**
>
> # Using the 6 F's to Address Polarizations
>
> Let's revisit Zoe to better understand using the 6 F's to address polarizations. Remember that Zoe is a 20-year-old woman who has been diagnosed with GAD and ADHD. In chapter 3, Zoe's therapist and Zoe used a visualization statement to create a parts map that revealed two protector parts—a "judge" part and a part that is scared of her feelings—and one exile: a younger part that felt overwhelmed.
>
> Zoe's therapist contracts to befriend these two parts. Zoe initially chooses to befriend the "judge" part first. Her therapist uses the 6 F's and asks Zoe how she feels toward the judge part, and Zoe responds that she is scared of it. Her therapist then shifts Zoe's focus to befriend the part that is scared of Zoe's judge part, again using the 6 F's.
>
> In doing so, Zoe's therapist discovers that these two parts—the judge part and the part that is scared of Zoe's feelings—are actually polarized and in conflict with each other, which Zoe had no conscious awareness of. Through befriending the scared part, Zoe learns that it is afraid that the judge part will overwhelm the system with harsh self-criticism, ultimately activating the young exile. Zoe's therapist uses the 6 F's to then learn that the judge part is working hard to try to protect the young part from feeling overwhelmed too. Thus, Zoe learns that they both have a shared concern of overwhelming and triggering the younger part. By using the 6 F's to befriend each of these polarized parts, the polarization weakens, Zoe gains self-compassion (access to Self) that she can share with these two protectors, and both parts ease their power struggle.
>
> This intervention helped the two parts to discover that they had the shared goal of not overwhelming the system and triggering the exile. They realized that they could work better as a team with Zoe's Self as the leader of the system.

The following therapist handout provides detailed directions for implementing this technique.

Therapist Handout

Using the 6 F's to Address Polarizations

This handout serves as a guide to using the 6 F's to address polarizations in clients' systems. Once you have identified the polarized parts, let both parts know that they will take turns sharing their fears and perspective. Follow the steps below to navigate the process of both parts hearing each other, and be sure not to favor either part (adapted from Schwartz & Sweezy, 2020).

Directions

- Ask the polarized parts to meet each other to be understood.
- Use the 6 F's *with each part* so each part feels validated and understood by the client's Self. Trust may need to be established between each part and Self before the parts are willing to meet each other.
  - **Find:** "Where do you notice this part in or around your body?"
  - **Focus:** "Bring your attention to this part."
  - **Flesh it out:** "How are you experiencing this part right now?" (If the client needs support to describe their experience of the part, it can be helpful to ask, "Do you have an image of this part, or are you experiencing this part as a felt sense or body sensation?")
  - **Feel toward:** "How do you feel toward this part?" (Schwartz & Sweezy, p. 132; you are checking for the client's access to Self anytime you ask this question.)
  - **Befriend:** "How is this part trying to help you? What is this part hoping to accomplish? How old does it think you are right now?" (You can guide the client to update the part, as needed, as to the client's current age.)
  - **Fears:** "What is it afraid would happen if it didn't do its job?" (This can organically reveal the exile, which can be added to the target list for potential EMDR reprocessing in phase 3.)
- Identify and appreciate what the two parts have in common. See how each part is responding to learning the other part's concerns.
- If protector parts are extremely polarized, you may need to mediate and negotiate the process of de-escalating the parts simultaneously (Krause et al., 2016).

In complex trauma systems, you may need to ask groups of protector parts to first meet with the client's Self in a protected imaginary location (e.g., around a campfire or in a stadium) so that trust can be established. This may need to happen several times before there is enough trust in Self and in the befriending process before you can have polarized parts meet to listen to each other (Krause et al., 2016; Schwartz & Sweeny, 2020). If that is not effective or if there are multiple parts in the polarization, you can use the conference table technique. Polarized parts soften when they see the other polarized part(s) soften and when they know the vulnerable part they are both protecting (the exile that will be targeted in EMDR) is cared for and healed (Schwartz & Sweezy, 2020).

Befriending Technique 3: Addressing Polarizations with the Conference Table Technique

The conference table technique—another strategy for addressing polarizations—was developed by Dr. Michi Rose, who was an early collaborator with Dr. Richard Schwartz as he developed IFS. You can use the conference table technique if using the 6 F's doesn't work, when there are multiple parts with fears or concerns, or when there are more than two polarized parts (Schwartz & Sweezy, 2020). For example, if you are using the 6 F's with two polarized parts and they do not soften or they have a difficult time taking in the presence of Self to be befriended, then use the conference table technique instead.

This IFS intervention has conceptual overlap with the commonly known ego state therapy interventions of the workplace or conference room (Forgash, 2010) and dissociative table technique (Fraser, 1991, 2003) used with clients with dissociative disorders and complex trauma. In the workplace or conference room technique, ego states (what IFS would call "parts") meet each other to make decisions and collaborate, using tools like microphones, speakers, or movie screens for communication between ego states. In the dissociative table technique, the client uses visual imagery to invite ego states to sit in empty chairs at an oval table.

Dr. Sandra Paulsen (2009) further developed Fraser's (1991) dissociative table intervention and brought it into EMDR therapy—the therapist says: "Take a glance into the conference room, and tell me what, if anything, you see" (p. 77). This can help clients access and distance internal ego states. The client can add various containment elements for distancing (e.g., a dimmer switch), and nurturing resources (e.g., a budding plant) for affect regulation in the conference room (Paulsen, 2009).

In contrast, in the IFS conference table technique, you invite the client's Self to be the leader of the meeting and to mediate conflicts through befriending the parts that are at the meeting, one at a time. As the parts share their hopes, fears, concerns, and needs, the client fosters Self-leadership, identifies commonalities among the parts, and attempts to strengthen the Self-to-part relationship. The following therapist handout provides detailed directions for implementing this technique.

Therapist Handout

Using the Conference Table Technique to Navigate Polarizations

This handout will guide you through the steps of the conference table technique, an IFS befriending technique to address polarizations. These directions come directly from the work of Dr. Schwartz and are intended to strengthen the client's Self-to-part relationship when there are many polarized parts in the client's system (adapted from Schwartz & Sweezy, 2020).

1. Ask the client to imagine a neutral meeting place for parts to meet, with the client present (as the client's Self will be the leader of the meeting). This meeting place can be formal (e.g., a conference room) or more casual (e.g., a kitchen table or campfire). It can be a real place the client has been or an imagined location.

2. Guide the client to invite protector parts, one at a time, into the conference room or other meeting place. Prompt the client to invite the protector parts to have a seat until the client has access to their own Self (i.e., demonstrates any of the 8 C's or 5 P's) and the relevant protector parts are all seated.

3. Once the client has access to their own Self, ask the client to enter the meeting place to be with these parts. Invite the protectors to take in Self's presence, and ask each part to take turns sharing their intentions while the other parts at the meeting place listen. Guide the client to go around the meeting place to each part, one by one, asking:
   ◦ What are you hoping to accomplish by doing what you do?
   ◦ What fears and concerns do you have?
   ◦ What are you scared would happen if you did not do your job?
   ◦ What do you need right now?

4. After a part has shared, invite the client to pause and see how the information shared is landing for the other parts in the meeting place. By asking each part, "What do you need right now?" and by checking for how the newly shared information is landing for other parts in the meeting place, you are guiding the client to foster Self-leadership.

5. As more parts share, guide the client to identify commonalities among parts and shared values (e.g., "Both of these parts are concerned about...") and also Self-to-part relationship (e.g., "How are these two parts responding to you now, knowing that you get that they both are concerned about...?"). If protectors think the client is much younger, have the client update the protector parts as to the client's current age and any other relevant current life updates.

6. Once commonalties are identified, guide the client to ask the parts if they have any specific fears or concerns about doing EMDR. You can provide more psychoeducation about the process of EMDR so these protector parts know what to expect.

7. Ultimately, you can have the client ask for the protectors' permission to do EMDR, inviting parts to share any other fears as they arise throughout the entirety of therapy.

Befriending Technique 4: Direct Access

When the client doesn't have access to their own Self due to being blended with a part, you can utilize your own Self for Self-energy by accessing a part directly. Direct access is an IFS befriending intervention in which you, the therapist, speak directly to a part in the client's system. The goal of direct access is to help the client ultimately unblend so that they can befriend the target part from their own Self.

There are three steps involved in direct access:

1. Gather information from the part and provide validation.
2. Provide a choice and an update of current information.
3. Invite the client's Self to be present and foster Self-to-part connection between the client's Self and this part.

Just as when working with common protector parts, respond directly to each answer to questions about the part's job and fears with validation and reassurance (step 1), and ultimately offer a choice to the part about its role (step 2). This helps the client's part feel understood and "seen" by you, which ultimately helps the part soften. Once the target part softens through direct access, you can invite the client's Self to connect with the target part to foster Self-to-part relationship within the client's system (step 3; Schwartz & Sweezy, 2020). The therapist handout "Direct Access in Three Steps" (on page 106) details these steps.

Remember: If parts feel heard and understood, they will soften. Direct access helps parts feel understood initially by the therapist's Self to ultimately elicit more internal space within the client for their own Self to emerge.

The direct access technique is an ideal example of IFS-integrative EMDR. From an IFS lens, you are embodying Self, offering relational attunement, and being a "hope merchant." From an EMDR lens, you are providing an update of current adaptive information through the neural network to the target part that is blended with the client to help it become unstuck from the past or a maladaptively stored state.

CASE EXAMPLE

Direct Access in Action

Let's return to our case example of Noah to see this technique in action. After identifying that Noah is blended with a protector part and does not have access to his Self-energy, his therapist moves into direct access.

THERAPIST: Is it okay if I speak directly to this protective part of you?

NOAH: Okay.

Step 1: Gather Information and Provide Validation

THERAPIST: Great, so just answer directly from this part. How do you protect Noah?

PROTECTOR: I help him by keeping his guard up and not trusting anyone.

THERAPIST: Okay, so you help him not to trust anyone. I hear that. What are you hoping to accomplish by helping him in this way?

PROTECTOR: I don't want him to get hurt.

THERAPIST: Okay, so you work hard because you don't want him to get hurt. That makes sense given all that he has been through. What are you scared would happen if you didn't do your job?

PROTECTOR: He'd fall apart and lose it.

THERAPIST: How old are you?

PROTECTOR: I'm the same age as Noah—11 years old.

THERAPIST: Okay, so you are 11 and you think Noah is 11 now; am I getting that right?

PROTECTOR: Yeah.

Step 2: Provide a Choice and an Update of Current Information

THERAPIST: Thank you for sharing all of this. Noah is all grown up now. He wants to get help to learn how to trust in relationships. What is it like to hear that?

PROTECTOR: Wow, that's hard to believe! I'm really surprised.

THERAPIST: So, knowing that Noah is all grown up now, you have a choice in what job you do to help Noah. If you didn't have to do this job, is there something else you would rather be doing?

PROTECTOR: Yeah, maybe. I'm so tired of doing this job. I'm exhausted.

Step 3: Invite the Client's Self to Be Present

THERAPIST: Would you like to meet Noah now?

PROTECTOR: Okay. It's hard to believe that he isn't the same age as me.

THERAPIST: We can invite present-day Noah, who is all grown up, to be here so that you can get to know him now. Would that be okay?

PROTECTOR: Okay.

THERAPIST: Noah, are you there? Did you hear all of that?

NOAH: Yeah, I'm here. I did hear everything that was said.

THERAPIST: How do you feel toward this part now?

NOAH: I really appreciate it and get where it's coming from.

THERAPIST: Great. Where are you noticing this part right now in and around your body?

NOAH: It's right here on my right side.

THERAPIST: Go ahead and share that appreciation and understanding with this part. See how it is responding.

NOAH: It likes the appreciation. I want to let it know that I can actually help it now.

The following therapist handout will guide you through the steps of direct access. Remember, when the part feels understood, it will soften. The direct access IFS befriending intervention may only be needed for part of a psychotherapy session or it may take the entire session. If this intervention takes the entire session, it is important for you to invite the client to connect with this target part before the end of the session. Ideally, this will help ensure that the client is leaving with some amount of Self-presence. When working with a client with complex trauma, it is wise to ask the client if they heard everything that the part shared. If the client states that they did not hear what was said, you need to consider that the client may have a dissociative system, which we'll discuss in chapter 5. You would then need to screen for dissociative disorders if you have not already done so in preparation to do EMDR reprocessing.

Direct access takes practice. It may be helpful to practice with a colleague before using this technique with a client. You also may notice your own parts emerge the first time you do this. For example, it is common for therapists first learning to use direct access to have parts that feel strange or have reactivity to referring to the client in the third person. The next therapist worksheet can be helpful in this case.

Therapist Handout

Direct Access in Three Steps

(Adapted from Schwartz & Sweezy, 2020)

This handout provides guidance on when to use the direct access intervention and walks you through the steps of this technique. First, it's important to understand the concept of "blending"—an IFS term that refers to when parts merge with Self. When a client is in a state of being triggered, or when a part takes over their system, the client is blended (Schwartz & Sweeny, 2020). When a client is blended, the client has difficulty differentiating parts in their system.

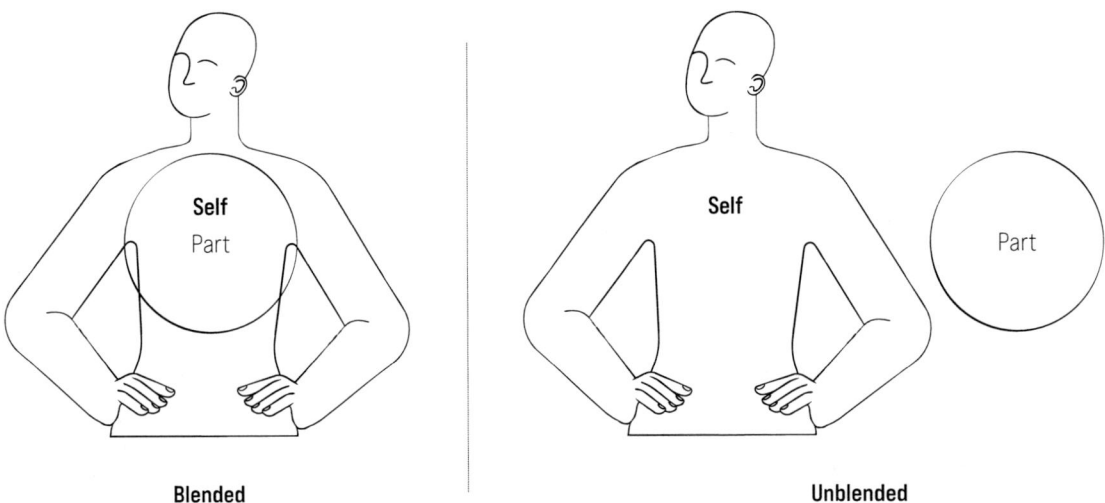

Direct access should only be used when the client is blended with a part and does not have much, if any, access to their own Self-energy. For example, direct access would be warranted if you ask, "How do you feel toward this part?" and the client responds, "This is me"; if the client is able to tell you they are blended with a part; or if the client can't access any of the 8 C's or 5 P's of Self. Direct access is only used for you to speak to one target part that is blended with the client, to help the client unblend from one part. If the client is blended with a part but has awareness of other parts also being present, you would use the conference table technique to help the client unblend and befriend multiple parts. You can use direct access anytime a client is blended with one part. Then, once the client is unblended, you guide the client to connect with the part directly, returning to befriending questions of the 6 F's.

There are three steps to implementing direct access.

Step 1: Gather Information and Provide Validation

- First, notice when a part of the client is blended with the client's system and the client is having difficulty accessing Self.
- Ask permission to speak directly to the target part (e.g., "Is it okay if I speak directly to this part of you?").
- If the client gives consent, ask the client to blend with the part so that they are speaking directly from the target part.
- Ask questions such as:
    - "How do you protect [*client's name*]?"
    - "How long have you been doing this job?"
    - "How do you feel about the job you are doing?"
    - "Are there other ways you protect [*client's name*]?"
    - "How old do you think [*client's name*] is now?"
    - "How old are you?"
    - "What are you afraid will happen if you do not do your job?"

As the part shares, provide reflective listening and validate whatever the part is sharing (e.g., "Okay, so I hear you are afraid that... Am I getting that right?"). With each response, you are validating, demonstrating compassion toward, and providing relational attunement to this part.

Step 2: Provide a Choice and an Update of Current Information

Once you have a sense of the part's job, you can provide an update to this part as needed (e.g., the client's current age). Then provide a choice to foster awareness that the part does not have to be stuck in this job for the client. For example, you might ask one of the following:

- "If you didn't have to do this job, is there something else you would rather be doing?"
- "Does your role come at some cost or have a downside?"
- "What difference would it make if you could have another job for [*client's name*]?"

Step 3: Invite the Client's Self to Be Present and Foster Self-to-Part Connection Between the Client's Self and this Part

- Ask the part for its consent to bring the client's Self into conversation with it. For example, you might say one of the following:
    - "Now that you have received an update about [*client's name*], how do you feel toward [*client's name*]? Would it be okay if we invite [*client's name*] back for you to get to know them now?"

- ○ "I hear that you are exhausted in this job for [*client's name*]. Knowing that [*client's name*] and I can help you so you don't have to work so hard, would it be okay if we invite [*client's name*] here to really get to know you?"
- If the part responds with a "yes" or any level of curiosity, then proceed with inviting the client to be present. Ask the client: "How do you feel toward this part of you?" If the client responds with any of the 8 C's or 5 P's, then proceed with traditional IFS befriending questions (from the 6 F's).
- If the part responds with negativity or hesitancy, you can respond with: "It sounds like you feel [*client's name*] is [*name the part's concern about the client*]. Am I getting that right? That may be another part in [*client's name*], but not present-day [*client's name*]. Do you have any fears or concerns about getting to know present-day [*client's name*]?" You can continue to befriend the part via direct access before asking again to invite the client to connect with this part.

Therapist Worksheet

The Therapist's Parts in Direct Access

(Adapted from Schwartz & Sweezy, 2020)

If you notice any of your own parts showing up when you are learning about or practicing direct access, feel free to acknowledge them here. Write your answers to the following questions.

What parts are you noticing right now?

_____
_____
_____
_____

Check in and ask these parts: What fears or concerns do you have? Do you have any specific fears or concerns about using direct access with clients?

_____
_____
_____
_____

Ask these parts: What do you need from me right now?

_____
_____
_____
_____

What are your intentions to care for these parts?

_____
_____
_____
_____

Befriending Technique 5: Self Tapping for Attachment Readiness & Repair

Self Tapping for Attachment Readiness & Repair (STARR) is a means of slow self-tapping, using a specific hand placement, that can be used to help clients initially communicate with a protector or exile. This initiates the attachment repair process that occurs through befriending and harnesses the IFS principle "The Self-to-part relationship is healing" (Fatter, 2023b).

STARR can help begin the befriending process in more complex systems. It is used with parts that have difficulty taking in Self-energy or are blended with the system. These could be protector parts that have a hard time receiving Self-energy or exile parts that are very young, are preverbal, or do not have an attachment template to know how to register the presence of Self. Because STARR is nonverbal and multisensory, parts that may not respond to the previously mentioned befriending interventions typically respond to STARR (Fatter, 2023b).

Butterfly Hug vs. STARR

Other techniques can also be used to enhance the attachment repair process. The butterfly hug, created by Lucina Artigas, is commonly used and paired with a positive resource during traditional EMDR phase 2 of resource development (Artigas et al., 2000; Jarero & Artigas, 2021). This technique involves guiding the client to do self-administered slow tapping briefly (e.g., six times) while focusing on a positive feeling, image, or body sensation so the working memory is not taxed (Jarero & Artigas, 2021). This supports the client to maintain vividness of the visceral experience of a positive resource (Jarero & Artigas, 2021). Research shows that when the butterfly hug is paired with positive imagery, it can increase relaxation and positive affect (Amano & Toichi, 2016). It has also been used with the elderly to naturally elicit relaxation (Girianto et al., 2021). In EMDR, you can use the butterfly hug to enhance the client's connection to a positive resource.

In contrast, STARR can be used as a "call and response" form of relational contact to help clients' parts relationally receive initial connection from Self (Fatter, 2023b). As discussed in chapter 2, some parts in more complex systems will initially only be able to take in Self through an integrative coping skill. After the client's part can receive Self from STARR, you can resume standard IFS befriending to support the Self-to-part relationship and co-regulation.

When providing directions for STARR, it is important to emphasize to the client to do slow (not fast) tapping, especially if the client feels anxious or fidgety and may tap faster than is therapeutically beneficial for them. If the client has mobility issues or cannot physically self-tap on their chest, then they can do self-tapping on the sides of their legs as an alternative.

When to Use STARR
(Adapted from Fatter, 2023b)

There are several clinical situations in which the use of STARR would be appropriate and beneficial. Here are some examples:

- **If the client is blended with dissociative parts:** STARR was originally created for working with dissociative parts to help them orient to the present moment and initiate the Self-to-part relationship. For example, if a client says they feel foggy, dizzy, or fuzzy (all indicators of a dissociative part), you can teach them the hand placement, then use STARR to help the part orient by taking in the sound, rhythm, and vibration of the slow tapping.

- **When the client is blended with a young or preverbal exile:** In working with complex trauma, it is common for younger parts to be frozen in time at the developmental stage they were at the time of the trauma. These young exiles can blend and overwhelm the system. For example, when the client suddenly starts intensely crying or is overtaken by a feeling of profound despair, you can use STARR to invite the part to take in the presence of Self. Given that the sound of STARR mimics that of a heartbeat, preverbal parts are responsive to this intervention. This is because they initially discern that there is a presence there and that they are not alone, and they perceive that what is present is the client's Self, enabling them to begin internal attachment repair. This is particularly helpful when working with clients who have a history of any form of neglect.

- **When the client is blended with a somatic part that is taking over the system:** It is not uncommon for clients with trauma histories to experience acute physiological sensations that are part of the unprocessed traumatic memory network. Fron an IFS lens, this means that a somatic part becomes blended with the system. If a client suddenly is taken over by a body sensation, you can use STARR to help the client's part receive the presence of Self.

- **When the client is blended with multiple parts are once:** For example, if the client is in acute shock or experiencing grief or loss, you can use STARR to help relationally invite connection between Self and the group of parts. You can say: "As you slowly tap, just invite these parts to take in that you are right here with them."

- **When two parts are in a polarization:** When the client communicates that they feel stuck in the middle of a power struggle between two parts, you can invite these two parts to initially take in Self's presence using STARR.

The following therapist handout provides detailed instructions for implementing this technique.

Therapist Handout

Self Tapping for Attachment Readiness & Repair (STARR)

(Fatter, 2023b)

STARR® intentionally uses slow self-tapping for relational connection within the internal system of the client.

What Is STARR?

- A multisensory form of relational communication for the target part to initially receive Self-energy from the client
- A means for the client's Self to communicate to parts
- A method of initiating an attachment repair process between Self and the IFS target part
- A "call and response" communication

When to Use STARR

- When a client is blended (merged with a part) and can't access Self-energy
- When protector parts have difficulty taking in the presence of the client's Self
- When exile parts have difficulty taking in the presence of the client's Self (exiles may be preverbal or have a history of neglect)
- When exile parts are taking over the session and the client is overwhelmed

Directions to the Client for STARR

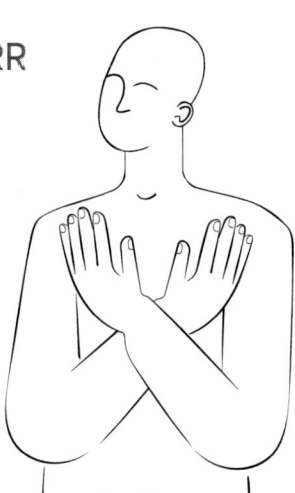

1. "Place your hands on your chest." You can demonstrate the placement of the hands and the slow self-tapping. The mechanics are the same as the butterfly hug (Artigas et al., 2000; Jarero & Artigas, 2021), but this is strategically used for relational connection between the client's Self and their parts.

2. "Let's try using slow tapping to send the part the message that you are right here with it, feel compassion toward it, and want to get to know it. Just invite the part to take in the rhythm, the sound, and the vibration of the tapping." Have the client slowly tap, alternating between their left and right hand with each tap.

3. Have the client use STARR for 20 seconds or less, during which both the client and you are quiet.

4. Then direct the client to pause the self-tapping to see how the target part received it and how it is responding to receiving the slow self-tapping as an initial form of communication from Self.

5. Parts usually need two rounds of STARR. Once the part senses Self, then befriend the part using the 6 F's or other befriending approaches.

Contracting to Receive Consent from Protectors to Proceed to Phase 3

After befriending protectors using whichever befriending strategy the client's system needs, you then can ask for permission from the protectors to proceed to phase 3. This question can further identify any other concerns protectors may have about doing EMDR, and further resources can be developed, as we'll discuss in chapter 5. Relationally, by asking for consent, you are showing respect to the client's protective system and giving the client the opportunity to receive internal consent from their own parts. This continues to communicate that the client has a choice in proceeding with EMDR, which can further strengthen their sense of empowerment and reinforce that what happens in therapy with you is consent-based.

You first want to ask if there are any parts with fears or concerns about doing EMDR, if you have not previously asked this. Here are some ways to approach this:

- "Do you have any fears or concerns about doing EMDR?"
- "Are there any parts of you with fears or concerns about doing EMDR?"
- "Check inside: Are there any parts of you that have fears or concerns about doing EMDR on [*name the trauma or focus of EMDR*]?"
- "Check inside: Are there any parts of you that have fears or concerns about doing EMDR on [*name the trauma or focus of EMDR*] with me?"
- "Take a moment and turn your attention inward. If it's helpful, you can use your breath to invite in curiosity as you breathe. Check and see if there are any parts of you that have fears or concerns about doing EMDR on [*name the trauma or focus of EMDR*] with me. If there are parts with fears, is it okay if we get to know them better? We can identify additional resources that would be helpful for them to feel included in treatment and further support stabilization."

If there are parts with fears or concerns, ask permission to get to know those parts through befriending. For example, you can say, "Thank you for describing these parts of you that have fears about doing EMDR. I want to make sure we have full consent from your system before we begin trauma reprocessing in EMDR. Would it be okay if we get to know the parts of you with these fears and concerns? Which one feels the closest to you right now?"

Once parts' fears are understood through befriending, you then can ask for consent to proceed with EMDR reprocessing. For example, you might say:

- "Ask this part: Do we have your permission to do EMDR on [*name the trauma or focus for EMDR*]?"
- "Knowing that EMDR can help your system release the emotional pain and charge from [*name the trauma or focus for EMDR*], ask this part if we have its permission to do EMDR."

For some systems, it will be enough to talk about the fears and concerns, then ask for permission to proceed with phase 3 of EMDR. For example, you can say: "Now that we have discussed these fears and concerns, do we have these parts' permission to do EMDR starting next session?" In other systems, new parts may emerge when asking about fears or concerns to proceed with EMDR. If this occurs, you can use parts mapping, as discussed in chapter 3, to explore protector parts, then guide the client to befriend these parts. By befriending protectors, the client can receive conscious consent from their protective system first, before activating the exile in phases 3 and 4 in EMDR.

In the context of EMDR treatment, contracting can also be used when parts agree to step aside to allow for EMDR reprocessing. After receiving consent, ask where the protector part(s) would like to be during EMDR before proceeding to phase 3 (Fatter, 2023b). Here are some ways you can ask the client to do so:

- "Where would these protector parts agree to be when you are doing EMDR reprocessing? Would they like to watch on the sidelines or go to a waiting room?"

- "Ask the part: 'Where would you like to be as we proceed with EMDR? You can watch on the sidelines or go to a waiting room.'"

- "The part is welcome to watch on the sidelines as we continue with EMDR. Let me know when it has moved to the sidelines to watch."

- "Thank this part for giving permission to do EMDR. Now ask it: 'Where would you like to be as we do EMDR?' If it has any more fears or concerns now or in the future, it is welcome to share them with us."

Protectors will likely be willing to proceed with EMDR after being befriended. The client has accessed enough Self to approach the protectors with curiosity and openheartedness. The client has listened to these parts' fears and expressed understanding, even appreciation, for their attempts to protect the client from these fears. The following case example shows the process of shifting from parts mapping to befriending and then asking protectors' consent to proceed with EMDR processing.

CASE EXAMPLE

Shifting from Parts Mapping to Befriending

Let's revisit Noah, who was diagnosed with PTSD from his military deployments, to see how Noah's therapist transitions from parts mapping in phase 1 to befriending in phase 2. As we saw in chapter 2, Noah's therapist learned that when Noah experiences anxiety, his nervous system goes into hyperarousal sympathetic activation (fight or flight). Consequently, the therapist noted that Noah needs to learn coping skills and resource development that includes helping his anxious part move out of hyperarousal to help him prepare for EMDR. As we saw in chapter 3, Noah's therapist worked with Noah to create a parts map connected to his symptoms.

Supporting Stabilization Through Befriending and Contracting

After talking about Noah's parts on the parts map to gain more clinical information, Noah's therapist contracts with Noah to get to know the parts better to help support his stabilization and prepare him to transition to EMDR reprocessing. Using the contracting intervention, Noah's therapist asks him which part he would like to start to get to know first: the anxious part or the suicidal part. (The therapist conceptualizes these as protector parts.)

With Noah's consent, Noah's therapist first uses the 6 F's befriending intervention to help Noah understand his anxious part. This can help create co-regulation—through his anxious part connecting with Self—and ultimately can help decrease his anxiety. When Noah's therapist then tries to use the 6 F's to befriend his suicidal part, Noah has a difficult time accessing Self and notices feeling anxiety and shame. Given that there are three parts present (the suicidal part, the anxious part, and the part that feels shame in response to the suicidal part), Noah's therapist then uses the conference table technique to help elicit Noah's compassion toward these three parts. Noah's therapist also identifies additional coping skills for Noah to use when he has suicidal thoughts.

Identifying Additional EMDR Targets

As Noah's anxious part is befriended, Noah's therapist asks: "What is this part scared would happen if it doesn't do its job?" Noah shares that the part is worried that he is bad. Noah immediately begins having flashes of multiple memories from his military traumas where he experienced and witnessed violence and caused harm to others in combat. Noah's therapist discusses adding this to the EMDR target list, and then focuses on further supporting this part through the Self-to-part relationship and resource development in phase 2.

Getting Consent from Protectors Before EMDR's Phase 3

After Noah has established coping skills and resource development in phase 2 and is able to practice coping skills on his own in between sessions to support his emotion regulation, his therapist guides him to ask the anxious part, the suicidal part, and the part that feels shame about the suicidal part if they give consent to proceed with EMDR reprocessing.

The following therapist handout describes the options for befriending protector parts in order to get consent to move to phase 3 to begin EMDR reprocessing on the agreed-upon EMDR target. Through befriending, protector parts may communicate potential additional resources that are needed before reprocessing in EMDR phase 3. Resource options are described in chapter 5.

Therapist Handout

Phase 2 Road Map to Protectors' Consent

The purpose of this handout is to guide you through the process of obtaining consent from protector parts. In short, this includes asking the client if they have any fears or concerns about doing EMDR, befriending the protectors that have fears and concerns, then asking for consent to proceed with EMDR. This is essential to do before proceeding to EMDR reprocessing in order to minimize backlash, address any specific concerns about EMDR reprocessing, and ensure that trauma reprocessing is consent-based.

Step 1: Ask About Fears and Concerns

Ask the client, "Do you have any fears or concerns about doing EMDR?"
Variations of this question include:

- "Do any parts of you have fears or concerns about doing EMDR?"
- "Do you have any fears or concerns about doing EMDR on [*name the EMDR target*]?"
- "Do you have any fears or concerns about doing EMDR on this issue with me?"

Step 2: Befriend Protector Parts with Fears or Concerns

If needed, you can map these parts on a parts map to specifically acknowledge each part with a fear and befriend these protector parts.

Step 3: Ask for Consent

Once fears have been named, use the contracting question to ask for consent to move to befriending. Ask the client: "Since there are parts of you with fears and concerns, would it be okay for us to get to know these parts of you?"

The following figure illustrates this process, including the specific befriending interventions to use for different circumstances.

CHAPTER 5

IFS Interventions for Attuned Resource Development During Phase 2

After IFS befriending interventions have been used and protectors' consent for proceeding with EMDR has been obtained, the next step is to apply IFS interventions to the resource development aspect of phase 2 to strengthen clients' coping skills and prepare them for later phases of EMDR. In this chapter we'll cover methods of integrating culturally based strengths; resource development methods for clients with complex trauma, including working with dissociative or numb parts; working with young parts; and IFS-informed EMDR exercises for resource development. A case example and therapist tools will help you apply the information in this chapter to your practice.

Integrating Culturally Based Strengths

Integrating IFS techniques to access culturally based strengths can enhance traditional EMDR resource development, particularly if clients embody a marginalized identity or if intergenerational or cultural trauma is the target for trauma reprocessing in phases 3 and 4 of EMDR (Fatter, 2023c; Nickerson, 2023d). The community cultural wealth framework defines cultural wealth as the "array of knowledge, skills, abilities, and contacts possessed and utilized by Communities of Color to survive and resist macro-and-micro forms of oppression" (Yosso, 2005, p. 77; Nickerson, 2023d). Applying this lens to integrating IFS into EMDR, you can invite in curiosity about what culturally based individual resources can be identified and strengthened to help support the client's connection with a sense of community (Venkatraman-Levis & Siniego, 2017; Venkatraman-Levis, 2017; Nickerson, 2023d).

Any access you have to your own curiosity can help you be Self-led in your own system. This will assist you in initiating conversation in session about cultural content: the client's lived experiences, how the client self-identifies, and how these identities relate to privilege and marginalization (Ashley & Lipscomb, 2023; Nickerson, 2023d). In chapter 10, you'll have an opportunity to explore your own parts related to *broaching*—intentional efforts to address the cultural, ethnic, and racial issues that are central to the client's presenting issues—during treatment (Day-Vines et al., 2007). According to Wendy Ashley and Allen Lipscomb (2023), broaching is a way to implement an anti-oppressive, anti-racist, intersectional lens with EMDR therapy with Black clients. An example of broaching would be asking the client: "Are there any culturally or spiritually relevant places or people that we can add to the list of resources to utilize if you are feeling destabilized?" (2023, p. 141). This also can include using resource development during phase 2 to identify and have the client connect with positive experiences of their own cultural identity and of inclusion (Nickerson, 2023d).

From an IFS lens, integrating culturally based strengths helps clients identify, acknowledge, and befriend parts that carry generational heirlooms, ancestral and cultural gifts, and blessings. In addition, this aids in supporting connection with parts that are adaptive and that support the client's system in navigating ongoing stressors (Fatter, 2023c). Fostering befriending between the client and parts that embody cultural wealth can strengthen resources for clients coping with current and ongoing stressors, including ongoing challenges due to systemic oppression and marginalization (Fatter, 2023c; Nickerson, 2023d).

Another useful framework to consider when integrating IFS interventions into phase 2 resource development is Yosso's (2005) six forms of resource capital. This strengths-based framework identifies six kinds of cultural capital that marginalized groups often possess but that are often underrecognized. These are listed next, along with directions on how to integrate them with resource development installation using slow BLS. This involves using slow BLS for a maximum of 6 to 12 sets, paired with a positive feeling and a positive cognition (i.e., what it means about the client that they were able to effectively navigate a challenging situation) or a cue word to describe the positive state (to help them reconnect to this resource and positive/empowered feeling in the future). Note that when utilizing this framework, you can choose to take an EMDR or an IFS approach with the intention of strengthening the client's access to these resources to prepare for EMDR trauma reprocessing. Descriptions and examples of both options are provided; the options from the EMDR lens are based on the work of Nickerson (2023d), Venkatraman-Levis (2017), and Yosso (2005).

Yosso's Six Forms of Resource Capital Applied to EMDR Resource Development

1. **Social capital:** This refers to social contacts, communal networks, and other resources that help emotionally support the client. These can be people or communities that help the client get through difficulty or problem-solve to progress in life.
    - For example, from an EMDR lens, you could ask the client: "What social connections and communities do you feel supported by or can you seek support from?" Then, to conduct resource development and installation (RDI), you could ask the client to imagine receiving support from specific people or communities, and if that feels positive for the client, they could strengthen that feeling with slow BLS. You can also ask them if there is a positive cognition that goes along with that feeling (e.g., *I am not alone*) that can be strengthened with this feeling and slow BLS.

- From an IFS lens, you might ask the client: "What parts of you have received support, a sense of connection, and belonging?" You then can ask the client to connect with those parts right now, guiding the client to ask the parts, "What do you need from me right now?" to support Self-leadership. If this process of connecting with these parts elicits a positive feeling, the client can use slow BLS for RDI, pairing the slow tapping and positive feeling with any images or sensations of connecting to these parts of themselves.

2. **Linguistic capital:** This refers to a client's understanding of in-group communication (including verbal and nonverbal communication, in formal and informal contexts) to foster connection and communication cross-culturally. This also refers to skills the client utilizes to navigate complex cultural and social situations, such as being bilingual or multilingual.

    - From an EMDR lens, you might ask a client: "What cross-cultural awareness and 'reading' the situation has helped you navigate life?" You could then ask the client to notice what it feels like to acknowledge their ability to navigate the situation. If the client can access a positive feeling or develop a positive cognition (e.g., "I am good at navigating hard situations; I am resourceful"), then the client can strengthen that feeling and positive cognition with slow BLS for RDI.

    - From an IFS lens, you might ask a client: "Would it be okay to acknowledge and send appreciation to the parts of you that helped you navigate complex social and cross-cultural situations?" If this elicits a positive feeling, the client can use slow BLS for RDI, pairing the slow tapping and positive feeling with any images or sensations of the client connecting to these parts of themself.

3. **Familial capital:** This refers to cultural wisdom and knowledge fostered by extended family, any family connection, or cultural or communal support. This may have potentially been left behind via immigration, differentiation, assimilation, or acculturation.

    - From an EMDR lens, you could ask a client: "What positive memories do you have of people you looked forward to seeing at family gatherings? If you have a family by choice, who would you want to be here right now with you?"

    - From an IFS lens, you might ask a client: "What people help your parts feel validated? This can be family, friends, or family by choice."

    - For either option, you then can guide the client to imagine being with preferred family members right now. If that feels positive for the client, ask if there are any accompanying positive cognitions that go with the positive feeling, and guide the client to use slow BLS to strengthen this positive state.

4. **Navigational capital:** This refers to the maneuvering skills—including internal resources and social and cultural skills learned through personal, collective, and communal wisdom—to navigate cultural and systemic challenges. This includes acknowledging learned competencies

that have been underrecognized that have helped the client navigate systemic oppression, such as systemic racism, homophobia, transphobia, sexism, classism, antisemitism, or xenophobia. According to Venkatraman-Levis (2017), acknowledging navigational capital can also involve "honoring the mastery of living and surviving in two worlds... acknowledging the distance traveled from place of birth and the resilience that allowed the client to navigate this dangerous journey [and recognizing] how clients negotiate for their basic needs in an unfriendly environment, including a place to live, employment, food, education, medical care, etc." (p. 106).

- From an EMDR lens, you might ask a client to recall a positive memory in which they effectively navigated a challenging cultural or systemic situation. Invite the client to notice what they feel as they recall that memory. If that is positive, then ask the client to identify a positive cognition. Once the client has a positive feeling, positive cognition, and positive image related to that experience, you can guide the client to strengthen this as a resource using slow BLS.

- From an IFS lens, you might ask a client: "What parts have helped you navigate living in two worlds or have helped you survive challenging systems? Would it be okay to send some gratitude and appreciation to these parts? How are they responding to you acknowledging them right now?" If this is a positive experience for the client, you can strengthen this positive state by guiding the client to do slow BLS. You can pair this with a positive cognition if the client can identify one as they acknowledge these parts of themself.

5. **Resistance capital:** This refers to the agency, skills, and knowledge acquired through one's own experiences, or those of one's community, challenging inequity.

    - From an EMDR lens, you could ask a client: "Who are your role models, or who are examples of people in your community advocating for social justice and equity?"

    - From an IFS lens, you could ask a client: "Who is a role model for you and your system in social justice and equity? These may be people in your community, ancestors, or anyone that serves as a role model for you in this way."

    - For either option, you then can guide the client to imagine receiving support or wise council from these role models. If that feels positive or empowering for the client, ask if there are any accompanying positive cognitions that go with the positive feeling, and guide the client to use slow BLS to strengthen this as a resource.

6. **Aspirational capital:** This refers to factors that activate a client's purpose and resilience. This may include connecting with the hopes and dreams of one's people.

    - For example, in EMDR, you could ask the client the following questions (Venkatraman-Levis, 2017, p. 102):

        – "During the hardest times before this, how did you keep going?"

- "Who, other than you, benefits from your being in this country/being out/being courageous/being alive?"
- "Are there other people whose dreams depend on you continuing to walk this path or for whom you are a role model?"

You can invite the client to notice where they feel their sense of purpose in their body, helping them identify if there is a cue word or positive cognition that describes this sense of purpose. You can invite the client to add any image, symbol, or color to help strengthen the client's access to this sense of purpose, and use slow BLS to pair these together and help the client access this resource in the future.

○ In integrating an IFS approach, you could ask the client the following series of questions:
- "What parts have helped you keep going during your hardest times?"
- "Would it be okay to connect with and acknowledge how hard those parts have worked to help you?"
- "Where is this part right now, in and around your body?"
- "How do you feel toward this part?"
- "What does this part need from you right now?"

You can guide the client to ask the parts if there is an image or symbol that helps connect to a sense of purpose. Then guide the client to identify a positive cognition or cue word to describe this sense of purpose, and use slow BLS as the client holds the image, positive cognition, or cue word with the positive feeling to strengthen this sense of purpose as a resource.

Applying this strengths-based approach using any or all of the cultural wealth resources can help the client identify resources they can access in the future, either between sessions or during EMDR reprocessing to support stabilization as needed.

Complex Trauma Tools for Resource Development

In applying phase 2 with clients with complex trauma histories, you will likely encounter clients who have dissociative parts or have parts that numb the client (either emotionally or physically). In this section, I'm going to discuss how to (1) identify dissociative or numb parts; (2) use IFS-informed integrative techniques to help the client become more oriented to the present, which supports stabilization; and (3) work with clients when they have parts that don't want to focus internally when doing IFS interventions. I also provide a therapist handout on sensory befriending to support your work with young parts that commonly, yet often unexpectedly, show up in session when working with clients with complex trauma histories. Last, I'll discuss tools to use if parts don't want the client to "go inside."

Identifying Dissociative or Numb Parts

Dissociation is a human experience; we all have parts that can and do separate us from the present moment in various ways. In applying the nonpathologizing IFS lens, you can invite in curiosity about how this may show up in clients' systems and in your own system. Dissociative and numb parts, like any parts in the client's system, have positive intentions for the client and are trying to help the system in the way they know how (Anderson, 2021; Marish, 2023; Schwartz & Sweeny, 2020; Twombly, 2022). In order to work with these parts, it's important that you understand how these parts function and what they represent. Dissociative parts may be operating in the client's system out of survival in ways that may make them harder to identify in a client's system than numb parts (Anderson, 2021; Marish, 2023).

In working with dissociative or numb parts in the system, it is vital to communicate the IFS principle "All parts are welcome." Dissociative parts may feel stigmatized or scared, or they may be part of a system of parts that had to keep trauma secrets or the truth of the traumatic event away from the rest of the system and from others for survival in the past.

Dissociation can be experienced in incremental degrees of being taken away from the present moment. In fact, a client can experience dissociation and be present at the same time (Marish, 2023). Additionally, dissociative parts or constellations of parts can express themselves in myriad ways (Anderson, 2021; Schwartz & Sweezy, 2020). Marish (2023) explains that dissociative parts may not emerge in all-or-nothing ways but can be more multidimensional in nature. While dissociative parts and parts that numb are not the same for each person, some common parts that emerge in complex trauma treatment include:

- Amnesic parts that take over, resulting in a temporary loss of time. This can vary from losing track of minutes or hours to losing track of days. The client may have gaps in memory or have amnesia about traumatic events or significant events, or may not remember several years of their life (Marish, 2023). Amnesic parts can also show up as a client not remembering what was focused on in the previous psychotherapy session, even after prompting.

- Parts that help the client feel foggy or dizzy (Fisher, 2021).

- Parts that help the client feel emotionally and/or physically numb (Fisher, 2021).

- Depersonalization parts, which can show up as a sense of being in a dream or watching oneself as though one is outside of one's body, or as parts feeling disconnected from the body (Gonzalez & Mosquera, 2012; Fisher, 2021; Marish, 2023).

- Derealization parts, which may describe feeling as though the world outside of themselves feels dreamlike, and may question "Is this real?" or whether other people outside of themselves are real (Gonzalez & Mosquera, 2012).

- Parts that have an unusual sensitivity to pain or a high pain tolerance. Clients may report that psychiatric medications are not effective or that the side effects are too intense. Clients may report not needing pain medications for medical procedures or, conversely, still feeling pain even when given high amounts of anesthesia (Fisher, 2021; Twombly, 2022).

- Parts that can communicate when dissociative states are happening and may say, "I see myself talking to you right now" or "I am floating above my body right now."

- Parts that may believe the trauma happened to someone else (Gonzalez & Mosquera, 2012; Paulsen, 2009).

- An absence of experiencing a part or the absence of a felt sense. For example, when describing Self, a client may say "nothing is there" or "nothing is inside" (Twombly, 2022, p. 82).

- Parts that respond, "I don't know" when the client is asked about their own feelings or body sensations (Gonzalez & Mosquera, 2012).

It is crucial to assess and screen for dissociation before beginning EMDR treatment in alignment with standard practice in EMDR therapy (Shapiro, 2018). This allows you to honor the client's integrative capacity to stay within their own window of tolerance during trauma reprocessing so that EMDR trauma reprocessing is therapeutic. A list of resources for complex trauma is provided at the end of this book (on page 230) to help you find specific assessments to screen for dissociation.

It is also important to assess dissociation during sessions. For example, you can consider using the Back of the Head Scale (Knipe, 2010, 2019) or the Scale of Presence, which can be used in telehealth or in person and integrates art therapy (Marchand & Simpson, 2023). Once a dissociative part is identified, you can guide the client to use integrative coping skills and IFS techniques to work with this part.

Integrative Techniques to Work with Dissociative or Numb Parts

Clinically, you will assess for the degree of emotional numbing, shutdown, or dissociation (i.e., signs of hypoarousal in the nervous system, as discussed in chapter 2). You and the client can collaboratively track the patterns of dissociative parts over time in therapy to help the client become more familiar with parts that may frequently emerge in therapy and in their daily life. Parts mapping to track sequences of parts, as discussed in chapter 3, can provide a practice structure and help the client become more conscious of their dissociative parts.

The following are five IFS techniques for working with dissociative or numb parts.

1. Befriend Dissociative or Numb Parts

First, acknowledge the dissociative or numb part(s). For example:

THERAPIST: [*Noticing a potential shift in the client*] What are you noticing now?

CLIENT: I'm feeling a bit foggy.

THERAPIST: Okay, so there is a foggy part trying to help you right now.

Next, give the part permission to help in the way it knows how:

THERAPIST: Invite that part to help you in the way it knows how for a few moments.

Finally, invite the part to take in appreciation from the client and therapist and unblend:

THERAPIST: Now that it has helped you, see if it can take in you and I both appreciating it trying to help. [*This is trying to extend Self-energy to the part.*]

THERAPIST: How is the part responding?

CLIENT: I'm feeling less foggy.

THERAPIST: Okay, so see if this part can take in your presence. Can it hear your voice right now? Ask it to give you a little more space for it to take in your presence.

2. Invite the Part to See Where It Is, Then Orient the Part

If the part won't unblend, invite it to look through the client's eyes and see where it is. This intervention comes from Dr. Paulsen (2009) and helps orient the part. Dissociative parts tend to respond to sensory input (bottom-up resources) as opposed to cognitive interventions (top-down strategies). Bottom-up strategies are recommended to help the client unblend (Anderson, 2021).

We know that based on neuroception, the nervous system has three channels of input for it to detect safety: internal cues (within the client), external cues (in the environment), and interpersonal cues (relationally between the therapist and the client; Porges, 2017). When a dissociative or numb part has blended with the system, you can focus on helping the system orient to external cues or interpersonal cues to establish a sense of feeling safe enough. With complex trauma, it's realistic that some clients have never had a sense of feeling fully safe in their lives. Thus, consider using language such as "feeling safe enough," rather than viewing safety as an all-or-nothing experience (Gonzalez & Mosquera, 2012; Marish, 2023).

CLIENT: I'm still feeling a little foggy—nothing is changing.

THERAPIST: Okay, so ask this foggy part just to look through your eyes and see where it is. [*Wait a few moments for this to happen. You are inviting the part to blend with the client.*]

THERAPIST: Can you hear my voice? [*Wait for a response.*] I want to introduce myself to you, foggy part. I'm [*client's name*]'s therapist. You are in a confidential session with me, [*client's name*], and you. Take some time to look around and see where you are. [*Give the client a few moments to do this.*] What's that like for you to see where you are now?

Dissociative parts may spontaneously unblend. If the client is still feeling blended with the dissociative part, you can continue to guide the client to help the part orient and unblend. Inviting the part to look at the client's hands can help it orient:

THERAPIST: You can also look at your hands to see the size of [*client's name*]'s hands now. [*Give the client a few moments to do this.*]

THERAPIST: What's that like for you to see [*client's name*]'s hands? [*Give time for the part to respond. If the part is still blended, offer it other present-day information*].

THERAPIST: [*Client's name*] is now [*client's age*] years old. Knowing that they are all grown up, you have a chance to get to know them now if you give them a little space. Is it okay if we bring [*client's name*] back so that they can get to know you?

3. Provide More Orienting Using Integrative Approaches

If the part needs more orienting, offer it more ways to orient to the present moment.

If a dissociative part won't unblend after various attempts of helping the part orient and be updated as to the present location and the client's current age, then you can use STARR or integrative approaches for hypoarousal. Dissociative parts that have blended with the client's system may have various abilities to talk with you—for example, some may be able to talk to the client, while others may communicate through the body or be nonverbal. Some dissociative parts may need more orientation to the present location. You can integrate classic orienting techniques from traditional psychotherapy to help offer the part data and connection with the environment, which harnesses neuroception.

THERAPIST: Take your time and as you look through [*client's name*]'s eyes, tell me things that you can see in the room . . . What things are closest to you that you can touch? . . . What are all the sounds that you are able to hear right now? . . . What smells are you noticing? . . . What are you tasting? [*Give the client a few moments to respond before offering each step of the orienting sequence.*]

You can integrate gentle movement, touch, or breathing to help orient the dissociative part. Bottom-up strategies also include somatic interventions, such as rocking from side to side, swaying, or touching one's chest or belly, which are well-known regulating strategies that you can integrate (Levine, 2010, 2018). Somatic practices such as using breath, movement, and self-touch can also be used in the befriending reprocessing (McConnell, 2013, 2020).

THERAPIST: Invite this dissociative part to be with you right now. Feel free to invite it to slowly rock from side to side to let it know that you are here with it right now. [*Demonstrate rocking.*] What are you noticing? [*Wait for the client to respond.*] Just invite the part to be with you as you rock from side to side; invite the part to take in the motion. [*Wait for the client to do this.*] If you like, you can place your hand on your chest or belly if that feels comforting to this part. [*Wait for the client to respond.*] What are you noticing now?

4. Use STARR

If the dissociative part is still blended, then you can use STARR. Be sure to use this before attempting direct access. This is because STARR is a multisensory intervention that nonverbal parts (such as emotionally numb or dissociative parts) are more likely to respond to. The directions for STARR are described in the handout on page 112.

THERAPIST: Let's invite this dissociative part to take in some slow tapping. [*Demonstrate the hand placement and invite the client to begin slow self-tapping.*] Invite this part to take in the sound, the vibration, and the rhythm of the slow tapping, letting it know that you get that this part is trying to help you.

5. Use Direct Access

If the dissociative part is still blended after implementing the previous interventions, you can use direct access. See the description for this intervention on page 106.

THERAPIST: Is it okay if I speak directly to this dissociative part? [*Wait for the client to consent.*] Okay, dissociative part, are you there? [*Wait for the part to respond.*] I'm aware you are trying to help [*client's name*]. How old do you think [*client's name*] is right now? [*Wait for response.*] What made you take over [*client's name*] a few moments ago? [*Wait for response.*] What fears or concerns do you have?

Continue befriending using direct access questions, then ask the part if they would be willing to step back and give the client some space so the client can get to know this part.

Once the client's dissociative part or numb part unblends, you can use the sensory befriending phrases described in the following section.

How to Work with Young Parts

It is important to know how to work with young parts that may spontaneously and unexpectedly show up in session, particularly as you're using the IFS befriending strategies discussed in chapter 4. These young parts may be protectors or exiles. Due to being developmentally frozen in time, young parts may not receive connection solely through verbal communication. For example, newborn or baby parts who are developmentally preverbal may first respond to the sound of the client's voice or the warmth of the client's presence. Dissociative parts are often young, so you can use these befriending phases with them after using any of the integrative techniques previously mentioned to work with dissociative or numb parts. You want to guide the client to use sensory input between the client's Self and the young part. You can use the phrases described in the therapist handout that follows.

> Therapist Handout

Sensory Befriending Phrases to Use with Young Parts

In traumatized clients, it is normal for both exiles and protectors to show up early in therapy in extreme roles or states. The younger the client was when they experienced any form of trauma, including attachment trauma, the more likely the client will have young parts. These young parts may be frozen in young developmental stages, including being preverbal. The client may need more support from Self to initially connect to a specific part.

Dissociative parts tend to respond to sensory input; therefore, using sensory language can be effective with these parts. This handout provides suggestions of sensory befriending phrases you can use to help the client connect with these young parts.

Use these phrases to support befriending:

1. "Where are you noticing the part in and around your body?" (This is the "find" question of the 6 F's.)
2. "How are you experiencing the part right now? For example, are you seeing it, sensing it, hearing it, et cetera?" (This is the "flesh out" question of the 6 F's.)

You can ask more specific questions to identify various sensations.

Touch/Sensing

- "How close is the part to you now? Can it sense you are with it right now?"
- "Invite it to take in your presence. Can it take in the warmth of being with you?"
- "If a baby or young part wants to be held, can it take in the warmth of your embrace and the rhythm of your heartbeat, knowing that you are right here with it?"

Vision

- "If you can see the part, let it know you can see it. What is it like for this part to be seen by you?"
- "Invite it to turn toward you and look at you, really taking in that you are right here with it."
- "If it feels okay, see if you can make some eye contact with this part. What is it like for this part to make eye contact with you?"

Hearing

- "If you can hear the part, let it know that you can hear it. What is it like for this part to be heard by you?"

- "Invite it to move closer to you so that it can hear your voice."
- "What is it like for this part to hear your voice and know who you are?"

It is not uncommon for young parts to initially blend with the client to receive Self from the therapist. If this occurs, you can gently invite the part to take in that both the client and you are there in the session with the part, as in this example:

> **THERAPIST:** Can the part hear my voice right now?
>
> **CLIENT:** Yes.
>
> **THERAPIST:** Great! Invite the part to notice your voice, too, as we get to know this part. You and I are both here with this part. [*Pause.*] How is the part responding to hearing both of us?

What If Parts Don't Want the Client to "Go Inside"?

In complex trauma, it is not uncommon for clients to initially present as being afraid of even bringing their attention inward or getting to know their internal world, or they may have difficulty initially noticing where a part is. These can be considered parts that don't want to "go inside" or have introspective awareness. In these cases, as mentioned in chapter 2, phase 2 resource development can be woven into phase 1 to help the client address these fears and difficulties by identifying the client's autonomic states. Teaching clients coping skills early in EMDR therapy helps support their stabilization (Gonzalez & Mosquera, 2012; Shapiro, 2018).

Using parts mapping to identify and explore parts that don't want to go inside can help clients identify fears and concerns about bringing their attention to their internal world. Additionally, the direct access befriending technique may be used if clients are blended with parts that have fears about even bringing attention internally or have difficulty noticing where parts are in or around their body. Integrating coping skills with parts work is essential for more complex systems. Sometimes parts need more time to develop trust in the therapeutic relationship and the treatment plan and to orient to the therapeutic process.

In complex trauma treatment, you can offer what Dr. Paulsen (2009, p. 79) calls "talking through" a part to get to know other parts' stories in the client's system. This stems from hypnotic interventions (Kluft, 1982), which Dr. Paulsen brought into EMDR therapy. In other words, you can befriend the part that doesn't want to go inside and that may have awareness of exiles that would be overwhelmed with inward attention. You can invite in curiosity about whether this is a manager part, approach it relationally with respect and compassion, and offer curiosity about how this part has helped the client adaptively survive and function.

If the client's system needs to talk about parts before shifting to being with their parts in befriending, respect this pacing and provide parts mapping. Ultimately, if the client does not want to go inside for exploration of their parts experientially, this is a clinical sign that you need to proceed slowly in trauma treatment, focusing on stabilization, building trust in the therapeutic relationship, and increasing the client's awareness of their own system.

IFS-Informed EMDR Exercises for Resource Development

In addition to accessing the client's culturally based strengths and implementing the complex trauma tools discussed previously, IFS can be integrated with traditional EMDR exercises for resource development.

IFS-Informed Container Exercise

The traditional container exercise in EMDR invites clients to intentionally set aside any residual disturbing material from EMDR reprocessing in an imaginary container between sessions (Hensley, 2021; Kluft, 1988; Shapiro, 2018). In integrating IFS, when there is an incomplete EMDR reprocessing session, you can guide the client to ask whatever parts (e.g., exiles) are present at the end of the session if they want to set anything aside in a container. After this, you can ask the client if that specific part would like to leave that scene and be connected to the client in a calm, safe, or healing place or in a place where the part can connect with the client's Self.

IFS-Informed Healing Place Visualization

To integrate IFS into the calm, safe, or healing place visualization traditionally used during phase 2 preparation (Hensley, 2021; Shapiro, 2018), invite the client to use the calm place as a location for the target part to be retrieved before the end of the session. This can be especially helpful for incomplete EMDR reprocessing sessions, as it supports continued relational repair with Self based on the IFS principle "The Self-to-part relationship is healing" (Fatter, 2023b). In essence, no parts are being left behind. Parts are given a choice to be in a healing place and are given the opportunity to connect with Self in that healing place.

The words "calm" and "safe" may not resonate with complex trauma clients and could even be activating for them. Therefore, it's been proposed that the term "safe place" be replaced with "healing place" (Turkus & Kahler, 2006) or "caring place" (Gonzalez & Mosquera, 2012), particularly when working with dissociative systems. This imagined location also can be a waiting area for parts to be between sessions as they are being befriended (Fatter, 2023b).

You can guide the client at the end of the session by saying: "As we prepare to end the session, ask the part in this scene, would it like to leave the scene and be with you in your healing place?" In IFS therapy, this is called the retrieval step, in which the client's Self invites exiles to leave the time period they are stuck in to be in a place of their choice where they can have access to Self (Schwartz & Sweezy, 2020). The exile may choose the healing place already established during phase 2 or may choose another place that feels healing to the part. This is a trauma-informed and client-centered invitation, as it gives the exile a choice of where it wants to be between sessions (Fatter, 2023b).

Active State or Active Place Visualization

Some parts may not want to be in a calm place or calm state to receive support from the client's Self, but would rather be in an active state or active place to do so. This is very common in clients with complex trauma and those with hyperarousal dominant systems. In this case, you can ask the client to retrieve the part and bring it to a place in which it connects with the client in the present day and in which the client and part are connecting through an activity, movement, or action (e.g., jogging, walking, bicycling, gardening, dancing, making art, cooking, climbing trees, rocking in a chair).

You can guide the client at the end of the session:

1. "As we prepare to end the session, ask the part in this scene, would it like to leave the scene and be with you in the present day?"

2. "Take your time and let me know when the part has fully landed in the present day."

3. "Where would this part like to be in your present-day life so it can feel your support between our sessions?"
4. "This part can be in a specific location in your present life or connect with you through a specific activity that feels restorative to the part."

Integrating Coping Skills for Parts to Strengthen Self-Leadership

As discussed in chapter 2, in an integrative approach, traditional coping skills can be used to help parts stabilize (Twombly, 2022), connect with the client's Self, and foster being in their window of tolerance. The intention of using a coping skill is not to make a part go away, but to foster connection and co-regulation between Self and the target part.

Whether it be journaling, movement, a grounding exercise, playing in the dirt, making art, exercising, breathwork, yoga, mindfulness and meditation practices, self-compassion practices, visualization, or any traditional EMDR resource development or stress management practice, you can invite the client to include the target part. This option can be introduced to the part after the part has been befriended. You and the client can identify coping skills that align with specific parts in the client's system, which the client can practice outside of session in preparation to do EMDR reprocessing and to foster Self-leadership. The therapist worksheet "IFS-Informed Practices Outside of Session to Support Stabilization and Integration" at the end of this chapter (page 140) provides many multisensory options.

The following examples illustrate the use of coping skills to strengthen Self-leadership.

THERAPIST: Now that you have gotten to know the angry part, ask it what helps it feel connected to you when it's upset. Would it like you to journal with it, do movement, or any specific coping skills to help it when it's upset?

CLIENT: It likes it when I journal.

THERAPIST: Great, so if the angry part feels activated between sessions, would the part like you to journal to feel connected to you?

CLIENT: Yes, that feels good to this part.

In complex trauma, different parts in a client's system likely will prefer different coping skills. The client can practice coping skills and see which resonate with specific parts in their system. These can become a regular way to end sessions throughout phase 2.

THERAPIST: Since we are coming to a place of closure for today's session, ask these two parts we have gotten to know today what helps them when they are upset, so they know that you are right here with them.

CLIENT: The sad part likes it when I garden.

THERAPIST: Great, so if you are feeling the sad part present between sessions, you can use gardening to help that part know that you are with it when it feels sad.

CLIENT: Yes, that feels good to the sad part.

THERAPIST: Great. Can you also ask the anxious part what can help it know that you are right there when it's feeling anxious?

CLIENT: The anxious part wants me to move my body. I can go on a walk or do some yoga at home.

THERAPIST: Okay, so in terms of helping these parts know that you are right there with them, if the sad part or the anxious part gets activated between sessions, you have a game plan of coping skills to practice.

> # CASE EXAMPLE
>
> ## Integrative Resource Development
>
> Let's return to our case example of Noah. During the befriending process, Noah's therapist offers parts of Noah specific coping skills that are attuned to his system. Specifically, Noah's therapist guides him to ask his protectors (his anxious part and suicidal part):
>
> - "What helps you feel connected to me? What helps you know that I'm right here with you?" (This helps support Self-to-part relationship, leading to stabilization.)
> - "What helps soothe you? What coping skill do you want me to practice helping you be soothed? I will be right there with you as we do the coping skills together." (Noah's therapist uses options from the therapist handout "IFS-Informed Practices Outside of Session to Support Stabilization and Integration." This helps parts practice being within the window of tolerance, which fosters stabilization.)
>
> Noah's therapist also assesses Noah's system's response by considering these questions:
>
> - Which coping skills help Noah access more Self-energy?
> - How well does Noah respond to traditional coping skills, such as the container exercise and the healing place visualization, in EMDR?
> - Is there any backlash (decompensation) in the system due to coping skills? Do specific parts get activated after using coping skills that initially seemed beneficial to Noah? If so, the therapist will befriend those parts and ask what helps them feel connected to Noah's Self.
> - What coping skills will help Noah down-regulate out of a state of hyperarousal activation to help his anxious part?
>
> ## Culturally Based Strengths
>
> Noah's therapist also asks questions about the six types of capital and strengthens these as resources using RDI. Particularly given that Noah's trauma history includes racial trauma, communal resources and navigational resources are identified using the IFS approach by asking, "What parts helped you navigate challenging situations?" (Note that the therapist could also have used the EMDR approach: "Imagine receiving support from a specific person or community right now.")
>
> Noah's therapist then invites him to notice any specific images or symbols that represent these resources and to notice any positive feelings and positive cognitions (i.e., what does this mean about him) or cue words (i.e., words that describe the feeling to help him return to it in the future). Then the therapist guides him to use slow BLS for a maximum of 6 to 12 sets for RDI. This gives him resources to practice connecting with on his own between sessions, as needed, for support and stabilization. These resources can be used in EMDR reprocessing as needed for stabilization.

Therapist Worksheet

Integrative Approach to Stabilization and Resource Development

The purpose of this worksheet is to help identify the parts that your client has befriended and what specific coping skills and resources support the client's parts. Use this worksheet in phase 2 when you guide clients to befriend parts and provide the client with more resources to help prepare them for EMDR reprocessing. How the client responds to the befriending process and how well their parts respond to coping skills—whether that be integrative culturally based strengths, the IFS-informed container visualization, or IFS-informed healing place visualization—will also help determine the timing of when to proceed with EMDR reprocessing in phases 3 through 8 of treatment.

Use the following guidelines to identify the client's parts that have been befriended, as well as coping skills and resources to support those parts:

- Consider what autonomic state parts are in during the befriending process.
- During befriending in phase 2, ask parts what helps them feel connected to Self. This might include activities, places, ways the parts like Self to connect with them, or times of day the part likes to connect with Self.
- Ask parts about what specific coping skills they like.
- Consider coping skills that align with the autonomic state each part tends to experience when activated (hyperarousal or hypoarousal). During befriending, parts can also be asked what triggers them, which can be added to the EMDR target list for current triggers.
- If parts get activated by the container exercise or healing place visualization, write those down (you can use the following worksheet) and guide the client to befriend those parts so that they feel included in treatment and specific resources for them can be identified.
- Ask the client what parts are showing up in response to any current constraints that client is experiencing. Those parts can be mapped and befriended to find resources and include them in treatment. While befriending these parts, guide the client to ask the parts on the parts map: (1) "What does this part want you to know?" and (2) "What does it need from you right now?"
- Consider what culturally based strengths were identified and used as RDI for the client.

Therapist Worksheet

Client's Identified Resources for Stabilization and Resource Development

Use the following table to document information for further treatment planning as to the client's readiness to proceed with EMDR reprocessing.

Client's Parts That Have Been Befriended	What Autonomic State Does the Part Experience? (Hyperarousal, hypoarousal)	What Helps the Part Feel Connected to Self? (Activities, places, time of day)	What Coping Skills Does the Part Like? What Coping Skills Align with the Part's Autonomic State?

What culturally based strengths were identified and used in RDI (e.g., social, linguistic, familial, navigational, resistance, or aspirational capital)?

_____

_____

Therapist Handout

IFS-Informed Practices Outside of Session to Support Stabilization and Integration

This handout describes IFS-informed practices clients can use between sessions to support stabilization and integration of therapeutic gains. It's important to offer the client choices and to not make IFS "homework" required. Giving traumatized clients choices is healing and empowering, and it helps clients take responsibility for caring for and relating to their own system in a Self-led way. An IFS-informed practice supports Self-to-part connection for co-regulation between the client's Self and a given part. This helps build a part's trust in Self being the leader of the client's system. Connection between a target part and the client's Self can also happen through sensory resources.

Options to offer clients include:

- **Asking the part, "How would you like to connect?"** To prepare for ending the session, guide the client to ask the target part (whatever part is present or activated) which coping skill and/or IFS-informed practice the part would like to use between sessions. The client can then make an intention with the part if they choose to connect to this part between sessions.

- **Asking the part, "What do you need from me right now?"** Checking in and connecting with the target part between sessions at least one time can help foster trust in the Self-to-part relationship and support stabilization. Invite the client to choose the time of day and where they would like to be if they would like to check in with the target part.

- **Self Tapping for Attachment Readiness & Repair (STARR)®:** If activated between sessions, the client can use STARR to help them unblend and invite the parts that are activated to take in the rhythm, sound, and vibration of the slow tapping. This can help parts move out of hyperarousal or hypoarousal.

- **Parts mapping:** Invite the client to notice what parts show up between sessions. This can be an opportunity for the client's curiosity and perspective taking (qualities of Self) to further develop. The client can create their own parts map of what parts showed up from being triggered, having conflict, having a hard day, or experiencing a good day or joy. Or they might just notice what parts show up throughout their daily routine.

- **Journaling:** Invite the client to journal between sessions. The client can intentionally choose a part to invite to express their feelings through writing. They can ask the part: "What would you like me to know about you? What is it like to be you? What do you need from me?" This can help the part feel welcome and seen by Self.

- **Art:** Invite the client to choose any type of art to help the part express itself and feel seen and understood by the client. Art can also be used to capture parts maps.

- **Meditation:** Invite the client to choose their favorite guided meditation. This can be an IFS-oriented meditation, mindfulness practice, self-compassion practice, or guided visualization. What parts did they notice showing up? What parts did they experience receiving the meditation? Did they discover any new parts?

- **Movement/exercise:** Invite the client to notice what parts show up when they move their body. What parts have fears or get triggered when the body moves? Are there certain movements or forms of exercise that feel good to the client's system? If movement feels foreign to the target part, the client can experiment by rocking, swaying, or using any rhythmic movement to connect with the target part. Exercise, even walking, naturally releases endorphins, which supports the client's stabilization and access to Self.

- **Breath:** The client can invite the target part to notice the client's breath or breathe with the client, using the breath as a relational bridge. This can be helpful for parts that have difficulty initially noticing the presence of Self. The client can also experiment with various forms of breathwork to help support the part in taking in support of the client's Self.

- **Music/sounds:** Invite the client to consider what sounds or music support the client's stabilization or help a target part feel seen or soothed. Music can also naturally calm the system by releasing endorphins. The client can explore what helps their system feel connected to Self.

- **Humming or singing**: Humming and singing help activate the ventral vagal social engagement system (Dana, 2018; Porges, 1995). The client can invite a specific part to sing with or hum with the client, which can support co-regulation between Self and activated parts.

- **Supportive touch:** Some parts prefer specific textures, such as soft or weighted blankets or a warm bath, to feel connected and supported by Self. The client can ask the target part what textures feel supportive and if there are any ways the client can use self-touch to help the part feel Self-support (e.g., hands on their own face, hugging themselves, or placing their hands on a particular part of the body).

- **Soothing through taste and smell:** The client can ask the target part or explore with their whole system: What smells and tastes feel good to the system? What smells and tastes help the client have more access to Self?

- **Images:** The client can ask the target part what images help this part feel connected to Self. These can be photographs, scenes from nature, or any other pictures that are engaging to the part or help the part feel seen or soothed. Young parts in particular sometimes benefit from having images to help them receive support of Self.

- **Identifying what part needs updating:** The client can choose a part that needs more updating and needs to get to know the client more in the present day. The client can invite the part to be with it throughout the week so that it can fully take in the client's current life. The client can ask the part what information it needs now about the client's current life.

- **Relational resources:** Parts can access Self-energy through other relationships as well as the client's Self. The client can ask the target part what other relationships (human and nonhuman) feel safe and nourishing for the part. This can include the client asking the target part to receive connection from a pet, another animal, the land, a star-filled sky, the ocean or another body of water, an ancestor, or any other spiritual resource that feels connected to something greater than the part.

CHAPTER 6

Assessment Options for Attuning to the Client's Internal System During Phase 3

We've covered the many ways you can integrate IFS principles and techniques into EMDR phases 1 and 2, and now we'll move on to phase 3. During this phase, the traumatic memory network is intentionally activated to begin EMDR trauma reprocessing in phase 4. As discussed in chapter 2, determining which target to start with will depend on the client's system, capacity, and treatment goals. You can identify EMDR targets for phase 3 using EMDR assessment methods alone (e.g., the worst part of the most recent trigger, the worst part of the specific trauma linked to the presenting symptoms, or the worst part of the touchstone memory tied to the presenting symptoms). Alternatively, you can use the IFS method of parts mapping the client's system in collaboration with the client, then befriending protector parts to identify EMDR targets connected to the client's presenting symptoms.

In this chapter, we will discuss two clinical decisions: (1) how to access the EMDR target and (2) how much to integrate IFS into asking the phase 3 questions. First, I'll address how to handle common scenarios therapists experience in accessing the target for phase 3, using case examples to illustrate these scenarios. Then I'll present three options for integrating IFS into phase 3 and provide a therapist handout that summarizes these options. Last, I'll cover how to identify legacy burdens (intergenerational trauma) that arise in befriending—which can become targets for EMDR reprocessing—and how to work with systemic and oppression-based trauma.

Common Scenarios for Accessing the Target

When integrating IFS techniques with EMDR phase 3, assessment, there are four common clinical scenarios you might experience:

1. You are using IFS interventions, and EMDR targets naturally emerge.
2. The client comes to therapy saying that they want to work on a specific trauma.
3. The client comes to therapy saying they want to work on a specific trauma or recent event and is highly activated and blended with multiple parts.

4. You are using IFS interventions to befriend protectors, which reveals an exile, and the client is able to maintain enough Self to access and befriend the exile.

Let's take a closer look at each of these scenarios and how to address them.

Scenario 1: When EMDR Targets Emerge Organically from Parts

As shown in the "Target Sequencing Chart for EMDR Reprocessing" table on page 38 in chapter 2, you identify potential EMDR targets through history taking and parts mapping. Targets can also naturally emerge from the client's system by befriending the client's protector parts connected to their presenting symptoms. The IFS approach of befriending protectors and asking these parts "What are you afraid would happen if you did not do your job?" can reveal an exile, which becomes the target for EMDR reprocessing. IFS interventions using the 6 F's and befriending questions leads to EMDR targets through the following process:

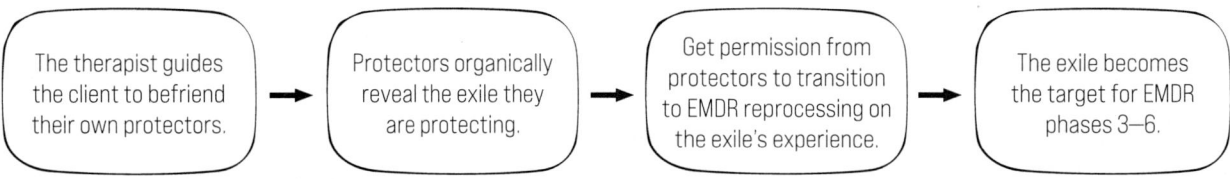

This IFS approach to identify EMDR targets through befriending protector parts that correspond with the client's symptoms aligns with EMDR's symptom-focused approach. This is because you are focusing on parts expressing themselves as the client's presenting symptoms, and the exile is holding the unprocessed traumatic memories from the past, which then become targets for EMDR reprocessing. The clinical decision of which of the three prongs (past, present, future) to focus on will depend on the client's treatment goals and also what exile emerges in befriending. Exiles are stuck in the past, so in this first clinical scenario, a trauma from the past (either the touchstone or the trauma that led to the present symptomology) is targeted. The most important IFS intervention to integrate into EMDR therapy is obtaining consent from protector parts to do EMDR during phase 2, as discussed in chapter 4. Befriending the exile is not required before transitioning to phase 3.

With clients with complex trauma, once the exile has been revealed, it will often blend with the client's system, and the client will experience intense feelings, body sensations, and memories from the exile. If this occurs, you can ask permission from the protectors that were befriended to begin EMDR reprocessing. You would then ask these protectors where they want to be during reprocessing, and begin phase 3 using the IFS-informed approach to phase 3 questions, described in the next section.

CASE EXAMPLE

When EMDR Targets Emerge Organically from Parts

Zoe, as you may remember, is a 20-year-old woman who was diagnosed with GAD and ADHD. Zoe experienced single-incident trauma from being sexually assaulted when she was 15 years old, precipitating her anxiety. Her current triggers are overwhelm from trying to get schoolwork done and relational triggers.

Earlier, Zoe's therapist guided her to befriend parts related to her symptoms and treatment goals. As you saw in her visualization statement parts map in chapter 3, Zoe ultimately wants to navigate her feelings with less overwhelm, and she identified two main protector parts (one that judges her feelings and another that is scared of her feelings). Zoe reported that when she experiences these two parts, she feels anxious. Through befriending, Zoe discovered that these two parts show up when she navigates relational triggers, and these parts confirmed that they were protecting a younger exile that was overwhelmed and anxious. Thus, in Zoe's system, there was a system of three parts connected to her clinical presentation (the judge, the part that is scared of her feelings, and the young exile that is overwhelmed and anxious).

Zoe and her therapist decide to target this exile as the first target in phase 3 for EMDR reprocessing. When assessing the worst image, Zoe is able to identify that this young exile was connected to her sexual assault. From an EMDR lens, the therapist would have added the single-incident sexual assault as a potential target as the touchstone memory from the intake process. Using the IFS interventions of first parts mapping and then befriending these parts connected to Zoe's feelings of overwhelm and anxiety confirms the sexual assault as the appropriate target to activate in phase 3 for EMDR reprocessing. Using the IFS-informed phase 3 approach, Zoe's therapist guides Zoe to ask for the consent of the two protectors to target the exile in EMDR and asks the protectors where they would like to be during EMDR reprocessing (e.g., watch on the sidelines, go to a waiting room). Zoe's therapist then proceeds with phase 3 standard EMDR questions.

Scenario 2: When the Client Says: "I Want to Work On..."

If the client is clear on the specific traumatic or stressful event they want to target in EMDR, then you can guide the client to ask their protectors: "Are there any fears or concerns any of you have about working on [*the target*]?" Befriend protectors as needed using the 6 F's, as discussed in chapter 4. After receiving consent from any protectors, you can ask the protectors where they would like to be during reprocessing and decide the best way to ask the phase 3 questions.

> **CASE EXAMPLE**
>
> ## When the Client Says: "I Want to Work On..."
>
> Noah, as you may recall, is a 32-year-old man who was diagnosed with PTSD following multiple military deployments. Noah came to therapy with the clear treatment goal of decreasing his PTSD symptoms.
>
> Through IFS befriending, Noah's therapist guides him to receive consent from his protector parts to do EMDR reprocessing on the agreed-upon target, which is the worst part of his military traumas. The therapist guides Noah to ask his protector parts where they would like to be during EMDR reprocessing, and they reveal that they want to watch on the sidelines. Noah's therapist then proceeds with asking IFS-informed phase 3 questions.

Scenario 3: When the Client Is Activated and Blended with Multiple Parts

It is very common when working with traumatized systems for the client to have difficulty accessing their own Self, to be blended with multiple parts, and to easily become dysregulated. This is also very common for any client who has experienced a recent traumatic event or loss. Even if the client is very activated, is blended with a part, or does not have any access to Self, you can still request consent of any protector parts by asking: "Are there any fears or concerns any parts of you have about working on [*the target*]?" You can befriend these parts using the 6 F's, the conference table technique, or direct access as needed to get consent to begin phase 3, trusting that phase 4 will activate the AIP system, which helps the client access Self. When a client is in a blended state, the SUDs rating will likely be high for a target, particularly if you are targeting a recent trigger or event. This process is illustrated in the following figure.

If the client is blended, you can still ask: "Are there any fears or concerns any parts of you have about working on [*the target*]?" Befriend protectors as needed using the 6 F's, the conference table technique, or direct access to receive consent.	After receiving consent from any protectors, welcome all the parts related to the target, knowing that the system will take the client where they need to go in EMDR for healing. Move into phase 3.	Phase 4 activates the AIP system, which helps the client access Self.

> ## CASE EXAMPLE
>
> ## When the Client Is Activated and Blended with Multiple Parts
>
> Let's return to Ava, the 55-year-old woman who was diagnosed with CPTSD and MDD stemming from frequent childhood sexual abuse from her father. Ava and her therapist already decided in phase 1 that due to the frequency and prolonged nature of her sexual abuse, her being in a long-term caretaker role with her father who was also her abuser, and her multiple current triggers, Ava's first EMDR target would be her most recent trigger.
>
> Ava's therapist uses befriending strategies to help Ava befriend her protector parts connected to her most recent trigger. Ava has difficulty maintaining Self-energy during this befriending process, but she is able to develop resources and coping using an integrative approach to bolster her ability to proceed to EMDR reprocessing. Even though Ava is in a blended state during befriending, her therapist still asks, "Are there any fears or concerns any parts of you have about doing EMDR on your most recent trigger?" Ava indicates that a part of her is afraid that she will be intensely emotional in EMDR, so the therapist uses the 6 F's to address that part's fears before receiving consent from that part. With consent of Ava's protectors, her therapist then proceeds to use IFS-informed phase 3 questions even when Ava is in a blended state.

Scenario 4: When the Client Can Maintain Enough Self to Connect with the Exile

Our last common clinical scenario is when the client can maintain enough Self to access and befriend the exile without being blended with the exile. In this scenario, after you use IFS interventions to befriend protectors and an exile is revealed, you guide the client to befriend the exile. You can then guide the client to ask the exile's permission to transition to EMDR reprocessing. You can use either an IFS-informed approach or a pure IFS approach in asking phase 3 questions.

In an IFS-informed phase 3 approach, you still do the pre-step of getting protectors' permission to do EMDR focused on the exile's trauma and ask the protectors where they would like to be during reprocessing, but you also guide the client to ask the exile for permission to do EMDR reprocessing. You would *not* ask the exile where it wants to be during reprocessing—in EMDR reprocessing, you want the exile to be present and have some level of activation because the unprocessed trauma it's carrying is what is being targeted.

Reasons for choosing the pure IFS approach include if you are working with attachment trauma or you are intentionally trying to limit arousal in the client's system. If you are targeting an exile that has experienced attachment trauma, and you want to foster internal repair between Self and the exile, it would benefit the exile to answer the phase 3 questions solely from its perspective. Another reason for choosing the pure IFS approach is if you are trying to limit the arousal in the client's nervous system and titrate the initial intensity and activation by solely asking the target exile the phase 3 questions. If it is the first time a client is doing EMDR reprocessing and you or the client has concerns about the level of intensity the client can tolerate, even with adequate resource development in phase 2, you could consider the pure IFS approach to asking the phase 3 questions to the target exile. If the client is used to pure IFS, this would offer a smooth transition for the first time they do EMDR reprocessing.

It is important to note that even with this intention of limiting the arousal by asking the exile to answer the phase 3 questions, EMDR reprocessing will, by its nature, take the client where they need to go for healing. Thus, the intensity level can still increase during phases 4 through 8 of EMDR reprocessing. Also, even though the pure IFS approach activates one exile's experience, EMDR reprocessing may take the client to other memories that activate other exiles. This is because EMDR reprocessing addresses the memory network of unprocessed traumatic memories, and there are multiple parts on a memory network, not just one.

> **CASE EXAMPLE**
>
> ## When the Client Can Maintain Enough Self to Connect with the Exile
>
> Out of our three case examples (Noah, Ava, and Zoe), Ava would be the most likely candidate for using a pure IFS approach due to the complexity of her trauma history and emotional dysregulation. If Ava had parts that did not trust the process or had concerns about EMDR, but her system wanted to try it, Ava's therapist could consider using the pure IFS approach. The key is that Ava would need to maintain enough Self to befriend one of her exiles in order to ask the exile the phase 3 questions using the pure IFS approach. This approach would limit the initial level of activation Ava may experience. Ava's therapist would still ask her protector parts for consent to proceed and where they would like to be during EMDR reprocessing. Then Ava's therapist would guide her to befriend one target exile to get permission to proceed with EMDR reprocessing on the traumatic memories the exile is carrying. After receiving consent, Ava's therapist would guide Ava to ask the target exile the phase 3 questions.

IFS-Informed Options to Ask Phase 3 Questions

There are three options for asking the EMDR phase 3 questions: the standard phase 3 approach, the IFS-informed phase 3 approach, and the pure IFS approach. With each of these options, you ask the phase 3 questions about the target you are reprocessing in EMDR to identify the worst image, the negative cognition, the positive cognition (desired state), specific emotions, and body sensations. The process of identifying these components of the EMDR target activates the client's memory network of unprocessed traumatic memories, and you then immediately begin phase 4. Let's discuss the three options.

The standard EMDR phase 3 questions use the original language from the standard EMDR protocol. This option elicits the most activation to process in EMDR.

The IFS-informed phase 3 approach adds two pre-steps before asking the standard EMDR phase 3 questions: (1) asking consent of protectors, and then (2) asking where the protectors would like to be during EMDR reprocessing. This gives you lots of clinical flexibility while upholding IFS's value on getting protector consent to help minimize backlash that can occur during EMDR reprocessing. So even though you may have targeted one exile's trauma to target in EMDR, asking the standard EMDR phase 3 questions allows openness in the client's system to let the answers emerge from their whole system, rather than just from one exile as in the pure IFS approach. Thus, the IFS-informed phase 3 approach potentially allows multiple exiles to respond to the question, not just one. This provides ample activation and arousal needed for EMDR reprocessing. You can use this approach even when the client has little access to Self, when the client is blended with multiple parts, or when multiple exiles are connected to the traumatic memory network (as in the case of Ava, who experienced childhood abuse that spanned multiple years).

The third option is using what I call a pure IFS approach. You still ask the standard EMDR phase 3 questions, but you are asking these explicitly from the perspective of the exile. This limits the activation and arousal the client experiences to start EMDR reprocessing, which may be helpful for some clients with complex trauma. You can consider this as a form of restricted EMDR reprocessing, because you are trying to access only one exile's perspective. To use this approach, the client must have enough Self-energy to stay present in order to connect with the target exile and ask the target exile the phase 3 questions. With this option, you are still guiding the client through the two pre-steps in IFS-informed phase 3 (asking for protector consent and asking protectors where they want to be during reprocessing), but you are then asking the standard EMDR questions to the exile they are protecting.

In using either the IFS-informed approach or the pure IFS approach to asking phase 3 questions, you want to be curious and aware that the part answering the question to identify the positive cognition and its validity (how true that cognition feels on a scale of 1 to 7) may be a manager. It is normal for manager parts to have views about what the desired state is and how the client should feel or what they should believe. Whether an exile or a manager is sharing their perspective, you still try to guide the client in matching the negative cognition and the positive cognition as you would using standard EMDR to maintain fidelity to the EMDR protocol. For example, if the client's exile reports that the negative cognition is "I am not good enough," the juxtaposed matching positive cognition would be "I am good enough."

The following therapist handout summarizes these three options for asking phase 3 questions.

Therapist Handout

IFS-Informed Options to Ask Phase 3 Questions

This handout explains the options regarding how much IFS you would like to integrate into asking phase 3 questions. The main factor to consider in making this decision is how much arousal the client's nervous system can tolerate. During IFS-informed phase 3, ask for protectors' consent to procced with doing EMDR, and ask protectors where they would like to be during reprocessing (e.g., if they want to watch on the sidelines), then proceed with the standard phase 3 questions. You can decide how much to integrate IFS into the standard EMDR phase 3 questions to assess a traumatic memory, using the following table to guide you.

The phase 3 questions can be seen as a telescopic image where, at the most open side, you ask the entire system (all parts) to weigh in, which will elicit the most arousal in the system. At the other side is the pure IFS method of asking only the exile the phase 3 questions. This is often appropriate in complex trauma systems if less arousal is needed for the client to proceed with EMDR reprocessing or if a very fragmented traumatic memory is being targeted.

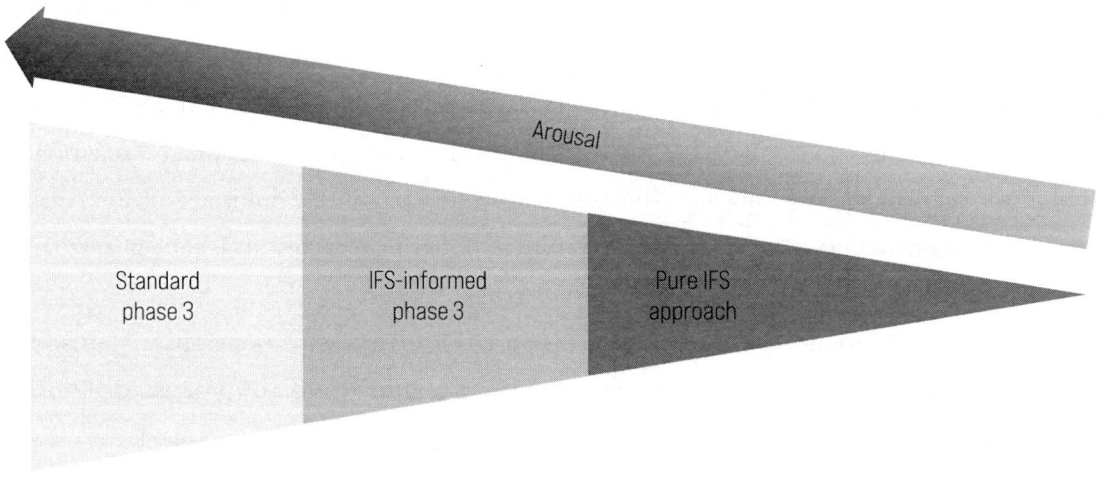

The Purpose of the Questions in Phase 3	Standard EMDR Phase 3 Questions (Shapiro, 2018) Use the standard approach of asking these questions to identify and activate various aspects of the target for EMDR reprocessing.	IFS-Informed Phase 3 Applying an IFS lens, ask protectors for permission, and then ask standard phase 3 questions.	Pure IFS Approach to Phase 3 The client directly asks the exile standard phase 3 questions; this helps limit arousal with complex trauma systems.
To access and activate the worst image of the target	"As you look back on that memory now, what image represents the worst part?"	Ask protectors for their consent to proceed with EMDR on the targeted trauma. Protectors can choose where they want to be during EMDR reprocessing. Then proceed with asking standard phase 3 questions (this potentially allows multiple exiles to respond, not just one).	Ask protectors for their consent to proceed with asking the exile and doing EMDR. Protectors can choose where they want to be during EMDR reprocessing. Guide the client to directly ask the target exile about the image they have that represents the worst part.
To identify and activate the negative cognition	"What words best go with the picture that express your negative belief about yourself now?" (p. 134)	Ask the standard phase 3 question to potentially allow for multiple exiles to respond, not just one.	The negative cognition is equivalent to the belief or burden in IFS. This comes directly from the exile.
To identify and activate the positive cognition	"When you bring up that picture/incident, what would you like to believe about yourself now?" (p. 136)	Holding an IFS lens, you can just be aware that this positive cognition may be coming from protector parts or the target exile.	Holding an IFS lens, you can just be aware that this positive cognition may be coming from protector parts or the target exile.
To measure the validity of cognition	"When you think of the incident (or picture), how true do those words [repeat the positive cognition] feel to you now on a scale of 1 to 7, where 1 feels completely false and 7 feels totally true?" (p. 137)	You can hold curiosity that this validity may be coming from protector parts or the target exile, just like the positive cognition may be coming from protector parts or the actual target exile.	You can hold curiosity that this validity may be coming from protector parts or the target exile, just like the positive cognition may be coming from protector parts or the actual target exile.

The Purpose of the Questions in Phase 3	Standard EMDR Phase 3 Questions (Shapiro, 2018) Use the standard approach of asking these questions to identify and activate various aspects of the target for EMDR reprocessing.	IFS-Informed Phase 3 Applying an IFS lens, ask protectors for permission, and then ask standard phase 3 questions.	Pure IFS Approach to Phase 3 The client directly asks the exile standard phase 3 questions; this helps limit arousal with complex trauma systems.
To activate the emotions connected with the traumatic memory	"When you bring up the picture (or incident) and those words [state the negative cognition], what emotion do you feel now?" (p.138)	Ask the standard phase 3 questions to potentially allow for multiple exiles to respond, not just one.	These are the exile's feelings.
To measure the subjective units of distress (SUDs)	"On a scale of 0 to 10, where 0 is no disturbance or neutral and 10 is the highest disturbance you can imagine, how disturbing does it feel now?" (p. 139)	Ask the standard phase 3 questions to potentially allow for multiple exiles to respond, not just one.	This is the SUDs rating according to the exile.
To identify the body sensations associated with the traumatic memory	"Where do you feel it (the disturbance) in your body?" (p.139)	Ask the standard phase 3 questions to potentially allow for multiple exiles to respond, not just one.	This identifies the location in the exile's body.

Identifying Legacy Burdens: Cultural and Intergenerational Trauma

From an IFS lens, parts can carry personal burdens (from one's own lived experience) and legacy burdens (from intergenerational trauma; Schwartz & Sweezy, 2020). Legacy burdens can be transmitted multiple ways, including through:

- Relationships (e.g., parent-child interactions)
- Epigenetics (how behavior and environment impact gene function)
- Culture (e.g., belonging to a specific culture, being a member of a marginalized community, in response to the dominant culture)
- Socialization
- Collective and historical trauma

Protector parts usually can't discern whether the exile they are protecting is carrying a personal burden, a legacy burden, or both (Sinko, 2017) until these parts are befriended. Typically, once parts become aware, through befriending, that they are carrying a legacy burden—one that does not belong to them but was handed down or absorbed in their system—then the parts become more ready to release the burden (Sinko, 2017). Once parts become aware they are carrying a legacy burden, you can add that to the potential target list for EMDR. In the remainder of this chapter, we'll cover key information to assist you in identifying and targeting legacy burdens in EMDR phase 3 using an IFS-integrated approach.

Befriending Techniques to Identify Legacy Burdens

By applying IFS befriending techniques, legacy burdens can be revealed and become the target for EMDR reprocessing in phase 3. From an IFS lens, you want to consider that a legacy burden may be present if a part is not softening using the standard befriending techniques described in chapter 4. To assess whether a client is carrying legacy burdens, guide the client to ask the target part these specific befriending questions:

- "How much of this belongs to you? How much was passed down?"
- "What percentage belongs to you? What percentage does not belong to you?"
- "How much does this belong to you and you alone?"
- "Where did this part learn or take on this belief/burden?" (Schwartz & Sweezy, 2020; Sinko, 2017)
- "What lineage does this part feel connected to?"
- "Which blood lineages are connected to the legacy burden?" (Fatter, 2023a)

The following therapist handout presents additional ways to identify legacy burdens through both an EMDR and an IFS lens.

Therapist Handout

Identifying Legacy Burdens

To assess whether a client is carrying legacy burdens, watch for clinical signs and use the IFS befriending questions specifically designed for legacy burdens, as described below.

Clinical Signs from the EMDR Lens	IFS Befriending Questions to Ask	Clinical Signs from the IFS Lens (Sinko, 2017)
• The client is having strong somatic reactions, images, beliefs/negative cognitions, dreams, or nightmares that are not from their own lived experience but what previous generations lived through (Alter-Reid & Heber, 2023; Robinson, 2023). • The client is having highly charged reactions to a collective or historic communal stressor. • The client is having a dissociative reaction (e.g., blank, spacey, "no feeling," emotional numbness, "I feel nothing") to a collective or historic communal stressor. • The client is presenting with a fractured cultural or family narrative and/or is having strong reactions or replaying images from family stories that were told (Alter-Reid & Heber, 2023). • The client experiences an ancestor show up–this could be when the client is awake, in dreams, perhaps in ceremony, spiritual, or ritual practice. The ancestor shares about traumatic things that happened or expresses that harm was done to them.	• "How much of this belongs to you?" • "How much was passed down? What percentage belongs to you? What percentage does not belong to you?" • "How much does this belong to you and you alone?" • "Where did this part learn or take on this belief/burden?" (Schwartz & Sweezy, 2020; Sinko, 2017) • "What lineage does this part feel connected to?" • "Which blood lineages are connected to the legacy burden?" (Fatter, 2023a)	Either organically or in response to the befriending questions, the client describes the burden using language like the following: • "I don't know where this comes from." • "It's always been there." • "I don't know when this started, but it's been there my whole life." • "This feels like it was handed down to me." • "This is so much bigger than me." • "My parent (or grandparent) had this too." (The client may also recognize that siblings, other extended family, or fellow people that share a specific identity share the same burden.)

Targeting a Legacy Burden in Phase 3

Once a legacy burden has been identified, you can receive consent from the protectors to do EMDR, and—if focusing on legacy burdens aligns with the client's treatment goals and the client has completed appropriate resource development in phase 2—proceed with phase 3 questions. If you are targeting legacy burdens in EMDR reprocessing, it is important to consider enhancing culturally based strengths by using RDI focused on the six forms of resource capital, as discussed in chapter 5. Be aware that any part in the system (managers, firefighters, and exiles) can carry legacy burdens. You have the choice to use specific EMDR protocols designed to address intergenerational trauma, such as a legacy-attuned protocol (Robinson, 2023) or a transgenerational approach (Alter-Reid & Heber, 2023); each offers a specific approach to asking the standard phase 3 questions to access and activate the memory network connected to intergenerational trauma. You can still provide an IFS-informed approach by asking if there are any parts with fears or concerns before proceeding with EMDR reprocessing, asking those parts for consent to proceed, and asking them where they would like to be during EMDR reprocessing. Sometimes legacy burdens show up as blocking beliefs during phase 4; we will discuss how to navigate this in chapter 7.

When legacy burdens are based on systemic oppression, careful attention is required to determine whether the threat is ongoing and to respond most effectively. We will turn next to this topic to close out the chapter.

Tools to Work with Systemic and Oppression-Based Traumas

From an IFS lens, blended systems are common when clients are experiencing ongoing systemic threat, harm, marginalization, or oppression. When there is an ongoing threat, protector parts realistically may not de-role from their jobs of protecting the system. The clinical goal when there is an ongoing threat in the client's life is to decrease acute distress within the client's system and help the client be Self-led. As discussed in chapter 2, from a nervous system perspective, the clinical goal is to support the client in having an adaptive nervous system to strengthen the client's sense of agency and enable the nervous system to continually adapt to any current threats or ongoing trauma exposure. Parts within the client's system may continually be adapting to present-day threats, stressors, and trauma exposure (whether experienced directly or vicariously from witnessing others' experiences). What this means is that realistically the SUDs level on the target may not go down to zero during EMDR reprocessing due to continued ongoing threat happening in the client's life. You can still use an IFS-informed approach to asking phase 3 questions by asking if any parts have fears or concerns about doing EMDR on the target and asking those protector parts where they would like to be during EMDR reprocessing.

As discussed in chapter 2, you want to assess any client for trauma exposure due to discrimination based on any aspect of the client's identity (e.g., race, sexual orientation, gender identity, socioeconomic class, faith, cultural identity, immigration status). Using a measure such as the Trauma Symptoms of Discrimination

Scale (Williams, Osman, et al., 2023) during the intake and asking about trauma history related to aspects of the client's identity is important.

You validate the client's lived experiences related to discrimination or ongoing exposure to systemic oppression just as you would other traumatic experiences that client has lived through. This also lends itself to developing a trusting therapeutic relationship and strong working alliance. In addition, be conscious of creating a less-hierarchical therapeutic stance when working with clients experiencing ongoing discrimination and/or ongoing trauma exposure due to oppression. This can help mitigate any potential power dynamics with clients if you embody identities that have sociopolitical privilege or are part of the dominant culture (Bartlett et al., 2022).

From an IFS lens, in identifying legacy burdens or EMDR targets with clients who are experiencing ongoing systemic threat, harm, marginalization, or oppression, you want to be Self-led in relating to the client and their parts. You also want to use broaching techniques to directly ask clients about cultural trauma, experiences of discrimination, and any ongoing trauma exposure due to systemic oppression. The therapist worksheet "What Parts Emerge in Broaching Cultural Content?" in chapter 10 (page 221) will help you to explore your parts that emerge in your efforts to address a client's cultural, ethnic, or racial issues that are central to their presenting issues or related to the client's EMDR target.

If a specific legacy burden is revealed or if you're working with a client who is targeting intergenerational trauma or ongoing systemic oppression, you want to make sure to include developing social capital during phase 2, prior to asking phase 3 questions. Let's discuss some options for this.

Bartlett and colleagues (2022) as well as Williams, Holmes, and colleagues (2023) recommend tailoring coping skills to the client's unique intersectional stressors, using empowerment-oriented approaches that support the client in accessing social capital (i.e., social support, whether online or in person). Research has shown that social support ameliorates mental health issues stemming from discrimination. This can include helping the client to strengthen their individual support system and to connect with other people who are marginalized through art making, sharing stories or similar experiences, and so forth. For marginalized groups, having physical or virtual space to be with each other in community for connection, celebration, or coalition-building is vital. Exploring the client's spiritual resources and practices has also been recommended. In working with clients with complex trauma that may embody multiple marginalized identities, like with any support plan, you and the client can determine an individualized approach to choose communal resources or strengthen social support that does not retraumatize the client or put them in harm's way. In addition to the benefits of social connection and fostering resilience, social capital can help the client access additional resources—from information, to childcare, to professional networking, to financial support for marginalized clients (Bartlett et al., 2022).

From an EMDR lens, as described in chapter 5, when the client has positive experiences of being connected to their support system or a specific community, you can enhance this as an ongoing internal resource for the client using RDI prior to beginning phase 3. These resources can then be accessed and used if there is blocked reprocessing or if more support is needed in session for stabilization throughout EMDR reprocessing.

Nickerson (2023a) provides a wealth of information on identifying specific themes or types of traumas that can be used as EMDR targets to activate in phase 3 for reprocessing when working with clients with cultural trauma and those in marginalized populations. These include considering the client's experiences of discrimination within systemic oppression; asylum seeking, immigration, and acculturation; social exclusion or being ostracized; stigmatization and being singled out; the impact on the client's social identity or cultural identity; prejudice, bias, and discriminatory behaviors toward others; societal neglect, lack of resources, and poverty; culturally shared adversity and trauma; intersectional challenges and in-group conflict; and cultural legacy traumas (Nickerson, 2023b). One way to make phase 3 adaptations when targeting a culturally based trauma with clients with ongoing systemic trauma exposure is to encourage the client to conjure an image of the target by asking: "If you were to paint a picture, what would that look like?" (p. 95). Using metaphors that the client uses to describe their lived experience can also be a helpful way to access an EMDR target (Nickerson, 2023c).

You can consider in phase 3 which treatment protocol would best serve the client—for instance, a protocol geared for recent events, the standard protocol, or a legacy-based protocol. If a client just had another traumatic event (e.g., a car accident, a house fire, a loss of a loved one) occur within the past three months, you would use the recent-events protocol. The EMDR standard protocol is very flexible and can be used in working with touchstone memories, the most recent trigger, or anticipated future events. A legacy-based protocol is specifically geared for targeting intergenerational trauma in EMDR. So, if the client's target is intergenerational trauma or a legacy burden, you want to use a legacy-based protocol.

It is important to note that regardless of what EMDR protocol you choose for a client, you can still use the IFS-informed approach to asking the phase 3 questions to receive protectors' consent and give protectors the choice of where they will be during EMDR reprocessing to minimize backlash. Trauma reprocessing begins in phase 4 of EMDR, which is the focus of the next chapter.

CHAPTER 7

IFS-Informed Desensitization During Phase 4

During phase 4 of EMDR, trauma reprocessing begins and desensitization occurs. This chapter describes this process through an IFS lens and discusses IFS interventions to use in session when clients get stuck. This chapter will provide you with clear directions for employing each IFS intervention, along with case examples illustrating when and how to use these interventions.

Bringing an IFS Lens to Phase 4 Trauma Reprocessing

During phase 4, the client receives fast alternating bilateral stimulation while focusing on the image, negative cognition, emotions, and body sensations of the target activated in phase 3 (Shapiro, 2018). When phase 4 trauma reprocessing is effectively progressing, there is movement and change in what the client is experiencing. From an IFS perspective, when phase 4 moves smoothly and ultimately reaches a zero or as close to zero as possible on a scale of 0 to 10 during EMDR reprocessing, parts (protectors and exiles) on the targeted memory network have been witnessed and unburdened, leading to an internal reorganization in the client's system. Phase 4 naturally results in the client having more access to Self, which holds adaptive information to help the client get unstuck from the past and heal traumatic wounds.

When a client is stuck in phase 4 reprocessing, it typically shows up as there being no change in at least two consecutive sets, which is called *looping* or *blocked reprocessing* (Shapiro, 2018). In applying the IFS lens, any looping or blocked reprocessing signals a lack of Self-to-part connection during EMDR reprocessing (Fatter, 2023b). Parts in either an exile or a protector role are blended with the system, leading the client to get stuck.

Thus, any IFS intervention used during phase 4 is focused on reestablishing Self-to-part connection in some way. For clients who are over-responders (over-accessing the traumatic memory), an exile is likely blended with the system, and the client will need support in accessing their own Self-energy first to reestablish Self-to-part connection. For clients who are under-responders (under-accessing the traumatic memory), a protector part is likely blended with the system and blocking access to the traumatic memory.

You can use the 6 F's to explore any blocking belief or fear the part may have to help the client increase their access to the target's (exile's) trauma-related content to resume BLS.

The IFS principle "The Self-to-part relationship is healing" underlies any IFS interventions used during phase 4. Traditional EMDR uses cognitive interweaves: interventions in which you offer new information or another perspective to help the client move through blocked reprocessing, enabling them to ascertain appropriate responsibility, the client's present-day safety, and choices the client has in the present day and in the future (Shapiro, 2018). In integrating IFS, this information can be provided organically—as connection with Self and the target part emerges in phase 4 reprocessing—to help the client become unstuck in their EMDR reprocessing. The following table illustrates how to use an IFS lens to interpret various client responses during EMDR phase 4 trauma reprocessing, along with IFS interventions to use in each case. Following the table, we'll discuss each IFS intervention in detail.

Clinical Signs During Phase 4 for Offering IFS Interventions

Client's Response to EMDR (Shapiro, 2018)	IFS Lens	IFS Interventions to Use
The client continues to respond with no change after two sets (the client is "looping").	The Self-to-part connection has been lost. • If a protector part is blended, this may clinically show up as the client under-accessing trauma material or blocking movement in reprocessing. • If an exile is blended, this may clinically show up as the client over-accessing trauma material, likely expressing overwhelm and high activation in reprocessing.	• Use STARR as needed to initiate befriending. • If a protector part is present, use the 6 F's or the IFS-informed two-hand interweave if there is a polarization between two parts in the client. • If an exile part is present, offer any of these options: witnessing, do-over, unburdening, updating, or retrieval.
The client expresses a blocking belief that contributes to reprocessing not changing after two sets.	A protector part is blended with the client.	• Befriend the part with the blocking belief. • Use the 6 F's. • Explore legacy burdens. • Update the part with the blocking belief through the Self-to-part connection. • Use the IFS-informed two-hand interweave if there is a polarization between parts in the client.

Client's Response to EMDR (Shapiro, 2018)	IFS Lens	IFS Interventions to Use
The client is not accessing information to help resolve reprocessing.	There is a lack of Self-to-part connection.	• Help the client access their Self-energy. • If a legacy burden emerges in reprocessing, invite in relational resources to help the client access Self-energy (e.g., ancestral guide, client-centered cultural and spiritual relational resources). • Befriend the part. • Use STARR as needed to initiate befriending.
EMDR reprocessing is not naturally generalizing to other channels.	The target exile may need more witnessing or a protector part may need to be included in reprocessing to integrate therapeutic gains.	• Use witnessing, do-over, retrieval, or unburdening.
During the last third of the EMDR reprocessing session, the client experiences high reactivity.	An exile is blended with the client.	• Use STARR as needed to initiate Self-to-part connection, then resume fast BLS. • Elicit the client's Self-energy through befriending. • Use updating. • To end an incomplete session: use retrieval, invite the part to use a container, and establish a healing place for the exile to have access to client's Self between sessions.
During the last third of the EMDR reprocessing session, a target emerges that will require more reprocessing than time allows for in the session.	Another exile on the memory network is uncovered.	• Use befriending. • To end an incomplete session: use retrieval, invite the part to use a container, and establish a healing place for the exile to have access to client's Self between sessions.

Client's Response to EMDR (Shapiro, 2018)	IFS Lens	IFS Interventions to Use
The client expresses emotional overwhelm, then exhaustion, falling asleep in session, and/or shutdown.	Potentially a group of exiles blended with the client, leading to a protector taking over the system. Clinically this may show up as the client moving outside of their window of tolerance in session.	• Slow down reprocessing by using STARR as needed to initiate befriending to groups of exiles and/or parts shutting the system down. • Utilize relational resources to bring in Self-energy connecting with the client as they are. (This can be anyone or anything in the client's life that brings in Self-energy, such as connecting with a pet or with cultural, communal, or spiritual resources.) This is intended to ultimately elicit a ventral vagal state to help the client move out of dorsal vagal shutdown, as described in chapter 5. • To end an incomplete session: use retrieval, invite the part to use a container, and establish a healing place for the exile to have access to client's Self between sessions.

Phase 4 IFS Interventions

As with any interweave used during phase 4 reprocessing, the intention of the intervention is to help the client get unstuck so they can resume EMDR reprocessing. You return the client back to reprocessing with fast alternating BLS once "the train is on the track," and then stay out of the way of reprocessing unless needed (Hensley, 2021; Shapiro, 2018). Thus, with any IFS intervention used in phase 4, you then resume fast alternating BLS for EMDR reprocessing, rather than proceeding with pure IFS therapy or changing the session to an IFS session (Fatter, 2023b).

Described next are nine IFS interventions you can use during phase 4, including when and how to use them and case vignettes demonstrating their use in session.

Befriending: Restoring the Self-to-Part Connection

Befriending is the IFS term that means getting to know a part from a place of curiosity. Befriending interventions help restore the connection between the client's Self and a given part. During phase 4, befriending interventions can help a client get unstuck in EMDR reprocessing by eliciting the client's Self to connect with a part. Befriending interventions were discussed at length in chapter 4 with regard to obtaining protector consent during phase 2. Please return to that chapter, if needed, to review the befriending techniques.

When to Use This

- Use befriending when the client is looping and there is a visual image of a memory or scene.

How to Use This

- Ask: "How do you feel toward this part of you in the memory?"
- If Self-energy is present (if the client feels one of the 8 C's: curiosity, compassion, calmness, creativity, connectedness, courage, clarity, confidence), then say: "Can you share that with the part? How is it responding?" This is based on the IFS principle "The Self-to-part relationship is healing." You can then resume BLS in phase 4 reprocessing.
- If Self-energy is not present, then proceed to an IFS-informed two-hand interweave.

CASE EXAMPLE

Using Befriending When a Protector Is Blended

A blended protector part can show up as underarousal or a blocking belief in reprocessing.

CLIENT: I'm not getting anything new. [*The client is looping.*]

THERAPIST: Check inside; do any parts of you have fears or concerns right now?

CLIENT: I don't think this is working for me. EMDR isn't working.

THERAPIST: Okay, so a part of you is questioning EMDR and is concerned this isn't working. Am I getting that right?

CLIENT: Yes.

THERAPIST: How do you feel toward this part right now? [*Assessing for the client's access to Self*]

CLIENT: I understand it.

THERAPIST: Does your heart feel open to getting to know this part? [*Assessing for the client's access to Self*]

CLIENT: Yes.

THERAPIST: Can you share that with this part of you? [*Pauses.*] How is it responding to your openheartedness right now?

CLIENT: It feels better.

THERAPIST: Okay. Be with this part and its feelings and go with that. [*Continues with BLS EMDR reprocessing.*]

If looping continues to occur with this part, the therapist can proceed as follows:

THERAPIST: Ask this part, what fears does it have if EMDR is not working? [*Befriending by asking about the part's fears*]

CLIENT: I'll never get better.

THERAPIST: Ask this part, if you never get better, then what would happen?

CLIENT: I'll be a failure.

THERAPIST: So this part is concerned that if you never get better with EMDR, then you will be a failure. Is there anything you want to say in response to this part's fear? [*Supporting Self-to-part connection*]

CLIENT: I get its concern.

THERAPIST: Then let it know that and see how it's responding to you really understanding it. [*Continues with BLS EMDR reprocessing.*]

> **CASE EXAMPLE**
>
> ## Using Befriending When an Exile Is Blended
>
> A blended exile can show up as overarousal, overactivation, and emotional overwhelm. The client may be moving out of their window of tolerance.
>
> In this example, the client paused the set early. They are crying profusely and extremely emotionally activated.
>
> **CLIENT:** I see a younger part of me screaming, "This person is dangerous!"
>
> **THERAPIST:** And how do you feel toward her right now?
>
> **CLIENT:** I love her.
>
> **THERAPIST:** Let her know that. [*Pauses.*] How is she responding to you loving her? [*Supporting Self-to-part connection and making sure the younger part is receiving the client's Self*]
>
> **CLIENT:** She's feeling relieved.
>
> **THERAPIST:** Go with that. [*Resumes fast BLS.*]

IFS-Informed Two-Hand Interweave

Robin Shapiro (2005) created the two-hand EMDR interweave to use when blocked reprocessing occurs. In this technique, the client is asked to "just notice" a feeling, belief, or ego state in one hand and an opposing feeling, belief, or ego state in the other hand. Two different ego states can interact with each other during this interweave, as needed, and you can ask the client, "What difference do you notice?" between the two ego states prior to returning to fast BLS (Shapiro, 2005, p. 161).

The IFS-informed two-hand interweave is intended to foster Self-to-part relationship. (That is, it is not designed for the parts to interact with each other, but rather for the parts to take in Self-presence and interact with Self.) This brings in the notion of multiplicity and enables the acknowledgment of parts that are dialectical, have different feelings from one another, and can coexist in the client's system with Self.

When to Use This

The IFS-informed two-hand interweave can be effectively used in the following scenarios:

- When you attempt to use befriending and the client is not in Self—for example, when you ask, "How do you feel toward this part in the memory?" and the client answers, "I don't like this part" or responds without one of the 8 C's
- When there is a polarization between parts that emerges during EMDR reprocessing

How to Use This

1. Invite one part to be in one hand and another in the other hand.

2. Invite in presence from the client's Self. You can say: "Invite these parts to turn toward you and take in your presence. You are here with both parts right now. Just notice how these parts are responding to you being with them right now." Then resume fast BLS.

    - If the opposing parts are not already clear or the looping does not resolve, you can also say: "Take turns and ask each part to share with you its fear or feelings." [*Pause while the client does this with no BLS.*] "Does that make sense to you? If so, then let it know you understand its feeling." [*The client does this with both parts.*] "Just invite these parts to take in that you understand both of them. How are they responding to you understanding both of them?" If the parts are responding positively, resume fast BLS.

    - If the parts are not responding positively to the client's presence, ask the client: "How do you feel toward each part right now?"

        – If at least one of the 8 C's is present, say: "Extend that compassion to both of these parts." Resume fast BLS.

        – If the client has difficulty accessing Self (i.e., does not respond with any of the 8 C's), invite in curiosity about whether there is another part that is present: "Let's invite whatever part does not like these two parts to also be here. Invite these three parts to take in your presence, knowing that each of these parts is important." Resume fast BLS.

3. If the IFS-informed two-hand interweave does not shift looping, then you can move to use the 6 F's with each part, further identifying the opposing part's fears or concerns. Ask the client, "What is this part scared would happen if it did not do its job?" before resuming fast BLS.

> ## CASE EXAMPLE
>
> # Using the IFS-Informed Two-Hand Interweave
>
> **CLIENT:** I feel anxious—it's just looming. [*This has occurred for two sets. The client is looping.*]
>
> **THERAPIST:** Where are you noticing this anxious feeling in and around your body?
>
> **CLIENT:** It's in my chest.
>
> **THERAPIST:** Focus on this part in your chest. How do you feel toward this part right now?
>
> **CLIENT:** I hate this anxiety. It doesn't go away. [*Since the client is not in Self, the therapist switches to use an IFS-informed two-hand interweave.*]
>
> **THERAPIST:** Okay. Invite the part that hates the anxiety to be in one of your hands. Let me know when you sense this.
>
> **CLIENT:** Okay.
>
> **THERAPIST:** Invite your anxious part to be in your other hand. Let me know when you sense this.
>
> **CLIENT:** Okay. Each one is in a different hand.
>
> **THERAPIST:** Invite these parts to turn toward you and take in your presence. [*Pauses.*] You are here with both of these parts right now. Just notice how these parts are responding to you being with them right now. [*Resumes fast BLS.*]

The 6 F's

As discussed in chapter 4, the 6 F's are used to help a client identify and understand a target part's perspective, including any fears and concerns. This intervention is particularly effective to use during phase 4 when the client is getting stuck in EMDR reprocessing because it elicits information from the part that the client was not aware of, helping the client be able to return to EMDR reprocessing with the new information shared by the target part.

When to Use

Use the 6 F's in the following scenarios during phase 4:

- When a blocking belief is causing the blocked reprocessing. Blocking beliefs are likely protector parts that have fears or concerns that get elicited through phase 4 trauma reprocessing. You can use the 6 F's to befriend parts that have any emerging blocking beliefs (Fatter, 2023b).

- When there is a polarization between two opposing parts that the IFS-informed two-hand interweave did not resolve. You can use the 6 F's to help the client identify each part's fear and concern and foster Self-to-part connection.

How to Use

Identify the target part and ask the 6 F's. If there are two opposing parts, prompt the client to take turns asking the 6 F's to each part. You can choose to use fast BLS after each question or pause BLS until Self-to-part connection is restored. For polarizations, the latter option is best.

Here are the 6 F's applied to phase 4 (Schwartz & Sweezy, 2020):

1. **Find:** "Where do you notice this part [*the part with the blocking belief*] right now in or around your body?" [*Wait for the client's response.*]

2. **Focus:** "Give your attention to this part."

3. **Flesh it out:** "How are you experiencing this part right now?" [*If needed, prompt:*] "For example, is this an image, a felt sense, a body sensation?" Once the client responds, say: "Let it know you can see it." (Use language that corresponds to the client's experience.)

4. **Feel toward:** "How do you feel toward this part?" (Schwartz & Sweezy, p. 132). This question is checking for the client's access to Self. It's okay if the part is blended with Self. The goal of using the 6 F's during phase 4 reprocessing is to have the fears of this part named, then to resume reprocessing.

5. **Befriend:** "What is this part hoping to accomplish? What is it scared would happen if it didn't do its job?"

6. **Fears:** "What are this part's fears and concerns?"

Neither you nor the client tries to get rid of or change the part with the blocking belief; rather, you invite in curiosity and invite the client to befriend this part and help this part feel understood. Using the 6 F's intervention during blocked or stuck reprocessing employs two IFS principles: "The Self-to-part relationship is healing" and "If parts feel understood, they will soften."

Common fears that emerge during EMDR reprocessing include the following (Hensley, 2021; Shapiro, 2018):

- Being stuck in a permanent state of overwhelm
- Going crazy
- Change
- Losing good memories
- Getting better in therapy—who will they be if they actually get better?

- Losing connection with the therapist
- Losing the respect of or positive regard from the therapist
- A worst-case scenario happening
- Being faced with even greater pain

These fears can usually be adequately addressed using IFS befriending and the 6 F's to resume BLS, helping the client become unstuck. If there is continued looping, then consider that the protector part with the blocking belief may be a legacy burden. As discussed earlier, the IFS term "legacy burdens" refers to trauma-related beliefs, feelings, or sensations that are handed down intergenerationally or due to collective or historical trauma. Legacy burdens can also stem from embodying a specific identity, one's membership of a specific cultural group and/or marginalized group, or in response to dominant culture. Any part (manager, firefighter, or exile) can carry a legacy burden (Schwartz & Sweezy, 2020).

Common fears that emerge when the blocking part is carrying a legacy burden include the following (Schwartz & Sweezy, 2020; Sinko, 2017):

- "Who would I be without this?"
- "This means I am disloyal to . . ."
- Fear of loss of community, identity, sense of belonging, duty, role in family
- Fear of success or failure (Shapiro, 2018)

If the blocking part continues to cause blocked reprocessing, invite curiosity about potential legacy burdens that the blocking part may be carrying. Review the therapist handout "Identifying Legacy Burdens" (page 154) for questions to ask the client and a list of clinical signs to note.

Guide the client to validate the part, fostering Self-to-part relationship that is healing, by asking: "Does this make sense to you? Let the part know that you get it and see how it is responding." Then resume fast BLS.

It is important to honor the IFS principle "All parts are welcome" when working with parts carrying legacy burdens. Honor that ancestral gifts and survival strategies likely show up within legacy burdens and should not be pathologized (or thought of as "all bad" or "all good"). Hold curiosity.

> ## CASE EXAMPLE
>
> # Using the 6 F's with a Blocking Belief
>
> During phase 4, a client is looping on a belief about needing to "push through."
>
> **CLIENT:** I just can't slow down. I have to push through.
>
> **THERAPIST:** Where do you notice this part in and around your body?
>
> **CLIENT:** It's on my left.
>
> **THERAPIST:** Give your attention to this part. How are you experiencing it right now? Is it an image, a sensation, a felt sense?
>
> **CLIENT:** It's a felt sense.
>
> **THERAPIST:** Let it know that you can sense it. Invite it to take in your presence. [*Pauses.*] How do you feel toward it right now?
>
> **CLIENT:** I don't understand it.
>
> **THERAPIST:** Okay. Ask this part, what is it hoping to accomplish if you don't slow down?
>
> **CLIENT:** It wants to help me stay functional so I can take care of my family.
>
> **THERAPIST:** Does this make sense to you?
>
> **CLIENT:** Yes.
>
> **THERAPIST:** Let it know that. [*Pauses while the client does this.*] See how this part is responding to being understood by you.
>
> **CLIENT:** It feels a little better.
>
> **THERAPIST:** Ask the part, what is it scared would happen if it didn't do its job?
>
> **CLIENT:** It's scared that if I let myself feel the grief, I'll feel an ocean of endless sorrow.
>
> **THERAPIST:** Ask the part, if you felt this ocean of grief, what is it scared would happen then?
>
> **CLIENT:** It will never stop.
>
> **THERAPIST:** And then what is that part afraid would happen?
>
> **CLIENT:** I'll become depressed again. I'll feel helpless and lose myself.
>
> **THERAPIST:** Does that make sense to you?
>
> **CLIENT:** Yes.
>
> **THERAPIST:** Let it know that you get it. [*Pauses.*] How is it responding to you understanding it?
>
> **CLIENT:** Now I'm seeing a memory of when I was depressed in the past. [*Indication of a shift out of the blocking belief*]
>
> **THERAPIST:** Notice that. [*Resumes fast BLS.*]

CASE EXAMPLE

Using the 6 F's with a Legacy Burden

The client is targeting a present stressor, leading to extreme anxiety and panic, and begins looping.

CLIENT: I can never feel settled. I must always be prepared to leave. [*The client is looping on this belief.*]

THERAPIST: Where do you notice this part right now in and around your body? [*Beginning the 6 F's*]

CLIENT: It's in my stomach and in my legs.

THERAPIST: Give your attention to this part. Let it know you can feel it in your stomach and legs. [*Pauses.*] How is it responding to you being with it right now? [*Supporting Self-to-part connection*]

CLIENT: It feels surprised to be acknowledged by me.

THERAPIST: How do you feel toward this part? [*Assessing for the client's Self-energy*]

CLIENT: I get it. This feeling of never feeling settled and needing to be prepared to leave feels familiar.

THERAPIST: Let the part know that you get it and see how it's responding to your compassion and understanding. [*Supporting Self-to-part connection*]

CLIENT: It's not sure that it can trust me.

THERAPIST: Okay. Ask this part what it is afraid would happen if you felt settled or weren't prepared to leave.

CLIENT: It's afraid of me being killed.

THERAPIST: Does that make sense to you?

CLIENT: Yes, it's the story of my people. We have to be ready to leave at any time. [*Indicating a culturally based intergenerational survival strategy*]

THERAPIST: Let it know you get that there is an intergenerational reason this belief is here. [*Pauses.*] How is it responding to you know really getting that?

CLIENT: It feels more understood and more trusting of me now.

THERAPIST: Ask this part how much of this belief that you have to be ready to leave belongs solely to you and how much of it was handed down. [*Further assessing for legacy burdens/intergenerational trauma*]

CLIENT: The part is saying that about 90 percent was handed down and a little bit belongs to me.

THERAPIST: How is the part responding to you getting that?

CLIENT: It feels lighter.

THERAPIST: Notice that. [*Continues with fast BLS EMDR reprocessing.*]

STARR

During phase 4, STARR can be used to help down-regulate arousal by providing a slow form of BLS and inviting a target part to receive the sound, vibration, and rhythm of the slow tapping to elicit Self-to-part connection. Please see the description of the STARR technique in chapter 4, if needed, for a review of this befriending technique.

When to Use

In phase 4, STARR is useful in the following scenarios:

- When there is blocked or stuck reprocessing
- When the client may be moving out of their window of tolerance

It is typically helpful to do at least two sets of STARR so that the target part can receive Self's presence. When the client gets unstuck, you can resume fast BLS.

How to Use

See the therapist handout "Self Tapping for Attachment Readiness & Repair (STARR)" from chapter 4 (page 112) for step-by-step directions.

> **CASE EXAMPLE**
>
> ## Using STARR with a Blended Exile
>
> STARR is helpful when an exile is blended, showing up as overarousal, overactivation, or emotional overwhelm, as in this example:
>
> **CLIENT:** I feel trapped and don't know what to do! [*The client is looping on this feeling. They are crying and visibly upset.*]
>
> **THERAPIST:** Tell the part that feels trapped that you are right here with it. [*Eliciting befriending through the Self-to-part connection. Alternatively, the therapist could say: "Tell the part that feels trapped that we are right here with it" to bring in the therapist's Self as a resource.*]
>
> **CLIENT:** It doesn't matter. I'm still trapped. I can't just sit around noticing my feelings—I need to find a way out of this! [*The client is continuing to loop. The therapist decides to bring in STARR, which they have already taught to the client during phase 2, to slow down reprocessing and elicit the target part to receive the client's Self-energy.*]
>
> **THERAPIST:** Let's have you send a message to this part through slow self-tapping. Do you remember how we did this before? [*Models the mechanics of the hand placement and tapping.*] Invite the part that feels trapped to take in the rhythm, the sound, and the vibration of the slow tapping. [*Pauses while the client does this.*] How is the part responding?
>
> **CLIENT:** It feels a little better.
>
> **THERAPIST:** Okay, invite this part to take in the slow tapping in whatever way it needs to so it knows that you are here with it and you are here to help it. [*Pauses while the client does this.*] How is the part responding to the slow tapping now?
>
> **CLIENT:** It knows that I'm here with it.
>
> **THERAPIST:** Great, so be with this part as we resume reprocessing. [*Resumes fast BLS.*]

CASE EXAMPLE

Using STARR When the Client Is Stuck on an Early Memory

In this example, a young exile is in a scene, and nothing is changing. The therapist has already taught the client to use STARR in phase 2.

CLIENT: I just keep seeing this image of me as a baby. [*The client is looping on this image.*]

THERAPIST: Let's have you send a message to this part through slow self-tapping, like we've done before. [*Models the technique again.*] Invite this baby part to take in the rhythm, the sound, and the vibration of the slow tapping. [*Pauses while client does this.*] How is the part responding to the slow tapping?

CLIENT: He can feel the vibration.

THERAPIST: Good. Invite him to take in the vibration, letting him know that he is not alone and you are right here with him. [*Pauses while the client does a second round of STARR.*] How is the part responding to the slow tapping?

CLIENT: He feels relieved.

THERAPIST: Go with that. [*Resumes fast BLS.*]

> **CASE EXAMPLE**
>
> ## Using STARR with a Blended Protector
>
> A protector being blended with the system can show up as underarousal, a blocking belief, or shutdown. As described in chapter 4, STARR can also be used to work with dissociative parts and parts that emotionally numb the system. In this example, like the previous cases, the therapist has already taught the client how to use STARR during phase 2.
>
> **CLIENT:** I feel nothing. [*The client is looping.*]
>
> **THERAPIST:** Where are you noticing this part that feels nothing in and around your body? [*Beginning the 6 F's*]
>
> **CLIENT:** It's all over. [*This indicates blending.*]
>
> **THERAPIST:** Let's have you send a message to this part through slow self-tapping. [*Models the technique as a reminder.*] Invite this part that feels nothing to take in the rhythm, the sound, and the vibration of the slow tapping. [*Pauses while the client does this.*] How is the part responding to the slow tapping?
>
> **CLIENT:** I feel a little heavier.
>
> **THERAPIST:** Okay, send a message to the heaviness through the slow tapping that you are here with it. [*Pauses while the client does a second round of STARR.*] What are you noticing now?
>
> **CLIENT:** I feel more intense sensation in my jaw now. [*This indicates that the part that was emotionally numbing has shifted and is not taking over the whole system.*]
>
> **THERAPIST:** Notice that. [*Resumes fast BLS.*]

Witnessing

Witnessing is an IFS intervention in which a target part is invited to share its story and what it has lived through. In essence, the exile is invited to share with the client the unprocessed traumatic memories it's carrying.

When to Use

Consider using witnessing in the following situations:

- If the SUDs rating is not moving or going any lower
- If the client is looping and nothing is changing in the scene or memory
- If you return to the target due to looping

How to Use

You can ask the client any of the following questions (adapted from Fatter, 2023b):

- "Does the part want to show you what it was like to be it?"
- "Is there anything else this part in the scene wants to show you or tell you about what this has been like?"
- "Are there any parts that want to share what this has been like?"

Then resume fast BLS.

> **CASE EXAMPLE**
>
> ### Witnessing When the SUDs Rating Is Not Decreasing
>
> The client is processing the sudden death of her mother, and the SUDs rating is not decreasing.
>
> **THERAPIST:** As you focus on that hospital scene with your mother [*the target*], check inside—are there any other parts that want to share more about what this was like to be them in that scene?
>
> **CLIENT:** I feel like I'm about to cry.
>
> **THERAPIST:** Invite this part to share all of its feelings. [*Resumes fast BLS.*]

Do-Over

The do-over is an intervention that provides an emotionally corrective experience to a part in the scene or memory that the part is still in. This provides emotional attunement and repair between the client's exile and Self and can be particularly effective when the client is reprocessing attachment or relational trauma in EMDR. The do-over gives the exile an opportunity to have a different experience within the traumatic memory by having the client be present with them in the memory.

When to Use

You can use this intervention when there is a visual image of a memory or scene and looping is occurring. This can be helpful if the part is overwhelmed or in a freeze state in the scene.

How to Use

You can say: "Ask the part if it wants you to be with it in the memory." If the part agrees, say to the client, "Be with this part in any way that it needed at the time." Then resume fast BLS.

If this intervention doesn't naturally help with stuck reprocessing, then you can move to updating, retrieval, and unburdening (described in the following sections) as potential IFS interventions.

CASE EXAMPLE

Do-Over

CLIENT: I see myself in shock in this memory [*The client is looping on this.*]

THERAPIST: Ask that part, do they want you to be with them in that scene?

CLIENT: Yes.

THERAPIST: Be with this part in whatever way it needed at the time. [*Waits to resume fast BLS until the client has established Self-to-part connection.*] How is the part responding to you being with them in the scene?

[*Alternatively, the therapist could have resumed fast BLS without further questioning.*]

CLIENT: They are relieved.

THERAPIST: Notice that. [*Resumes BLS.*]

Updating

Updating involves providing a part in the client's system with current information about the client's life. This usually happens naturally when there is Self-to-part connection. You can think of this intervention as asking the client to share any adaptive information that the target part needs to know.

When to Use

Use updating when reprocessing is blocked or when the client is looping and reprocessing is getting stuck due to lack of current information. While this is not a step in the traditional IFS protocol, updating happens naturally when Self-to-part connection occurs.

How to Use

Ask the client: "What information does this part need updating on? Provide this part with any information about your life now that would be helpful for it to know."

> **CASE EXAMPLE**
>
> ## Updating
>
> **CLIENT:** I feel terror. It's not changing. [*The client is looping.*]
>
> **THERAPIST:** What information does this part need to be updated on?
>
> **CLIENT:** That we aren't in that place anymore.
>
> **THERAPIST:** Let the part know this. [*Pauses.*] How is the part responding to learning that?
>
> **CLIENT:** It doesn't believe me.
>
> **THERAPIST:** What else about your life now would be helpful for this part to know?
>
> **CLIENT:** That my perpetrator is dead.
>
> **THERAPIST:** Let the part know this. [*Pauses.*] How is the part responding to learning that?
>
> **CLIENT:** He's crying now. [*This indicates a shift within the part.*]
>
> **THERAPIST:** Notice that. [*Resumes fast BLS.*]

Retrieval

The retrieval intervention invites the target part to leave the traumatic scene or time period from the past to go to a different location. This different location can be the present day or a place (real or imagined) that feels safe or healing for the target part. This intervention can significantly help the client decrease arousal and bring in adaptive information to the target part that they have choice and that the trauma is not happening in this moment.

When to Use

You can use the retrieval intervention in any of these situations:

- If the client is looping
- If the client is getting overactivated—for example, if the scene or memory is too distressing—and is moving out of their window of tolerance during reprocessing
- If the part was unable to take in an update from Self as an interweave when looping
- At the end of any reprocessing session to help close the session

How to Use

You can offer this intervention in a number of ways, including one of the following:

- "Let's invite this part to come be with you in the present day."
- "Would the part like to leave that scene? Where would it like to go?"
- "Does the part want to go somewhere else, to be with you in the present day, or to go to a healing place to be with you?"

Note that giving the part a choice of where to go can help bring adaptive information to the part.

Then say: "Take your time and let me know when this part has fully landed in the present day. Invite it to orient to you now and where you are right now."

You can use fast BLS as the retrieval is happening. Once the part is in the present day, you do not need to use BLS if the retrieval step is being used at the end of session.

CASE EXAMPLE

Retrieval

In this example, the client is moving out of their window of tolerance during EMDR reprocessing, as they are looping on emotional overwhelm during a specific traumatic scene.

THERAPIST: Ask the part of you in that scene—does this part want to go somewhere else or be with you in the present? [*Giving the part a choice*]

CLIENT: She wants to go to a playground.

THERAPIST: Take your time and let me know when this part has fully landed at a playground.

CLIENT: Okay, she's there. It's a playground I played at when I was a kid. [*The client looks calmer.*]

THERAPIST: Be with this part at the playground so she knows you are with her right now. Let me know when you are with her. [*Inviting Self-to-part connection after the part is retrieved from the traumatic scene.*]

CLIENT: I'm there with her.

THERAPIST: How do you feel toward her as you are with her right now?

CLIENT: I have so much love and care for her. [*Indicative of the client's Self-energy*]

THERAPIST: Invite her to orient to you. [*Pauses.*] How is she responding to you being with her right now? [*Checking to see that the part can take in the presence of the client's Self-energy.*]

CLIENT: She's happy that I'm with her.

THERAPIST: Ask her if it's okay with her if we continue with EMDR reprocessing. She can share any more about what it's like to be her. [*Ensuring consent of the exile that is the focus for phase 4 reprocessing.*]

CLIENT: Yes, we can continue.

[*The therapist then resumes fast BLS.*]

Unburdening

Unburdening is a powerful intervention you can use to invite the target part to intentionally release any negative belief or burden it is carrying. You also can give the part a choice of how much it feels ready to intentionally release the trauma-related feelings, beliefs, or sensations it is carrying by offering what is called a *partial unburdening*.

When to Use

You can use this intervention when:

- The client is underaroused or underactivated
- The SUDs rating is not moving or going any lower (Fatter, 2023b)

How to Use

Ask: "Are there any parts with fears or concerns about releasing this?" You can resume BLS after asking this or wait until the client responds before resuming BLS.

If the client affirms that there is fear about releasing this burden in reprocessing, then ask: "What is the part afraid would happen if it let it go?" You can resume BLS after asking this or wait until the client responds before resuming BLS.

Then you can ask, "What does the part need in order to release the burden?" You can resume BLS after asking this or wait until the client responds before resuming BLS.

Partial Unburdening

Healing is not all or nothing; it is a process. Sometimes parts need to release a little bit at a time to slowly release the negative belief, burden, or emotional pain they are carrying. You can say: "Ask the part if they are willing to release any amount of the belief or emotional pain they are carrying." You can prompt the client to reassure the part that it can decide how much it wants to release (e.g., 10 to 15 percent of the emotional pain).

CASE EXAMPLE

Partial Unburdening

THERAPIST: Check inside and see—are there any parts with fears or concerns about releasing this belief?

CLIENT: I have a feeling of fear right now.

THERAPIST: Where are you noticing this in and around your body? [*Locating where the part is can help the client become more conscious of the part in order to move into connection with it.*]

CLIENT: It's in my chest. There's a part there who's so scared. He wants me to stop trying to release this.

THERAPIST: Bring your attention to this part and invite him to take in your presence. [*Pauses.*] How is the part responding to you acknowledging him this way?

CLIENT: He feels more scared.

THERAPIST: Ask this part what he is scared of.

CLIENT: Scared of change.

THERAPIST: What is he scared will happen if change were to occur?

CLIENT: He doesn't know.

THERAPIST: What is he scared of if he released the fear of change? [*The therapist keeps exploring the fear.*]

CLIENT: This part doesn't know who he will be without this belief.

THERAPIST: Does this make sense to you?

CLIENT: Yes.

THERAPIST: Then let him know that you get that. [*Pauses.*] How is he responding to you getting it?

CLIENT: He feels better but still a little scared. He doesn't know any different.

THERAPIST: Is there anything you want to say to him in response to that? [*Checking whether the client's Self has wisdom to share.*]

CLIENT: I understand.

THERAPIST: Let the part know that he can explore, if he wants to, what it's like to even feel a little less of the fear. [*Given that the client didn't have more to share with the part, the therapist had the client give the part a choice.*]

CLIENT: He's interested to see what you mean.

THERAPIST: Ask him, is there any amount of the fear of change that he feels ready to release?

CLIENT: He is okay to let go of 10 percent of it.

THERAPIST: Great. Invite him to release 10 percent of it and see how that feels. [*Resumes fast BLS.*]

> **CASE EXAMPLE**
>
> # Legacy Unburdening
>
> The client is looping on a fear of being blindsided.
>
> **THERAPIST:** Where are you noticing this part with a fear of being blindsided right now in and around your body?
>
> **CLIENT:** I see it in the scene [*referring to the target*].
>
> **THERAPIST:** Let it know you can see it. [*Pauses.*] How is it responding to you seeing it?
>
> **CLIENT:** It's confused.
>
> **THERAPIST:** How do you feel toward it? [*Checking for how much Self the client has access to*]
>
> **CLIENT:** I care about it. [*Indicative of some amount of Self-energy*]
>
> **THERAPIST:** Share that with it.
>
> **CLIENT:** It likes that.
>
> **THERAPIST:** Good, ask this part to tell you more about the fear of being blindsided. [*This is bringing in the witnessing intervention to see if the part has more to share.*]
>
> **CLIENT:** It doesn't know much more about it. [*This suggests that this fear, or some amount of this fear, may be handed down intergenerationally or potentially absorbed culturally or in response to the dominant culture.*]
>
> **THERAPIST:** How long has it had this fear of being blindsided? [*Assessing for a legacy burden*]
>
> **CLIENT:** It doesn't know. It's always been there. [*As discussed chapter 6, this indicates a legacy burden.*]
>
> **THERAPIST:** Ask the part, how much of this belongs to it and how much of this was handed down?
>
> **CLIENT:** Ninety percent does not belong to it.
>
> **THERAPIST:** Ask it what it needs from you to help it release the amount that doesn't belong to it.
>
> **CLIENT:** It just wants to know I'll still be here.
>
> **THERAPIST:** What is your response to that request?
>
> **CLIENT:** I'm telling it—I will be here with it no matter what.
>
> **THERAPIST:** Great. Invite the part to release the 90 percent that does not belong to it. [*Resumes fast BLS.*]

As discussed earlier, anytime IFS interventions are integrated as interweaves during stuck or blocked reprocessing in phase 4, resume fast BLS once the client gets unstuck to continue trauma reprocessing. In chapter 9, we'll discuss IFS interventions to use during phase 7 when there is an incomplete or complete EMDR reprocessing session, including optional interventions of intention setting and appreciation.

The next therapist handout summarizes how to use the nine phase 4 interventions we've just explored.

Therapist Handout

Phase 4 IFS Interventions

(Adapted from Fatter, 2023b)

This handout provides brief directions for each IFS intervention to use during phase 4 when a client is looping or blocked (i.e., nothing is changing after two sets of EMDR reprocessing). The intention of any IFS intervention is to help the client have some level of Self-to-part connection—to help access the AIP model—so the client gets unstuck and then can proceed with fast BLS.

1. **Befriending:** "How do you feel toward this part?" (Schwartz & Sweezy, 2020, p. 132). If Self-energy is present (i.e., if the client feels one of the 8 C's—curiosity, compassion, calmness, creativity, connectedness, courage, clarity, or confidence—toward the part), say, "Can you share that with the part? How is it responding?" This restores the Self-to-part connection. If Self-energy is not present, then proceed to an IFS-informed two-hand interweave.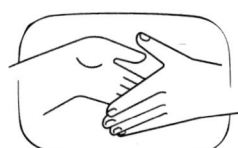

2. **IFS-Informed Two-Hand Interweave:** Use this when there are two parts present during blocked reprocessing. This brings in the notion of multiplicity and enables the acknowledgment of parts that are dialectical and have different feelings from one another. This is an IFS adaptation to Robin Shapiro's (2005) two-hand interweave that fosters Self-to-part relationship and elicits awareness that both Self and parts are present in the client.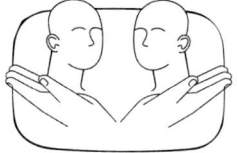

   For example, when you ask the client: "How do you feel toward this part of you?" and the client responds without one of the 8 C qualities, have the client invite one part (the one that doesn't like the target part) in one hand and the target part in another hand. Then say, "Invite these parts to turn toward you and take in your presence. You are here with both of these parts right now. Just notice how these parts are responding to you being with both parts right now."

3. **Use the 6 F's for Blocking Beliefs:** Blocking beliefs are likely protector parts that have fears or concerns that get elicited through Phase 4 trauma reprocessing. Use the 6 F's to befriend parts that have whatever blocking belief that is emerging (Fatter, 2023b; Krause & Gomez, 2013; O'Shea Brown, 2020; Schwartz & Sweezy, 2020; Twombly & Schwartz, 2008).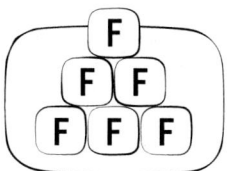

   a. **Find:** "Where do you notice this part in or around your body?"

   b. **Focus:** "Bring your attention to this part."

   c. **Flesh it out:** "How are you experiencing it right now?" (Is this an image or felt sense?)

d. **Feel toward:** "How do you feel toward this part?" (Schwartz & Sweezy, 2020, p. 132)

e. **Befriend:** "How is this part trying to help you? What is this part hoping to accomplish? What is its job? How does this part feel about doing its job?"

f. **Fears:** "What are this part's fears and concerns?"

We do not try to get rid of the part with the blocking belief; we invite in curiosity and invite the client to befriend this part and help it feel understood. Use the IFS principle "If parts feel understood, they will soften."

4. **Self Tapping for Attachment Readiness & Repair (STARR)®:** This can be used to change the BLS to slow tapping for a set or two as another means to foster Self-to-part connection.

"Let's try using slow tapping to send the part the message that you are right here with it, feel compassion toward it, and want to get to know it." Provide directions for the hand placement and slow tapping—the mechanics are the same as the butterfly hug (Artigas et al., 2000; Jarero & Artigas, 2021). "Just invite the part to take in the rhythm, the sound, and the vibration of the tapping."

5. **Witnessing:** "Does the part want to show you what it was like to be it? Is there anything else this part wants to show you or tell you about what this has been like?"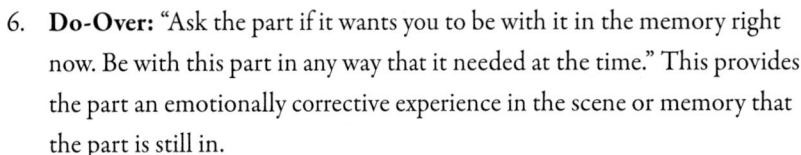

Use witnessing when the SUDs rating is not moving or going any lower. "Are there any parts that want to share what this has been like?"

6. **Do-Over:** "Ask the part if it wants you to be with it in the memory right now. Be with this part in any way that it needed at the time." This provides the part an emotionally corrective experience in the scene or memory that the part is still in.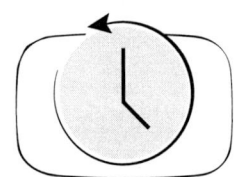

7. **Updating:** "What information does this part need updating on? Provide this part with any information about your life now that would be helpful for it to know." This happens naturally in phase 4 reprocessing, but when reprocessing is blocked or looping, the system can benefit from an information update.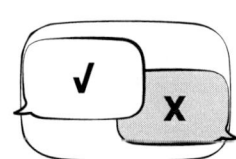

8. **Retrieval:** This interweave is very helpful if the part was unable to take in an update from Self or if the part is in a distressing scene in the past.

a. "Let's invite this part to come be with you in the present day."

b. "Would the part like to leave that scene? Where would it like to go?"

c. "Does the part want to go somewhere else, be with you in present, or go to a safe place to be with you?" [*Pause.*]

d. "Take your time and let me know when this part has fully landed in the present day. [*Pause.*] Invite it to orient to you now and where you are right now."

9. **Unburdening:** Use this when the SUDs rating is not moving or not going any lower.

   a. "Are there any parts with fears or concerns about releasing this?"

   b. If the target part doesn't feel ready to release, ask, "What is it afraid would happen if it let it go? What does the part need in order to release the burden?"

   c. Consider partial unburdening. "Is there any amount that it feels ready to release?"

   d. Assess for legacy burdens if the part is not willing to release. Ask: "How much of this belongs to you or was handed down to you?" (Schwartz & Sweezy, 2020; Sinko, 2017).

Other Options to Integrate IFS Interventions with EMDR's Phase 4

This chapter covered several methods of integrating IFS with EMDR phase 4, along with case vignettes illustrating their use. The following are additional scenarios that might arise, with instructions for using IFS interventions in these situations:

- If the client reports a dissociative response when you check in between sets during phase 4 EMDR reprocessing, invite in curiosity and clinical discernment, as follows:
    - Is this dissociative response a clinical indication of the client moving out of their window of tolerance (e.g., the client is reporting dizziness, feeling "out of it," going "blank," or finding themselves unable to focus on the target)?
    - Or is this dissociative response a part that is on the traumatic memory network that you are targeting? In this case, the dissociative response is the system sharing its story of what happened during the traumatic event being processed in EMDR.

    In this situation, you can also assess how much access the client has to Self. Indications that the client is out of their window of tolerance would include the client saying, "I don't know," reporting dizziness or mental fogginess, and having difficulty focusing in the session. If the client has access to Self and awareness of the dissociative response being part of the traumatic event, the client may say: "I can tell this happened in the past" or "That is how I responded then."

- After a SUDs rating is 0 per the EMDR protocol for phase 4's completion, you can invite the client to do an unburdening of anything else that needs to be released or a retrieval of parts from the past. These options can help further deepen therapeutic gains from EMDR and enable you and the client to attend to any other burdens the target parts may be carrying.

- If a burden comes back in pure IFS therapy, you can explore with the client whether this may be a legacy burden. Alternatively, the client can transition to EMDR reprocessing, which may address more aspects of the burden that have not yet been revealed in the system.

- As discussed in chapter 1, there are many indicators in pure IFS therapy that the client would benefit from transitioning to EMDR reprocessing. You can provide psychoeducation on the benefits of EMDR, discuss what a treatment plan that includes EMDR would look like, and obtain informed consent for EMDR. You would still guide the client to ask their protector parts for their permission to transition to EMDR and provide EMDR resourcing.

CHAPTER 8

IFS-Informed Installation and Body Scan During Phases 5 and 6

By now you've seen how IFS interventions can be integrated with EMDR therapy during phases 1 through 4. In this and the following chapter, you'll learn how to integrate IFS into the final four phases of EMDR. The format of this chapter will be similar to that of the previous one: specific IFS interventions will be presented, including guidance for when and how to use each one, along with case vignettes illustrating their use.

Using IFS Interventions During Installing the Positive Cognition in Phase 5

Phase 5, installation, occurs after the client experiences the target at a SUDs rating of 0 or as low as is ecologically valid (i.e., realistic given the context of the trauma or given the client's ongoing trauma exposure). From an EMDR lens, when all the channels associated with the targeted memory network are "cleared," the client experiences little to no disturbance when focusing on the original traumatic event targeted in EMDR reprocessing. You then re-check if the originally identified positive cognition in phase 3 still fits with how the client is experiencing the original EMDR target now. For example, you can ask: "As you focus on the original event, do the words [*name the original positive cognition*] still fit or is there a positive statement that feels like a better fit?" The positive cognition is then installed and strengthened by pairing it with the original event using fast BLS (Shapiro, 2018).

The client continues installing the positive cognition with sets of fast BLS until there are no more changes. Then you re-check the validity of cognition (VOC) by asking: "As you focus on the event, how true do the words [*name the positive cognition*] feel now on a scale of 1 to 7, with 1 being completely false and 7 being completely true?" The client continues to strengthen the positive cognition until the VOC is at a 7 (or a 6, if 6 is ecologically valid). If the VOC does not increase to a 7 after repeated sets of fast BLS, then the positive cognition needs to be re-checked to see if there is an alternative positive cognition that is a better fit for the client. The positive cognition is fully installed when the VOC is a 7 and there are no longer functional shifts with any additional fast BLS (Shapiro, 2018).

From an IFS lens, phase 5 is similar to the IFS invitation intervention. In the invitation intervention, the client asks the target part that has unburdened to invite in whatever positive qualities it needs now or in the future. This helps further transform a target exile from being in a burdened role to being just a part in the client's system that can share its naturally valuable gifts.

EMDR phase 5 has many therapeutic functions. It can help improve the client's general self-esteem and sense of empowerment. Since phase 4 processes an entire traumatic memory network, phase 5 can also potentially generalize the installed positive cognition to other associated memories on the targeted memory network. The installed positive cognition can also potentially generalize to present triggers that may be EMDR targets in the future as part of the client's treatment plan. Phase 5 also supports integration of therapeutic gains by stimulating adaptive neuro networks (the AIP system that organically resides in the client; Shapiro, 2018).

Let's consider a common clinical scenario that occurs when phase 5 gets stuck, which is when a client's VOC is not increasing to a 7. This is a sign for you to check for blocking beliefs. From an IFS lens, this means there is a part that stepped in the process that has a blocking belief that needs to be identified so further healing can occur. The main IFS intervention to use in this scenario is the 6 F's.

Using the 6 F's When the VOC Is Not Increasing

The 6 F's befriending intervention has been discussed extensively in previous chapters. For a review, please see the section in chapter 4 titled "Befriending Technique 1: Using the 6 F's" (page 88). This intervention also lends itself well to phase 5 of EMDR if the VOC is not increasing after trying to install the identified positive cognition by pairing it with the original event that was targeted in phase 4. The 6 F's is a very effective intervention to use when phase 5 gets stuck, as it helps the client access new information from whatever part has a blocking belief, which then can be focused on for further reprocessing with fast BLS.

When to Use

When the VOC rating is not naturally increasing to a 7 (on a scale of 1 to 7, where 7 means that the client believes that the positive cognition is completely true), the 6 F's IFS intervention relationally guides the client to befriend any part that has a blocking belief that might be preventing the VOC from increasing.

How to Use

- Say any of the following:
    - "Check inside—are there any parts with fears or concerns about the positive cognition being completely true?" (This can identify a blocking belief.)
    - "Check inside—what parts are preventing the positive cognition from being a 7?" (This can identify a blocking belief.)

- "Check inside—are there any other parts that need to be included here to help make this a 7?" (This is another way to invite unaddressed parts into the phase 5 process.)
- "Check inside—are there any parts that want to add on to this positive cognition? Does this positive cognition fit for all parts of you? If not, what words go best now for all parts of you?" (In more complex systems, sometimes a positive cognition fits for some parts, but not all. This invites exploration to confirm that the positive cognition fits for the system of parts. It can also invite in the option to continue to tweak the positive cognition so that it feels true for the client's internal system.)

- Once parts are identified, use the 6 F's to help the client befriend any parts with blocking beliefs, fears, or concerns, and then resume fast BLS for any additional reprocessing needed. In more complex systems, parts may be identified through this intervention that can become the target for future EMDR reprocessing if they do not naturally resolve with additional fast BLS sets in phase 5.

- Sometimes parts in more complex systems are unfamiliar with, or have fears about, feeling good or having positive feelings or beliefs. If this emerges as a block during phase 5, you can invite parts to "try on" the positive cognition, a positive quality, or both.

- If parts have fears of having positive feelings or are simply unfamiliar with experiencing positive feelings, beliefs, or cognitions, you can invite these parts to try on an incremental degree of the positive cognition to experience what it feels like. Similar to the partial unburdening intervention discussed in chapter 7 that's used during phase 4, this IFS intervention gives identified parts an option to partially take in the positive cognition and gradually see what it feels like. You can ask: "Would this part like to try any amount of this positive feeling to see what it's like?"

CASE EXAMPLE

Using the 6 F's When the VOC Rating Is Not Increasing

Let's return to our case example of Ava. Ava's positive cognition of "I am enough" is at a VOC of 5 and not increasing, so her therapist uses the 6 F's (indicated in bold).

THERAPIST: Check inside—are there any parts with fears or concerns about believing that you are enough is completely true? [*Reiterating the positive cognition; asking for protector parts*]

AVA: Yeah, I'm noticing this feeling of "I'm just not buying it."

THERAPIST: Where are you noticing this part in and around your body? [***Find***]

AVA: It's in my head.

THERAPIST: Okay, so ask this part if it can separate from your body to be right next to you, to get to know it better. [*This is helping the client unblend from the part in order to befriend it—**focus** and **flesh out**.*]

AVA: It's a little unsure, but it's right next to me.

THERAPIST: How do you feel toward this part? [***Feel toward***; *checking for Self-energy*]

AVA: I'm curious about it.

THERAPIST: Okay, so let it know that. [*Pauses.*] How is this part responding to your curiosity? [*This confirms there is Self-to-part connection.*]

AVA: It's glad I'm noticing it.

THERAPIST: Ask the part, what does it want you to know about it not buying that you are enough when you think about this event? [*Referencing the target event;* ***befriend***]

AVA: It's wanting me to know that it's not sure I deserve to feel good and to be so kind to myself.

THERAPIST: Ask the part, what is it afraid would happen if you deserve to feel good and be kind to yourself? [***Fears****; this supports further befriending.*]

AVA: It's afraid that this bad thing will happen again if I let myself feel good. [*Referring to the target for reprocessing*]

THERAPIST: What is your response to this part's concern? [*This supports Self-leadership.*]

AVA: I get that and I'm aware we can't control the future.

THERAPIST: How is the part responding to hearing you say that?

AVA: It feels sad.

THERAPIST: Go with that. [*Resumes fast BLS reprocessing.*]

When Parts Are Unfamiliar with Feeling Good

Sometimes when the VOC is not increasing, it is due to parts not being familiar with feeling good. Clients with complex trauma histories commonly have parts that protect them from, or are unfamiliar with, feeling good. If the client communicates this at all in phase 5, it is indicative of the need for more reprocessing. Clients may communicate hesitancy or distrust of taking in the positive cognition. You can use the 6 F's to find the part with the fear of or unfamiliarity with experiencing positive feelings, facilitate Self-to-part connection, and then invite the part to slowly let in the positive cognition and/or positive qualities so it can have a choice to titrate the positive feeling. This is used prior to returning to fast BLS reprocessing for further installation of the positive cognition.

CASE EXAMPLE

When Parts Are Unfamiliar with Feeling Good

Let's stay in the same session with Ava, where her VOC is stuck at a 5. Ava expresses how unfamiliar she is with believing that she is enough (her positive cognition). Here is how the 6 F's and an invitation for the part to "try on" the unfamiliar positive cognition might play out for Ava.

THERAPIST: Let's check inside and see what part is experiencing this as unfamiliar. Where are you noticing this part now in and around your body? [*Find*]

AVA: She's right next to me.

THERAPIST: Great. Bring your attention to her. [*Focus*] How are you experiencing her right now? Do you have an image of this part, a body sensation, or a felt sense? [*Flesh out*]

AVA: I sense her. It's a felt sense.

THERAPIST: Great. Just invite her to take in your presence. How is she responding to you being with her right now? [*Checking for Self-to-part connection*]

AVA: She likes that I'm here.

THERAPIST: How do you feel toward her right now? [*Checking for Self-energy; feel toward*]

AVA: Lots of love.

THERAPIST: Great—let her know that. What else does this part want you to know about the belief that you are enough? [*Elicits more befriending*]

AVA: She just has never felt that way. It feels really unfamiliar and that scares her.

THERAPIST: So, the part is scared because its unfamiliar and doesn't know what that feels like? [*Confirming that this is the part's fear*]

AVA: Yes.

THERAPIST: Would the part like to try on that feeling to see what it's like? The part can decide how much she wants to try on.

AVA: Hmm . . . she's curious about that.

THERAPIST: How much of that belief "I am enough" would she like to try on now? The part can choose a percentage of this belief to try on.

AVA: She'd like to try 10 percent of it on.

THERAPIST: Great, invite her to try on 10 percent of the belief "I am enough" and see what that's like for her. [*Pauses.*]

AVA: That feels okay to her.

THERAPIST: Okay, give the part a choice—would she like to try on any more right now?

AVA: Yes, 5 percent more for now.

THERAPIST: Okay, invite her to try on 5 percent more and see what that's like for her. [*Pauses.*]

AVA: That feels good. The part just wants to stay with this amount for now.

THERAPIST: Okay, ask the part if there are any other positive qualities that she would like that she needs now or in the future. [*This is the IFS invitation intervention to support this part. This is essentially asking if there are any other positive cognitions that are a better fit.*]

AVA: Actually, she'd like to invite in that it's okay to think about the future. This part has a gift of foresight.

THERAPIST: Great, invite the part to let that in and let me know when that feels complete.

AVA: That feels good. The part feels really good.

THERAPIST: Great. See if there is anything else this part needs from you right now.

AVA: No, she feels good.

THERAPIST: All right, ask the part if we have her permission to return to our EMDR process now to help strengthen this good feeling. [*Getting permission from the system to return to EMDR phase 5 protocol*]

AVA: Yes. [*Therapist resumes fast BLS.*]

The therapist would continue fast BLS until there are no more changes in reprocessing, then would reassess the VOC of the positive cognition by asking, "As you focus on the event, how true do the words [*name the positive cognition*] feel now on a scale of 1 to 7, with 1 being completely false and 7 being completely true?"

Now that we have discussed IFS interventions to use during phase 5, let's discuss intervention options for phase 6.

Using IFS Interventions During the Body Scan in Phase 6

After the positive cognition reaches a 7 or the highest rating that is ecologically valid on the VOC scale, you initiate phase 6 by inviting the client to focus on the original memory and the positive cognition while scanning the body. You say to the client: "Close your eyes and keep in mind the original event and the words [*repeat the positive cognition*]. Starting with your head and working downward, bringing your attention to different parts of your body, tell me if you notice any place you feel tension, tightness, or an unusual sensation." Any physical sensations that are uncomfortable, tense, or unusual are indicative of associated networks that need to be reprocessed with fast BLS until the body scan is "clear." Phase 6 is complete when the client focuses on the original targeted event from phase 4 and the positive cognition from phase 5, and, when they scan their body from head to toe, they find no negative sensations or tension. During this phase, fast BLS is used to strengthen positive or comfortable sensations reported by the client (Shapiro, 2018).

From an IFS lens, the body scan is an opportunity to directly attend to parts that may express their experience through the body if they did not previously emerge organically in EMDR reprocessing. As discussed in chapter 2, parts can express themselves through the nervous system (e.g., hyperarousal, hypoarousal, and blended states); through body sensations, tension, tightness, pain, and other physical symptoms (e.g., headaches, lump in the throat, chronic numbness, dizziness); through body urges, instincts, and the breath; and through specific parts of the body.

Even if the client does not have any residual body sensations when holding the positive cognition and targeting event through the body scan, you can still bring in an IFS intervention to explicitly invite any other parts that express themselves through the body. For example, you can ask: "Are there any other parts held in the body that hold anything else related to this event?" You can proceed with fast BLS as needed for any remaining reprocessing for somatic-based parts.

Let's explore situations that may arise during the body scan for which IFS interventions are particularly well suited.

Blocked Reprocessing During the Body Scan: What Parts Need to Be Known?

From an IFS perspective, if there is blocked reprocessing during the body scan, either (1) protector parts have fears or concerns about releasing the trauma-related feelings, beliefs, and burdens from the body or (2) exiles need more witnessing to share their story. IFS interventions can be used during the body scan to help the client's system slow down. This can create space for these parts to be known more, as needed, before resuming fast BLS to continue reprocessing during phase 6.

In more complex systems or if the client is reprocessing intergenerational trauma in EMDR, parts may not have words and may only know how to communicate through the body. In applying what we know about the nature of traumatic memory to IFS, body sensations are parts that are not encoded with context and not yet connected to the language part of the brain (van der Kolk, 2014). Current scholarship indicates that historical and intergenerational trauma also shows up in decontextualized form and emerges through body sensations, the body's instinctual reactions, or a somatic urge (Menakem, 2017). Thus, IFS interventions during phase 6 may help the client put words to the texture, temperature, and weight of parts that are showing up through body sensations.

When to Use

If there is blocked reprocessing during phase 6, explore the possibility of additional parts that need to be known.

How to Use

Hold curiosity about whether there is a protector part or an exile that needs befriending and is trying to communicate through the body.

You can use any of the following IFS interventions:

- "If we approach this body sensation as a part of you, what does it want you to know?"

- "If this [*body sensation*] could talk, what would it say?" Or "Are there any words that go with that [*body sensation*]?" (adapted from McConnell, 2013, 2020).

- "Check inside: Is there a feeling that goes with that [*body sensation*]? What is the temperature or texture of this part? Is there any movement or behavior that goes with this [*body sensation*]?" (Examples include pushing with hands, grinding of the teeth, running away, hiding, or trying to disappear.)

- Further befriending: "Let's invite this [*body sensation*] to share more. Bring your attention to this part of you. [*Pause.*] Notice the texture, the weight, and the temperature of this sensation. [*Pause.*] How is this part responding to you really being with it right now? [*Pause.*] What else does it want to show you or tell you?" [*Pause.*] You have a choice either to invite the part to share with the client—which may be through an increase, decrease, or shift in the body sensation—or to resume fast BLS for continued reprocessing.

- "Check inside—ask [*body sensation*], does it have any fears or concerns about releasing what the body is holding from this memory?" [*Pause.*] If there's no response: "Check inside your entire body; are there any other parts with fears or concerns about letting this [*body sensation*] go?" [*Pause.*] "How is the body responding? What is the body scared would happen if it let go of this sensation that goes with the memory?"

- "What parts are keeping the body scan from being clear? Let's make space for those parts. Where are you noticing those parts right now in and around your body? [*This is the find question from the 6 F's.*] How are these parts of the body responding to you acknowledging them in this way? [*This checks for Self-to-part connection.*] Be with these parts right now, inviting them to share any way they would like—through images, sensations, feelings, and so on—anything they want you to know."

- If there are numb parts: "Let's invite in curiosity. Does the numb part have fears about feeling sensations in the body? What does it want you to know about that?" For numbing parts or parts that are taking away any feeling or sensation from the client or preventing the client from being present in their body, you can use STARR. (For detailed instructions, see chapter 4, particularly the therapist handout "Self Tapping for Attachment Readiness & Repair (STARR)" on page 112.)

Integrating Somatic Approaches to Befriend Parts in the Body

Susan McConnell's (2013; 2020) somatic IFS approach involves using the wisdom of awareness, breath, resonance, touch, and movement to elicit the client's presence to the body's moment-to-moment changes, whatever the body is communicating.

When to Use

In addition to using the previous IFS interventions during blocked phase 6 reprocessing, you can integrate somatic IFS into the body scan by inviting the use of breath, movement, and touch to invite parts to share and befriend them.

How to Use

There are two options here: (1) You can invite the client to befriend any part of the body that has tension or is dysregulated during the body scan by inviting the body part to take in the presence of Self. From an IFS lens, this body sensation is how a part is expressing itself, so you befriend the body sensation or body part using IFS interventions. (2) Alternatively, you can also use the breath, movement, or self-touch as a form of the client's Self-energy to connect with the dysregulated part.

Let's look at two different case vignettes to see what these IFS interventions look like in action.

CASE EXAMPLE

Befriending the Breath as a Body Part

Noah's body scan is blocked. His therapist can see that Noah is breathing quickly, his breath dysregulated. The therapist approaches the breath as a part.

THERAPIST: Let's invite in some curiosity about what's happening in your body right now. Let's start with your breath. What are you noticing about your breath right now?

NOAH: It's hard for me to notice it.

THERAPIST: Take your time and bring your attention to your breath. [*Pauses.*] You can place one hand on your chest and the other below your navel. [*Pauses.*] What are you noticing now?

NOAH: My breathing is fast.

THERAPIST: Let's get to know this part of you. Let's first see if you can ask it to slow down so it can take in your presence.

NOAH: Okay.

THERAPIST: Begin to make your exhale a little longer. [*The therapist demonstrates an elongated exhale, which will activate the parasympathetic nervous system to move out of sympathetic activation. The therapist then pauses while Noah does this.*] Now invite this part to take in your presence, knowing that you are right here with it and it's not alone. [*Pauses.*] How is this part in your breath responding now?

NOAH: It's surprised. It's like now I'm feeling a strange sense of embarrassment.

THERAPIST: Notice that. [*Resumes fast BLS.*]

CASE EXAMPLE

Befriending with the Breath
(Using the Breath as an Aspect of Self)

Zoe's body scan is blocked during phase 6, and she reports shakiness in her chest, though she appears calm with regulated breathing. Her therapist initially uses traditional IFS befriending to elicit Self-to-part connection, and then uses the client's regulated, calm breathing as an aspect of Self because the somatic part has difficulty taking in the presence of the client's Self. Sometimes somatic-based parts respond well to somatic-based expressions of Self (e.g., regulated breathing or STARR). Self can communicate with parts through regulated, calm breathing.

THERAPIST: Is it okay if we get to know this part of you in your chest that is shaky?

ZOE: Yes.

THERAPIST: Invite that part to take in your presence. [*Pauses.*] How is it responding to you being with it right now?

ZOE: It doesn't know I'm here. It's having a hard time.

THERAPIST: How do you feel toward it right now? [*Assessing for Self-energy*]

ZOE: I feel compassion toward it.

THERAPIST: Share that with the part. See if it can take in your calm breathing as a resource to know it's not alone. Invite it to notice your breath. [*Pauses while Zoe does this.*] How is this part in your chest responding to sensing your breath? [*The therapist is using the client's calm breath as a way for the part to connect with the presence of the client's Self.*]

ZOE: It's feeling almost shocked . . . and I'm now feeling teary.

THERAPIST: Notice that and invite this part to share anything it wants to about the shock and tearfulness. [*Resumes fast BLS.*]

The body scan is considered complete when the client has no remaining negative or uncomfortable body sensations connected to the targeting event when holding the positive cognition and the target event (Shapiro, 2018).

CHAPTER 9

IFS-Informed Closure and Reevaluation During Phases 7 and 8

This chapter will round out the portion of the book teaching you how to integrate IFS techniques into the eight phases of EMDR. First we'll discuss using IFS interventions during phase 7, including interventions for closing incomplete sessions, IFS-informed practices the client can practice between sessions to support stabilization, and ways to support integration and therapeutic gains for complete sessions. Case vignettes will illustrate the use of these interventions, and a therapist handout is provided to reinforce how to end an incomplete session. Following this, we'll discuss IFS interventions to use during phase 8 for reevaluation and identifying future targets, and, finally, how to handle backlash in the client's system.

Using IFS Interventions During Phase 7: Closure

Phase 7 is focused on debriefing, assessing the client's safety, and helping the client stabilize prior to the session ending. IFS interventions can enhance these components for both incomplete and complete sessions, as we'll discuss in the following sections. Whether the client has an incomplete session or a complete session, you are ensuring that the client ends the session in a stable emotional state. At the end of the session, fast BLS has stopped and you are inviting the client to focus on either neutral or positive networks not connected with the memory network targeted in phase 4. Then you describe how to manage triggers that may arise between sessions by discussing the TICES log (for recording triggers, images, cognitions, emotions, sensations, and the SUDs level for each trigger; this will be discussed later in this chapter). You also review coping skills the client learned in phase 2 that they can practice to manage triggers or emotion dysregulation in between sessions (Shapiro, 2018).

Closing Incomplete Sessions

If an EMDR reprocessing session is "incomplete," it means that the SUDs rating is not the lowest it can go during phase 4, or that the client has not yet fully completed phase 5 or phase 6 (Shapiro, 2018). IFS interventions can be integrated in phase 7 to close incomplete sessions. This would occur prior to providing the client standard debriefing about the TICES log. To close an incomplete session, you use IFS-informed resource development options that the client should already be familiar with, since they practiced them during phase 2 prior to beginning EMDR reprocessing.

The sequence of IFS interventions to close an incomplete session is as follows:

1. Use the IFS-informed **container exercise** by asking if the client or any part of them wants to intentionally set anything into a container to be held for them between sessions. Ask: "Is there anything this part of you wants to intentionally set aside to hold for you until we meet again next session?"

2. Use the **retrieval** intervention by inviting any parts in the traumatic scene or memory to move to the client's calm/safe/healing place that they practiced accessing during phase 2. Say: "Invite the part to be with you in the present day or to go to your healing place to be with you."

Steps 1 and 2 should be familiar to the client, as they have already practiced them during phase 2. These two steps follow standard EMDR practice of using a container and safe place visualization to end an incomplete session. This is sufficient for many clients doing EMDR reprocessing to close an incomplete session. For more complex systems, the next step might be necessary.

3. Use the IFS **integration** intervention to support integration of therapeutic gains and stabilization within the system of parts. To do this, you guide the client to check back in with any protector parts that gave permission for EMDR reprocessing, who stepped aside or watched on the sidelines during phase 4.

    Say: "Check in with any protector parts that stepped aside, gave permission, and watched on the sidelines to see the transformation that happened during the reprocessing session, including [*name any change that happened for the target exile(s)*]. What do these parts need from you right now?" This fosters Self-leadership and helps update protector parts as to changes that occurred in the system if they weren't naturally updated during EMDR reprocessing.

    Sometimes, clients may have difficulty accessing those protector parts because the parts have changed through the EMDR reprocessing. An indication of this is if the client reports, "They are gone" or "I'm not getting anything." If that is the case, then you can end the procedure for incomplete sessions by describing the TICES log. From an EMDR lens, if the client can't access the protectors that originally gave consent, it presumably means that the memory network targeted in EMDR reprocessing has significantly changed, which would be considered therapeutic progress.

    If the client *can* access the protectors that gave consent, you guide the client to briefly invite those protector parts to see how the system has transformed or changed. You also ask the client: "What do these protector parts need from you right now?" This helps support Self-leadership and integration of therapeutic changes to the system. If the client is targeting oppression-based trauma or anticipated continued trauma exposure, it is normal for protector parts to remain in their roles of protecting the client's system, since there is ongoing threat. Asking what these protectors need for support strengthens teamwork and allyship between the protectors and the client's Self in navigating the client's ongoing stressors.

The final IFS-informed interventions to use for incomplete sessions are optional.

4. Use **intention setting** and **appreciation** by inviting the client to (a) set any intention for in between sessions and (b) send appreciation to all the parts that arose during the session, which supports Self-leadership. In some systems, clients will feel more stable by checking in on a part one time between sessions or practicing specific IFS-informed coping skills outside of session. Parts also respond well to being appreciated and acknowledged for their hard work in session, so inviting the client to send appreciation to their parts as closure for an incomplete session can help support the client ending an incomplete session feeling good and stable.

   a. Ask: "Is there any intention or commitment to checking in on any of these parts that came up in the session before we meet again?" This supports parts' development of trust in Self-leadership and clients' being accountable for their own ongoing healing.

   b. Say: "Send appreciation to all the parts that we focused on in the session today, acknowledging their hard work."

You also describe the TICES log and review coping skills the client can practice between sessions. You can prompt the client to use any of the IFS-informed practices outside of session to support stabilization and integration during phase 7. The client will have already practiced these during phase 2. For a refresher, refer to the therapist worksheet "Integrative Approach to Stabilization and Resource Development" in chapter 5 (page 138).

The following therapist handout summarizes the four interventions described previously for closing incomplete sessions.

Therapist Handout

How to End an Incomplete Session

This handout describes how to integrate IFS interventions into phase 7 at the end of an incomplete session to help stabilize the client and offer target parts resources. An incomplete session is when the target of the EMDR reprocessing is not yet at a zero or not yet as low as it will go on a SUDs scale of 0 to 10.

Integrating IFS into EMDR to end an incomplete session is a multistep process that involves the following interventions: (1) container (practiced during phase 2 as described in chapter 5), (2) retrieval, (3) integration, and, optionally, (4) intention setting and appreciating the parts that showed up. Instructions for these interventions are as follows:

1. **Container:** Invite the target part (whatever part is present for the client at the end of the session) to use the container exercise. Say: "Is there anything this part of you wants to intentionally set aside to hold for you until we meet again next session?" (Sometimes parts need to be retrieved first before they can do the container exercise.)

2. **Retrieval:** Move the target part to a calm place outside of the traumatic scene where the part can connect with the client's Self. Say: "Invite the part to be with you in the present day or to go to your healing place to be with you. [*Pause.*] Let me know when this part has landed there."

3. **Integration:** Ask protector parts that stepped aside for trauma reprocessing to see any shifts in the system (i.e., integration). Say: "Check in with any protector parts that stepped aside, gave permission, and watched on the sidelines to see the transformation that happened during the reprocessing session, including any change that happened for the target exile(s). What do these parts need from you right now?" This fosters Self-leadership, helps update protector parts as to changes that occurred in the system, and helps stabilize the system as the session is closing.

4. **Intention setting and appreciation (optional):** You can ask: "Would you like to set any intention or commitment to checking in on any of these parts from our session before we meet again?" This supports parts' development of trust in Self-leadership and clients' taking accountability for their own ongoing healing. Say: "Send appreciation to all the parts that we focused on in session today."

5. **TICES log and coping skills:** Describe the TICES log and review coping skills the client can practice between sessions, based on what felt good for the client's system when the client practiced various coping skills and used client-centered resources in phase 2.

Let's look at how Zoe's therapist uses the IFS-informed interventions to close an incomplete session.

> ## CASE EXAMPLE
>
> ## Ending an Incomplete Session
>
> **THERAPIST:** Knowing that we are coming to the end of our session soon, ask the younger part in the scene if there is anything she would like to intentionally set aside in your container to hold for you until we meet again next session. [*This is the **container** exercise.*]
>
> **ZOE:** Yes, this part wants to set aside the idea that she's selfish and weak. She's *not* selfish or weak.
>
> **THERAPIST:** Take your time and let me know when the younger part has set this aside and the container is closed.
>
> **ZOE:** It's closed.
>
> **THERAPIST:** Okay, invite this part to be with you now in the present day or to be in your healing place with you. [*Pauses.*] Let me know when this part has landed there. [*This is the **retrieval** intervention. If the client had previously used a term like "beach" or "cabin in the woods" to describe the healing place, the therapist would have used this same language.*]
>
> **ZOE:** She's with me here.
>
> **THERAPIST:** Great. Ask her, is there anything that she needs from you right now? [*This supports Self-to-part connection to continue to restore Self-leadership in the client's system.*]
>
> **ZOE:** No, she feels good to be with me.
>
> **THERAPIST:** Okay. Let's circle back to the anger part that wanted to watch the session on the sidelines. Where is this part right now in and around your body? [*This elicits Self-to-part connection and begins the **integration** intervention.*]
>
> **ZOE:** The angry part is right next to me.
>
> **THERAPIST:** Okay, ask the angry part to see the young part that is with you now. What is it like for this angry part to see that? [*This helps update the protector part in case it did not see the changes in the system from reprocessing.*]
>
> **ZOE:** It feels better seeing that and feels much less angry. It's like it can trust this process more now.
>
> **THERAPIST:** What does this part need from you right now? [*This supports Self-to-part connection to continue to restore Self-leadership in the client's system.*]
>
> **ZOE:** The angry part just wants me to remember that the anger is still there.
>
> **THERAPIST:** Okay, send these two parts appreciation for all their work today. Is there any intention or commitment you'd like to make to check in on the angry part or the younger part between our sessions? [*This is the **appreciation** and **intention-setting** intervention.*]
>
> **ZOE:** Yes, I'd like to check in with each of these parts once between our sessions.

Closing Complete Sessions

A completed target in EMDR reprocessing means that the client reaches a zero or as close to zero as possible (e.g., a low SUDs rating of 1 to 3) and has completed phases 5 and 6 (Shapiro, 2018). For complete sessions, before reviewing the TICES log, discussed later in this chapter, you use the IFS integration intervention, setting any intentions and sending appreciation to parts as discussed in the previous section. You do this by inviting the client to reconnect with the protector parts that gave consent to do EMDR reprocessing, asking them to see the system now. This will help further stabilize the client's system and deepen therapeutic gains. Guide the client to ask the protectors what they need from the client by saying: "Ask this part, what does it need from you right now?" This helps support a Self-led system and assures protector parts that Self is still there.

For complete sessions, you can also guide the client to ask the part if there is anything it needs to release and what new role it would like in the system. This helps further reorganize the system to be Self-led by helping protector parts move out of protective roles and just be parts sharing their natural gifts in the client's system.

Not all protectors will be available or ready to de-role out of being a protector for the system. It is common in complex systems, or when targeting an oppression-based trauma or anticipated ongoing trauma exposure, for the client's protector parts to remain in protective roles to help the client navigate ongoing threat. And, as discussed earlier, sometimes clients cannot locate the protector parts that originally gave permission; if this is the case, proceed with describing the TICES log as described later in this chapter.

After the client has reconnected with and potentially reassigned the protectors, ask the client if they would like to set any intention or commitment to checking in on a specific part in between sessions. When there is a complete session, intention setting may also include noticing what the client's experience is of feeling good given the progress in therapy the client has made with a completed target. Lastly, you invite the client to send appreciation to all the parts that they focused on in session today. The following therapist handout provides additional guidance on integrating IFS interventions to close a complete session.

Therapist Handout

How to End a Complete Session

This handout describes how to integrate IFS interventions into phase 7 at the end of a complete reprocessing session (i.e., in which the client reached a SUDs rating of 0 or as low as it will go and phases 5 and 6 are completed). The purpose of these interventions is to deepen and reinforce therapeutic gains from successful phase 4 reprocessing. Use the IFS integration intervention to invite any protector parts to be included in the healing process and take in the transformation that occurred from reprocessing.

While completed EMDR reprocessing may naturally include shifts in protector parts on the targeted memory network for trauma reprocessing, this is not always the case, particularly when working with more complex systems.

To use these interventions, say:

1. **"Let's circle back to the parts that gave permission for us to do EMDR."** These parts were identified and befriended in phase 2.

2. **"Where are you noticing these parts right now in and around your body?"** This is the *find* question of the 6 F's. If the parts went to a specific location during reprocessing, like a waiting room, you would name that by saying: "Let's invite the parts that were in the waiting room during reprocessing to be here with you now."

3. **"How do you feel toward this part?"** You are checking for Self-energy. For a completed target, the client demonstrates Self-energy as they are feeling a sense of resolution of the EMDR target from reprocessing; they feel good from the positive cognition and body scan.

4. **"Invite the part to take in your presence."** This invites Self-to-part connection.

5. **"Ask these parts to notice the shifts in your system since reprocessing."** If there was a specific exile that shifted during reprocessing, you can address that by saying: "Ask the protector parts to notice the transformation that has happened for the younger part we focused on in reprocessing."

6. **"What's that like for these parts to see the shifts?"** This is eliciting Self-to-part connection, giving protectors a chance to have a voice, and ensuring that these protectors are taking in the changes in the client's internal system. Pause to hear whatever the client shares about the parts' experience.

7. **"Is there anything these parts need to release now that they have seen this transformation?"** This invites protector parts to unburden if that did not happen naturally during phase 4 reprocessing.

8. **"What job would these parts like now?"** This supports reorganization of the internal system toward parts sharing their natural gifts within the system.

9. **"What do these parts need from you right now?"** This further supports a Self-led system.

10. **(Optional) "Would you like to set any intention or commitment to checking in on any of these parts from our session before we meet again?"** This supports parts' development of trust in Self-leadership and the client's taking accountability for their own ongoing healing. Also say: "Send appreciation to all the parts that we focused on in session today."

11. **Describe the TICES log and review coping skills the client can practice between sessions.** This is based on what felt good for the client's system when the client practiced various coping skills and used client-centered resources in phase 2.

CASE EXAMPLE

Ending a Complete Session

Since we last checked in on Noah, he has not only done EMDR reprocessing on the worst of his traumatic military experiences (the initial focus of his treatment plan) but also reprocessed racial traumas related to the bullying he experienced in his youth. Although his SUDs rating for the bullying has not gone to a 0, and his positive cognition has decreased to a 6 and not fully a 7, his therapist considers this realistic given that Noah may experience racial trauma again due to ongoing systemic racism. Noah's body scan revealed some level of alertness in his body, which did not feel uncomfortable or distressing to him, but rather felt adaptive as he focused on the original event, with his positive cognition, during the body scan.

Let's see how Noah's therapist uses the IFS integration intervention for a complete session.

THERAPIST: Okay, so now that we've completed the body scan, let's return to the protector that originally gave you consent to do EMDR. That protector part originally agreed to watch on the sidelines. Check inside—where are you noticing this part right now in and around your body? [*Circling back to the protector and using the find question of the 6 F's*]

NOAH: It's on my left side.

THERAPIST: Great. Bring your attention to this part and invite it to take in your presence. [*Focus*]

NOAH: I see an image of the part next to me. This part helps me keep alert. [*Noah naturally fleshed out the part and shared how he is experiencing the part as an image.*]

THERAPIST: How is the part responding to knowing you get how this part helps you? [*Checking for Self-to-part connection*]

NOAH: It appreciates it. It feels respected.

THERAPIST: How do you feel toward it right now?

NOAH: I feel compassion toward it. It keeps working so hard.

THERAPIST: Share that compassion with the part and see how it is responding to you.

NOAH: It's feeling really appreciated.

THERAPIST: Great. Ask this part to notice the shifts in your system since we completed all of the steps of reprocessing with the events we started with. [*Pauses. Note that if there was a specific exile that shifted during reprocessing, the therapist could have addressed that by saying: "Ask this part to notice the transformation that has happened for the younger part we focused on in reprocessing."*]

THERAPIST: What's that like for this part to see the shifts? [*This is eliciting Self-to-part connection, giving protectors a chance to have a voice, and ensuring that they are taking in the changes in the client's internal system.*]

THERAPIST: [*Pauses to hear whatever the client shares about the part's experience.*]

NOAH: It's feeling relieved.

THERAPIST: Great. Is there anything these parts need to release now that they have seen this transformation? [*This invites protector parts to unburden if that did not happen naturally during phase 4 reprocessing.*]

NOAH: This part wants to release that it doesn't have to care for me all by itself.

THERAPIST: Great. Invite it to release that in whatever way feels right. [*This is not done with BLS.*] Just let me know when that feels complete.

NOAH: Okay. It feels complete.

THERAPIST: What job would it like now for you?

NOAH: It will still be vigilant for me, watching out for danger, but it knows I'm here too.

THERAPIST: Okay. Ask this part, what does it need from you right now? [*This question helps support Self-leadership.*]

NOAH: It wants me to just know that it's here.

THERAPIST: Great, let it know that. [*Pauses.*]

THERAPIST: As we come to closure for today's session, is there any intention or commitment you'd like to make to this part to check in on it in the future, on your own, to see if it needs anything from you? [*This reinforces Self-leadership in the client's system.*]

NOAH: Yes, I'd like to check on it regularly so it knows I'm right here.

THERAPIST: Great. Let the part know that and see how it is responding to your intention.

NOAH: It really likes that. It feels like we're working as a team and knows I'm right here.

THERAPIST: Great! Send this part appreciation and let it know that you'll be checking on it regularly.

Explaining the TICES Log

Whether the client has an incomplete or complete session, after guiding the client through the IFS-informed interventions described previously, you then provide standard debriefing. During standard debriefing in EMDR you say to the client: "The reprocessing we have done today may continue after the session. You may or may not notice new insights, thoughts, memories, or dreams. If you do, just notice what you are experiencing. Take a snapshot of it (what you are seeing, feeling, thinking, and the trigger), and keep a log. We can work on this new material next time" (Hensley, 2021, p. 133). Then give the client a TICES weekly log and explain that after recording any triggers on the TICES log, the client can practice coping skills (e.g., the container or healing place visualization described in chapter 5), as needed, between sessions. The client can also begin to write down what helped them cope after they recorded the trigger on the TICES log. This will help them become more aware of coping skills that help regulate their nervous system after being triggered.

When the client comes to their next session (whether from an incomplete or complete previous session), they are in phase 8, where you are assessing the client as to what has changed since the last EMDR reprocessing session.

Using IFS Interventions During Phase 8: Reevaluation and Options for Future Targets

During phase 8, you assess the client's stability, ask the client about the TICES log to identify future targets, and inquire about any changes the client has experienced since the last session. In this phase, you determine how much the target resolved through EMDR reprocessing. You then re-access the target if it is unresolved or choose a new EMDR target—in collaboration with the client—using the standard three-pronged approach (addressing targets from the past, current triggers, and anticipated future scenarios). For clients with complex trauma, it is normal for reevaluation to include continued reprocessing of incomplete targets over many months until targets are resolved (Shapiro, 2018).

Reevaluation

An IFS approach considers the client's parts to naturally reveal themselves if there are clusters of similar traumatic events that may be on the same memory network. This may show up as parts that share the same burden, are the same developmental age, or are from the same time period. From an IFS lens, new parts realistically are discovered on the targeted memory network, which may naturally resolve (and unburden) through EMDR reprocessing or may need to be their own target in EMDR. In phase 8, you can apply the IFS principle "All parts are welcome" and trust the client's system with what is emerging to identify potential future targets.

If the client's TICES log did not reveal current triggers, you can ask the target part or use standard EMDR questions to identify where the part gets triggered in the present day, as well as any other concerns it has for the future. You can ask the target part: "What do you need from the client for support for present-day triggers?" before proceeding to EMDR reprocessing on them.

An IFS-informed approach to reevaluation includes asking the client again: "Are there any parts of you with fears or concerns about returning to this target and continuing EMDR?" This supports a consent-based approach to trauma reprocessing and respecting the client's protective system before returning to a target or beginning a new target. If the client accessed a target by befriending a specific part, you can guide the client to return to the exile to reevaluate the target. Given that phase 4 reprocessing helps elicit more Self in the client, you can ask more standard EMDR reevaluation questions as the client's system can tolerate more arousal. This will include more parts in the client's system and not just the target exile's assessment of the SUDs level.

Anticipated Future Scenarios and a Future Template

After past and present targets are resolved in EMDR, you'll want to support the client's ability to navigate anticipated situations, people, and choices the client will face in the future. This helps support Self-leadership in the system and applies therapeutic gains from therapy to potential future scenarios. A future template in EMDR—in which the client runs a "movie" of how they would like to navigate a future situation—helps the client's system imagine their response in that scenario (Shapiro, 2018). A future template can be seen as a Self-led system rehearsing with parts how the client wants to respond in the future.

Focusing on anticipating future scenarios and conducting a future template may reveal parts with fears that are future-oriented or more global in nature. These parts may need more befriending using the techniques described in chapter 4. With the consent of the client's system, you may be able to proceed using the standard EMDR approach to reprocessing anticipated future scenarios and a future template.

What Happens If There Is Backlash in the System?

Backlash refers to the client experiencing an increase in mental health symptoms due to protector parts taking over the system (Schwartz & Sweezy, 2020). This typically shows up as firefighter parts trying to regulate the system in the way they know how—by increased suicidality, substance abuse, self-harm, or high-risk behavior. From an IFS lens, backlash is a clinical indicator of potentially needing to slow down the treatment.

When backlash occurs, you can return to using befriending techniques as discussed in chapter 4 to befriend the parts activated in the client's system, beginning with firefighter parts before befriending other protector parts. You and the client may collaboratively decide to alternate EMDR reprocessing sessions with sessions focused on using IFS befriending to support stabilization and integration as needed, with the intention of returning to EMDR reprocessing.

The steps for managing backlash are illustrated in the following therapist handout.

Therapist Handout

How to Navigate Backlash

1. Befriend Firefighters First
- Befriend any firefighters (parts exhibiting suicidality, substance abuse, self-harm, or high-risk behavior) in the system first.
- Use the 6 F's.
- If there are polarizations or multiple parts, use the conference table technique.
- Ask the protector parts, "What do you need right now?"

2. Befriend Any Protectors Activated
- Once firefighters soften, assess if there are any other parts with fears or concerns.
- Address all protector parts' concerns so they feel heard. This will soften them.
- Use befriending interventions to support client stabilization.

3. Assess Client Stability
- Assess client stability and, if protectors give consent, reevaluate the EMDR target to proceed with EMDR reprocessing.
- If client doesn't receive consent or is not stable, continue with befriending focused on fostering Self-to-part connection, using direct access as needed.
- Utilize integrative coping skills that help the parts that are activated.

As clients resolve EMDR targets and meet their treatment goals, it is a natural time to collaboratively decide with clients what closure and terminating therapy look like. An IFS-informed decision process about termination is client-centered and consent-based, inviting the client to reflect on the therapeutic gains they have experienced in therapy. The process of terminating EMDR therapy can include the IFS-informed process of inviting clients to speak for their parts about their feelings related to ending therapy, closure of their therapeutic work, and saying goodbye. It's also helpful to let the client know that integration of therapeutic gains often continues to occur after therapy ends and to remind the client that they now have valuable tools—such as parts mapping and relating self-compassionately to their parts—to navigate future stressors.

CHAPTER 10

Exploring Our Own Therapist Parts

You have now learned how to integrate IFS therapy into the eight phases of EMDR. You've explored numerous IFS interventions and clinical situations in which this integrative approach can benefit your clients. You've reviewed therapist handouts and case examples to reinforce your learning. But there's one more step to cover before ending this book. To effectively apply IFS interventions, it is helpful for us as therapists to also become familiar with our own parts that may show up as we provide psychotherapy. This chapter consists of several worksheets for you to explore your system of parts for your self-care, which will allow you to be more Self-led in your own system when providing mental health services. I encourage you to complete all the worksheets prior to implementing IFS-integrative EMDR therapy with your clients.

Therapist Worksheet

Our Own Parts That Show Up in Providing Therapy

This worksheet will help you explore and understand your own parts that show up in your work treating clients. Common burdened parts that show up in therapists include feeling overly responsible for clients or having specific countertransference reactions with a particular client.

Check the box if any parts of you resonate with the statement:

- ☐ I am betraying my client if they don't get better.
- ☐ I did something wrong or it's my fault if my client isn't getting better.
- ☐ I need to feel all of my client's feelings so I can help them.
- ☐ I repetitively dream about my clients or a particular client.
- ☐ I feel significant relief when clients or a particular client cancels their appointment.
- ☐ I dread my sessions with clients or a particular client.
- ☐ If my client abruptly terminates therapy with me, I feel rejected and hurt.
- ☐ If my clients are not getting better in therapy with me, then they will never get better.
- ☐ If my clients are not getting better in therapy with me, that means I'm broken.
- ☐ I am the only person that can help my clients or a particular client.
- ☐ I must save my clients.
- ☐ I frequently feel overwhelmed by my clients' feelings in general or by a particular client's feelings.
- ☐ It's hard for me to tell what feelings are mine and what feelings belong to my client.
- ☐ I feel held hostage by my clients or by a particular client.
- ☐ I feel I am constantly grieving for my clients or for one particular client.
- ☐ If my clients don't like me or get angry with me, that means I am a bad person or a bad therapist.
- ☐ If my client doesn't follow the treatment plan, then I feel like a failure.
- ☐ It is hard for me to tolerate hearing my clients' feelings or pain in general, or a particular client's feelings or pain.
- ☐ I can barely stand to be with my clients or a particular client.
- ☐ I want to ignore or avoid a particular client.
- ☐ I feel nothing or have a hard time having empathy for a particular client.

❏ I feel I'm not enough when I'm in session with my clients.

❏ I regret being a therapist or sometimes feel resentment about being a therapist.

Pick one of the beliefs you checked to explore. First, take some big breaths with long exhales. Invite in curiosity to get to know this part better. Then answer the following questions.

When do you notice this part of you showing up? For example, is there a particular behavior or tone of voice in another person that activates this part?

_____
_____

How does your body respond when this part is activated?

_____
_____

What fears or concerns does this part have?

_____
_____

What does this part need from you right now?

_____
_____

See what it's like to offer this part your heart-centered presence, acknowledgment, and understanding. How is this part responding to you?

_____
_____

If you are able to offer the part what it needs from you, how is the part responding to receiving this from you?

_____
_____

Therapist Worksheet

Signs of Being Self-Led and Signs of Being Triggered

Polyvagal theory proposes that when people are in ventral vagal states, they are calm and not in survival mode (Dana, 2018; Porges, 1995). This worksheet can help you better identify when you have access to Self, what helps you return to Self, and what moves you out of being Self-led.

When have you noticed being Self-led? Remember, you are Self-led when you experience any of the 8 C's (compassion, calmness, courage, curiosity, creativity, connectedness, clarity, confidence) and 5 P's (presence, perspective, persistence, playfulness, patience).

_____
_____

Some people experience being Self-led as being in a flow state, feeling more grounded or centered. What helps you experience this or return to this experience after being triggered?

_____
_____

What signs are you aware of that indicate that you are triggered?

_____
_____

What triggers are you aware of? What situations or scenarios are activating for you?

_____
_____

What does your body do when you are triggered or activated?

_____
_____

What feelings or fears emerge?

_____

_____

What do you notice thinking or believing?

_____

_____

Now let's put this all together in the following table. In the first column, list what you learned from completing this worksheet about how your Self shows up—in other words, signs that your system is being Self-led. In the second column, list what you learned about how parts in your system show up when you are triggered (i.e., What do you feel? What do you fear? What do you think? How does your body respond?).

Signs of Being Self-Led	How Your Parts Show Up When You Are Triggered

Therapist Worksheet

Get to Know Your Protector Parts

Protector parts are more likely to show up for therapists when we are stressed. This worksheet is an invitation to get to know your own protector parts.

How do you know when you have reached your stress limit?

_____
_____

What do you notice in your body?

_____
_____

What do you do or say?

_____
_____

What do you feel?

_____
_____

What do you think?

_____
_____

What do others notice about you?

_____
_____

Pick a part that you would like to get to know that shows up for you when you are stressed. Take some big breaths with long exhales. Invite in curiosity. Where do you notice this part right now in and around your body?

_____
_____

What fears or concerns does it have?

_____
_____

What is it hoping to accomplish by showing up in the way it does?

_____
_____

What does it need from you right now?

_____
_____

What else does this part want you to know about what it's like to be this part?

_____
_____

What do you want to tell this part in response to what it has shared?

_____
_____

How is the part responding to receiving your heart-centered attention, presence, and acknowledgment?

_____
_____

If you can offer this part what it needs from you right now, how is the part responding to your giving it what it needs?

_____
_____

See what it's like to offer this part some gratitude for trying to help you in the way that it does. What do you notice inside? How is this part responding to your gratitude?

_____
_____

Are there any other parts of you that have fears or concerns about this part that shows up when you are stressed?

_____
_____

If so, what fears or concerns do these other parts have?

_____
_____

What do those parts need from you right now?

_____
_____

What intention or commitment would you like to make to any part that shows up when you are stressed to help it receive support from you?

_____
_____

Therapist Worksheet

What Parts Emerge in Broaching Cultural Content?

Developed by Norma Day-Vines, PhD, and colleagues (2007), "broaching" refers to the therapist's intentional efforts to address the cultural, ethnic, or racial issues that are central to the client's presenting issues. This worksheet is an opportunity to get curious about what parts show up in your own system when broaching cultural content as a therapist.

Imagine any client (past, present, or imaginary) who differs from you in one or more aspects of their identity—this may be in their cultural, racial, or ethnic identity, sexual orientation, gender identity, immigration status, political orientation, health status, socioeconomic class, or faith, spirituality, or religious orientation. Perhaps you are unfamiliar with the culture of this client, or you may notice hesitancy or reactivity inside when thinking about intentionally discussing the client's identity and how it impacts their presenting concerns. Take some big breaths with long exhales and invite in curiosity.

What fears or concerns do you have about directly and intentionally discussing important aspects of the client's identity?

_____

_____

What fears or concerns do you have about exploring how the client's cultural content or identity relates to their presenting concern?

_____

_____

How do these parts show up in your body?

_____

_____

When do you notice these parts show up in sessions with this client?

_____

_____

What do you do or say when these parts are activated?

_____
_____

Are there any parts of you that want to avoid exploring this with a client? What are you scared would happen if you explored this with a client?

_____
_____

Turn toward a part of you that you are aware shows up in your broaching process with this client you are imagining. Ask this part, what is it scared is going to happen?

_____
_____

If the part's response makes sense to you, internally let the part know that you are understanding it right now.

How is this part responding to you acknowledging it?

_____
_____

What does this part want you to know about itself?

_____
_____

What does this part need from you right now?

_____
_____

See what it's like to offer this part your heart-centered presence, acknowledgment, and understanding. How is this part responding to you?

_____
_____

If you can offer the part what it needs from you, how is the part responding to receiving this from you?
_____
_____

What do you want to tell this part in response to what it has shared?
_____
_____

Give the part a choice to go to an alternative location (e.g., a waiting room or your own healing place, real or imagined, that you can visualize) during the session with the client. See how the part responds knowing that you can lead the session with the client (not this part).
_____
_____

Let this part know that you can also gain more skills, practice your skills, and become more at ease inside with ways to effectively broach cultural content in session. How is the part responding to receiving this support from you?
_____
_____

Ask this part what it needs to be in a different location (e.g., waiting room, healing place visualization) during the session with the client.
_____
_____

See if you can offer what it needs. What are you noticing? How is the part responding?
_____
_____

What intention or commitment would you like to make to this part to help it receive support from you?
_____
_____

Therapist Worksheet

Exploring What It Means to Have Needs

This worksheet is an invitation to identify parts in your own internal system that show up regarding having self-care needs. For each prompt, complete the sentence.

If I put myself first, then I'm afraid that...

_____
_____

If I put my needs for self-care first, then I'm afraid that...

_____
_____

If I slow down, then I'm afraid that...

_____
_____

If I say no, then I'm afraid that...

_____
_____

If I do less for others, then I'm afraid that...

_____
_____

If I ask for help, then I'm afraid that...

_____
_____

If I don't feel some of my client's feelings, then I'm afraid that . . .

_____
_____

If I set boundaries for how much I take on, then I'm afraid that . . .

_____
_____

If I tell myself "I'm doing enough," then I notice inside that . . .

_____
_____

And my body's reaction is . . .

_____
_____

If my body could tell me what it needs for self-care, it would say:

_____
_____

If I listen deeply within, I need . . .

_____
_____

Pick one of the beliefs you just identified to explore. Take some big breaths with long exhales. As you breathe, invite in curiosity to get to know this part better.

When do you notice this part of you showing up?

_____
_____

How does your body respond when this part is activated?

_____
_____

What do you do (behaviorally) when this part is activated?

_____
_____

What fears or concerns does this part have?

_____
_____

What does this part need from you right now?

_____
_____

Ask this part, does its role come at a cost or have a downside?

_____
_____

What difference would it make if this part could get some support in your system or have another job in your system?

_____
_____

See what it's like to offer this part your heart-centered presence, acknowledgment, and understanding. How is this part responding to you?

_____
_____

If you are able to offer the part what it needs from you, how is the part responding to receiving this from you?

_____
_____

What intention or commitment would you like to make to this part of you to ask it what it needs from you for support?

_____
_____

Therapist Worksheet

Exploring Legacy Burdens

Every one of us carries legacy burdens passed down from our families, communities, and systems we belong to and navigate. This worksheet is an invitation to explore what legacy burdens your system may be carrying related to your being a therapist. For each prompt, complete the sentence.

According to my profession and my professional creed/code of ethics, being a therapist means . . .

_____

_____

_____

According to cultures and communities I belong to, being a therapist, a healer, a change maker, a helper, or an advocate means . . .

_____

_____

_____

According to my family, being a therapist, a healer, or a helper means . . .

_____

_____

_____

My family's story and history about self-sacrifice and giving to others says that . . .

_____

_____

_____

My family's story and history about putting others' needs above my own says that . . .

_____

_____

_____

My family's story and history about what it means to work, to have a work ethic, and to push yourself says that . . .

_____
_____
_____

My family's story and history about self-care says that . . .

_____
_____
_____

Check inside—what parts do you notice inside as you reflect on these beliefs and values?

_____
_____
_____

What does your body need from you right now as you uncover parts that may carry legacy burdens?

_____
_____
_____

Conclusion

Trauma treatment is not one-size-fits-all. Some parts will be more easily accessible through using IFS interventions, while others will be more easily discovered through EMDR trauma reprocessing. By integrating IFS interventions into EMDR therapy, your clients can attune to, understand, and respect their parts, which will decrease their mental health symptoms and help them stabilize.

As discussed in this book, through an IFS lens, you consider the client's symptomology as parts trying to help the client in the way they know how. These parts can be stuck in specific autonomic states that will benefit from an integrative approach that considers polyvagal theory, external and internal factors, and the impact of trauma on the client's nervous system. Some parts may initially take in the relational presence of Self before receiving the benefits of coping skills. Other parts may only be able to receive the presence of Self after first receiving the benefits of coping skills. Be flexible!

IFS interventions, such as parts mapping and befriending protectors, can help clients experience being understood in the therapeutic relationship, support their access to Self, and proceed with trauma reprocessing with consent of their system. If the client experiences blocked or stuck reprocessing in phases 4 through 6 in EMDR therapy, IFS interventions can help them get unstuck and restore the Self-to-part connection in a multitude of ways.

The five IFS principles, emphasized throughout this book, can serve as a guide to navigate the integration of these two models: *We all have Self and parts. All parts are welcome. Receive consent from protector parts first. The Self-to-part relationship is healing. If parts feel understood, they will soften.*

Remember that IFS slows down the pace and EMDR speeds it up. Considering the distinct speeds of these two therapies can help inform clinical choices to support your client's system capacity and window of tolerance in any given session.

At the end of the day, you, as the therapist, being Self-led will also support clients' trust in the therapy process. Get curious about any parts in your own system that have strong agendas for what the path toward emotion regulation or healing needs to look like. It is normal for our own parts to get activated in providing psychotherapy. Care for your own nervous system and parts that show up in response to working with complex trauma. This will help you be Self-led, which can help you sustainably support the communities you serve.

May you continue to guide your clients toward healing, bolstered by your new knowledge and understanding of an IFS-integrative approach to EMDR therapy.

Resources for Complex Trauma

> For your convenience, worksheets from this book are available for download at **www.pesipubs.com/IFSnEMDR**

EMDR Resources for Complex Trauma

- Gonzalez, A., & Mosquera, D. (2012). *EMDR and dissociation: The progressive approach* (1st ed., rev.). Authors.

- Hase, M. (2021). Instant resource installation and extensive resource installation: Two novel techniques for resource installation in EMDR therapy—Theory, description and case report. *European Journal of Trauma & Dissociation, 5*(4), Article 100224. https://doi.org/10.1016/j.ejtd.2021.100224

- Hofmann, A., Ostacoli, L., Lehnung, M., Hase, M., & Luber, M. (2022). *Treating depression with EMDR therapy: Techniques and interventions.* Springer Publishing.

- International Society for the Study of Trauma and Dissociation (https://www.isst-d.org)

- Knipe, J. (2019). *EMDR toolbox: Theory and treatment of complex PTSD and dissociation* (2nd ed.). Springer Publishing Co.

- Leeds, A. M. (2023). Foundations of the Positive Affect Tolerance Protocol: The central role of interpersonal positive affect in attachment and self-regulation. *Journal of EMDR Practice and Research, 17*(3). https://doi.org/10.1891/emdr-2023-0006

- Luber, M. (Ed.). (2010). *Eye Movement Desensitization and Reprocessing (EMDR) scripted protocols.* Springer Publishing.

- Manfield, P. E., Taylor, G., Dornbush, E., Engel, L., & Greenwald, R. (2024). Preliminary evidence for the acceptability, safety, and efficacy of the flash technique. *Frontiers in Psychiatry, 14,* Article 1273704. https://doi.org/10.3389/fpsyt.2023.1273704

- Manfield, P., Lovett, J., Engel, L., & Manfield, D. (2017). Use of the Flash Technique in EMDR therapy: Four case examples. *Journal of EMDR Practice and Research, 11*(4), 195–205. http://dx.doi.org/10.1891/1933-3196.11.4.195

- Nickerson, M. (Ed.). (2023). *Cultural competence and healing culturally based trauma with EMDR therapy: Innovative strategies and protocols* (2nd ed.). Springer Publishing Company.

- Parnell, L. (2013). *Attachment-focused EMDR: Healing relational trauma.* W. W. Norton & Company.
- Paulsen, S. L. (2017). *When there are no words: Repairing early trauma and neglect from the attachment period with EMDR therapy.* Author.
- Shapiro, F. (2018). *Eye Movement Desensitization and Reprocessing (EMDR) therapy: Basic principles, protocols and procedures* (3rd ed.). The Guilford Press.

IFS Resources for Complex Trauma

- Anderson, F. G. (2021). *Transcending trauma: Healing complex PTSD with Internal Family Systems therapy.* PESI Publishing and Media.
- Fisher, J. (2017). *Healing the fragmented selves of trauma survivors: Overcoming internal self-alienation.* Routledge.
- Fisher, J. (2021). *Transforming the living legacy of trauma: A workbook for survivors and therapists.* PESI Publishing and Media.
- Riemersma, J. (Ed.). (2023). *Altogether us: Integrating the IFS model with key modalities, communities, and trends.* Pivotal Press.
- Schwartz, R. C., & Sweezy, M. (2020). *Internal Family Systems* (2nd ed.). The Guilford Press.
- Twombly, J. H. (2022). *Trauma and dissociation informed Internal Family Systems.* Author.

References

Ally, D., Tobiasz-Veltz, L., Tu, K., Comeau, A., Bumpus, C., Blot, T., Rice, F. K., Orr, B., Soumerai Rea, H., Sweezy, M., & Schuman-Olivier, Z. (2025). A pilot study of an online group-based Internal Family Systems intervention for comorbid posttraumatic stress disorder and substance use. *Frontiers in Psychiatry, 16,* Article 1544435. https://doi.org/10.3389/fpsyt.2025.1544435

Alter-Reid, K., & Heber, R. (2023). The transgenerational impact of antisemitism. In M. Nickerson (Ed.), *Cultural competence and healing culturally based trauma with EMDR therapy: Innovative strategies and protocols.* (2nd ed., pp. 225–237). Springer Publishing Company.

Amano, T., & Toichi, M. (2016). The role of alternating bilateral stimulation in establishing positive cognition in EMDR therapy: A multi-channel near-infrared spectroscopy study. *PLoS One, 11*(10), Article e0162735. https://doi.org/10.1371/journal.pone.0162735

American Psychiatric Association. (2022). *Diagnostic and statistical manual of mental disorders* (5th ed., text rev.). https://doi.org/10.1176/appi.books.9780890425596

American Psychological Association. (2021). *APA guidelines on evidence-based psychological practice in health care.* https://www.apa.org/about/policy/psychological-practice-health-care.pdf

Anderson, F. G. (2021). *Transcending trauma: healing complex PTSD with Internal Family Systems therapy.* PESI Publishing and Media.

Artigas, L., Jarero, I., Mauer, M., López Cano, T., & Alcalá, N. (2000, September). EMDR and traumatic stress after natural disasters: Integrative treatment protocol and the butterfly hug. Poster presented at the EMDRIA Conference, Toronto, Ontario, Canada.

Ashley, W., & Lipscomb, A. (2023). Strategies for implementation of an anti-oppressive, antiracist, intersectional lens in EDR therapy with Black clients. In M. Nickerson (Ed.), *Cultural competence and healing culturally based trauma with EMDR therapy: Innovative strategies and protocols* (2nd ed., pp. 135–147). Springer Publishing Company.

Bartlett, A., Faber, S., Williams, M., & Saxberg, K. (2022). Getting to the root of the problem: Supporting clients with lived-experiences of systemic discrimination. *Chronic Stress, 6,* Article 24705470221139205. https://doi.org/10.1177/24705470221139205

Bilbao Bourke, J., Dobrovolny, J., Eaton, M., Ferrante, T., & Smith, M. (2021). Complex trauma care pathway: Results of a 12-month pilot. *The Permanente Journal, 25*(3), https://doi.org/10.7812/TPP/20.147

Bongaerts, H. Voorendonk, E. M., van Minnen, A., & de Jongh, A. (2021). Safety and effectiveness of intensive treatment for complex PTSD delivered via home-based telehealth. *European Journal of Psychotraumatology, 12*(1), Article 1860346. http://dx.doi.org/10.1080/20008198.2020.1860346

Bongaerts, H., Voorendonk, E. M., van Minnen, A., Rozendaal, L., Telkamp, B. S. D., & de Jongh, A. (2022). Fully remote intensive trauma-focused treatment for PTSD and complex PTSD. *European Journal of Psychotraumatology, 13*(2), Article 2103287. https://doi.org/10.1080/20008066.2022.2103287

Catanzaro, J. (2017). IFS and eating disorders: Healing the parts who hide in plain sight. In E. Zeskind & M. Sweezy (Eds.), *Innovations and elaborations in Internal Family Systems therapy* (pp. 10–28). Routledge.

Christiansen, C., & Martinez-Dettamanti, M. (2023). Embodying IFS with neurodivergent clients: A neuro-inclusive approach for therapists. In J. Riemersma (Ed.), *Altogether Us: Integrating the IFS model with key modalities, communities, and trends* (pp. 315–358). Pivotal Press.

Cloitre, M. (2020). ICD-11 complex post-traumatic stress disorder: Simplifying diagnosis in trauma populations. *The British Journal of Psychiatry, 216*(3), 129–131. https://doi.org/10.1192/bjp.2020.43

Cloitre, M. (2021). Complex PTSD: assessment and treatment. *European Journal of Psychotraumatology, 12*(Suppl. 1). https://doi.org/10.1080/20008198.2020.1866423

Comeau, A., Smith, L. J., Smith, L., Soumerai Rea, H., Ward, M. C., Creedon, T. B., Sweezy, M., Rosenberg, L. G., & Schuman-Olivier, Z. (2024). Online group-based Internal Family Systems treatment for posttraumatic stress disorder: Feasibility and acceptability of the program for alleviating and resolving trauma and stress. Psychological Trauma: *Theory, Research, Practice, and Policy.* Advance online publication. https://dx.doi.org/10.1037/tra0001688

Courtois, C. A., & Ford, J. D. (2016). *Treatment of complex trauma: A sequenced, relationship-based approach.* The Guilford Press.

Dana, D. (2018). *The polyvagal theory in therapy: Engaging the rhythm of regulation.* W. W. Norton and Company.

Darker-Smith, S., & Clarke, A. (2024). Coping with "difference": Neurodiversity-affirming eye movement desensitization and reprocessing therapy for autistic and attention deficit hyperactivity disorder clients with eating disorders. In A. Seubert & P. Virdi (Eds.). (2024). *Trauma-informed approaches to eating disorders* (2nd ed., pp. 400–410). Springer Publishing Company. https://doi.org/10.1891/9780826147981.0031

Day-Vines, N. L., Wood, S. M., Grothaus, T., Craigen, L., Holman, A., Dotson-Blake, K., & Douglass, M. J. (2007). Broaching the subjects of race, ethnicity, and culture during the counseling process. *Journal of Counseling and Development, 85*(4), 401–409. https://doi.org/10.1002/j.1556-6678.2007.tb00608.x

de Boer, K., Arnold, C., Mackelprang, J. L., Williamson, D., Eckel, D., & Nedeljkovic, M. (2023). Outcomes from a pilot study to evaluate phase 1 of a two-phase approach to treat women with complex trauma histories. *Australian Psychologist, 58*(5), 346–356. https://doi.org/10.1080/00050067.2023.2192335

Ecker, B. (2018). Clinical translation of memory reconsolidation research: Therapeutic methodology for transformational change by erasing implicit emotional learnings driving symptom production. *International Journal of Neuropsychotherapy, 6*(1), 1–92. https://doi.org/10.12744/ijnpt.2018.0001-0092

Ecker, B., & Bridges, S. K. (2020). How the science of memory reconsolidation advances the effectiveness and unification of psychotherapy. *Clinical Social Work Journal, 48*(3), 287–300. https://doi.org/10.1007/s10615-020-00754-z

Ecker, B., Ticic, R., & Hulley, L. (2012). *Unlocking the emotional brain: Eliminating symptoms at their roots using memory reconsolidation.* Routledge.

Ecker, B., & Vaz, A. (2022). Memory reconsolidation and the crisis of mechanism in psychotherapy. *New Ideas in Psychology, 66,* 1–11. https://doi.org/10.1016/j.newideapsych.2022.100945

Eitan, A., & Torem, M. S. (2018). The roots and evolution of ego-state theory and therapy. *International Journal of Clinical and Experimental Hypnosis, 66*(4), 353–370. https://doi.org/10.1080/00207144.2018.1494435

Fatter, D. (2023a). Ancestral lineage healing: Restoring belonging and reconnection with ancestral wisdom and collective Self-energy. In J. Riemersma (Ed.), *Altogether us: Integrating the IFS model with key modalities, communities, and trends* (pp. 595–623). Pivotal Press.

Fatter, D. (2023b). IFS and EMDR: Transforming traumatic memories and providing relational repair with Self. In J. Riemersma (Ed.), *Altogether us: Integrating the IFS model with key modalities, communities, and trends* (pp. 81–110). Pivotal Press.

Fatter, D. (2023c, October 27). *Integrating IFS and EMDR: Transforming traumatic memories and providing relational repair with Self* [Conference presentation]. International Internal Family Systems Conference, Denver, Colorado.

Fatter, D. (2024). Integrating Internal Family Systems into EMDR therapy's 8 phases. *Go With That Magazine, 29*(2), 13–21. EMDR International Association.

Finley, E. P., Mader, M., Bollinger, M. J., Haro, E. K., Garcia, H. A., Huynh, A. K., Pugh, J. A., & Pugh, M. J. (2017). Characteristics associated with utilization of VA and non-VA care among Iraq and Afghanistan veterans with post-traumatic stress disorder. *Military Medicine, 182*(11–12), e1892–e1903. https://doi.org/10.7205/MILMED-D-17-00074

Fisher, J. (2017). *Healing the fragmented selves of trauma survivors: Overcoming internal self-alienation.* Routledge.

Fisher, J. (2021). *Transforming the living legacy of trauma: A workbook for survivors and therapists.* PESI Publishing and Media.

Fisher, N., van Diest, C., Leoni, M., & Spain, D. (2023). Using EMDR with autistic individuals: A Delphi survey with EMDR therapists. *Autism, 27*(1), 43–53. https://doi.org/10.1177/13623613221080254

Forgash, C. (2010). Workplace or conference room. In M. Luber (Ed.), *Eye Movement Desensitization and Reprocessing (EMDR) scripted protocols* (pp. 221–224). Springer Publishing.

Fraser, G. A. (1991). The dissociative table technique: A strategy for working with ego states in dissociative disorders and ego state therapy. *Dissociation, 4*(4), 204–213.

Fraser, G. A. (2003). Fraser's "dissociative table technique" revisited, revised: A strategy for working with ego states in dissociative disorders and ego state therapy. *Journal of Trauma and Dissociation, 4*(4), 5–28.

Girianto., P. W. R., Widayati., D., & Agusti, S. S. (2021). Butterfly hug to reduce anxiety on elderly. *Journal Ners dan Kebidanan 8*(3), 295–300. https://doi.org/10.26699/jnk.v8i3.ART.p295-300

Gonzalez, A., & Mosquera, D. (2012). *EMDR and dissociation: The progressive approach* (1st ed., rev.).

Haddock, S. A., Weiler, L. M., Trump, L. J., & Henry, K. L. (2017). The efficacy of Internal Family Systems therapy in the treatment of depression among female college students: A pilot study. *Journal of Marital and Family Therapy, 43*(1), 131–144. https://doi.org/10.1111/jmft.12184

Hensley, B. J. (2021). *An EMDR therapy primer: From practicum to practice* (3rd ed.). Springer Publishing.

Herman, J. L. (1992a). Complex PTSD: A syndrome in survivors of prolonged and repeated trauma. *Journal of Traumatic Stress, 5*(3), 377–391. https://doi.org/10.1002/jts.2490050305

Herman, J. (1992b). *Trauma and recovery*. W. W. Norton.

Hodgdon, H. G., Anderson, F. G., Southwell, E., Hrubec, W., & Schwartz R. C. (2022). Internal Family Systems (IFS) therapy for posttraumatic stress disorder (PTSD) among survivors of multiple childhood trauma: A pilot effectiveness study. *Journal of Aggression, Maltreatment and Trauma, 31*(1), 1–22. https://doi.org/10.1080/10926771.2021.2013375

Hofmann, A., Ostacoli, L., Lehnugn, M., Hase, M., & Luber, M. (2022). *Treating depression with EMDR therapy: Techniques and interventions*. Springer Publishing.

Jarero, I., & Artigas, L. (2021). The EMDR therapy butterfly hug method for self-administered bilateral stimulation. *Iberoamerican Journal of Psychotraumatology and Dissociation, 10*(1). https://www.revibapst.com/volumen-11

Jones, E. R., Lauricella, D., D'Aniello, C., Smith, M., & Romney, J. (2022). Integrating Internal Family Systems and solutions focused brief therapy to treat survivors of sexual trauma. *Contemporary Family Therapy: An International Journal, 44*, 167–175. https://doi.org/10.1007/s10591-021-09571-z

Kluft, R. P. (1982). Varieties of hypnotic interventions in the treatment of multiple personality. *The American Journal of Clinical Hypnosis, 24*(4), 230–40. https://doi.org/10.1080/00029157.1982.10403310

Kluft, R. P. (1988). Playing for time: Temporizing techniques in the treatment of multiple personality disorder. *American Journal of Clinical Hypnosis, 32*, 90–98.

Kluft, R. P. (1993). Basic principles in conducting the psychotherapy of multiple personality disorder. In R. P. Kluft & C. G. Fine (Eds.), *Clinical perspectives on multiple personality disorder* (pp. 19–50). American Psychiatric Press.

Knipe, J. (2010). Back of the head scale. In M. Luber (Ed.), *Eye Movement Desensitization and Reprocessing (EMDR) scripted protocols* (pp. 233–234). Springer Publishing.

Knipe, J. (2019). *EMDR toolbox: Theory and treatment of complex PTSD and dissociation* (2nd ed.). Springer Publishing Co.

Kolodny, P., & Mazero, S. (2022). The interweave of Internal Family Systems, EMDR, and art therapy. In E. Davis, J. Fitzgerald, S. Jacobs, & J. Marchand (Eds.), *EMDR and creative arts therapies* (pp. 208–240). Routledge.

Korn, D. (2009). EMDR and the treatment of complex PTSD: A review. *Journal of EMDR Practice and Research, 3*(4), 264–278.

Krause, P., & Gomez, A. (2013). EMDR therapy and the use of Internal Family Systems strategies with children. In C. Forgash & M. Copeley (Eds.), *Healing the heart of trauma and dissociation with EMDR and ego state therapy* (pp. 295–311). Springer Publishing Company.

Krause, P. K., Rosenberg, L. G., & Sweezy, M. (2016). Getting unstuck. In M. Sweezy & E. L. Ziskind (Eds.), *Innovations and elaborations in Internal Family Systems therapy: New dimensions* (pp. 35–54). Routledge.

Kredler, V. (2023). How does Internal Family Systems therapy lead to transformational change through memory reconsolidation? *Counselling Australia, 24*(2), 26–36. www.theaca.net.au/counselling-australia.php

Levine, P. A. (2010). *In an unspoken voice: How the body releases trauma and restores goodness*. North Atlantic Books.

Levine, P. A. (2018). Polyvagal theory and trauma. In S. W. Porges & D. Dana (Eds.), *Clinical applications of the polyvagal theory: The emergence of polyvagal-informed therapies* (pp. 3–26). W. W. Norton & Company.

Lobenstine, F., & Courtney, D. (2013). A case study: The integration of intensive EMDR and ego state therapy to treat comorbid posttraumatic stress disorder, depression, and anxiety. *Journal of EMDR Practice and Research, 7*(2), 65–80. https://doi.org/10.1891/1933-3196.7.2.65

Lucero, R., Jones, A., & Hunsaker, J. (2017). Using Internal Family Systems theory in the treatment of combat veterans with post-traumatic stress disorder and their families. *Contemporary Family Therapy, 40,* 266–275. https://doi.org/10.1007/s10591-017-9424-z

Marchand, J., & Simpson, M. (2023). Inviting the body, movement, and the creative arts into telehealth: A culturally responsive model for online EMDR preparation. In E. Davis, J. Fitzgerald, S. Jacobs, & J. Marchand (Eds.), *EMDR and Creative Art Therapies* (pp. 64–101). Routledge.

Marish, J. (2023). *Dissociation made simple.* North Atlantic Books.

Maxfield, L. (2019). A clinician's guide to the efficacy of EMDR therapy. *Journal of EMDR Practice and Research, 13*(4), 239–246. http://dx.doi.org/10.1891/1933-3196.13.4.239

McConnell, S. (2013). Embodying the internal family. In E. Zeskind & M. Sweezy (Eds.), *Internal Family Systems therapy: New dimensions* (pp. 90–106). Routledge.

McConnell, S. (2020). *Somatic Internal Family Systems therapy: Awareness, breath, resonance, movement and touch in practice.* North Atlantic Books.

Mehrad Sadr, M., Borjali, A., Eskandary, H., & Delavar, A. (2023). Design and validation of a therapy program based on the Internal Family Systems model and its efficacy on internet addiction. *Journal of Psychological Science, 22*(121), 19–36. http://dx.doi.org/10.52547/JPS.22.121.19

Menakem, R. (2017). *My grandmother's hands: racialized trauma and the pathway to mending our hearts and bodies.* Central Recovery Press.

Miller, B. J., Cardona, J. R. P., & Hardin, M. (2007). The use of narrative therapy and Internal Family Systems with survivors of childhood sexual abuse: Examining issues related to loss and oppression. *Journal of Feminist Family Therapy: An International Forum, 18*(4), 1–27. https://doi.org/10.1300/J086v18n04_01

Nickerson, M. (Ed.). (2023b). *Cultural competence and healing culturally based trauma with EMDR therapy: Innovative strategies and protocols* (2nd ed.). Springer Publishing Company.

Nickerson, M. (2023c). Culturally-based trauma and adversity: Recognition, definition, and implications. In M. Nickerson (Ed.). *Cultural competence and healing culturally based trauma with EMDR therapy: Innovative strategies and protocols* (2nd ed., pp. 36–52). Springer Publishing Company.

Nickerson, M. (2023d). Healing and resilience building with EMDR reprocessing: Target selection and EMDR phases 3 to 6. In M. Nickerson (Ed.). *Cultural competence and healing culturally based trauma with EMDR therapy: Innovative strategies and protocols* (2nd ed., pp. 84–105). Springer Publishing Company.

Nickerson, M. (2023a). Opening the door: Exploring social and cultural experiences and building resources – EMDR phases 1 and 2. In M. Nickerson (Ed.). *Cultural competence and healing culturally based trauma with EMDR therapy: Innovative strategies and protocols* (2nd ed., pp. 66–83). Springer Publishing Company.

Novo Navarro, P., Landin-Romero, R., Guardiola-Wanden-Berghe, R., Moreno-Alcázar, A., Valiente-Gómez, A., Lupo, W., García, F., Fernández, I., Pérez, V., & Amann, B. L. (2018). 25 years of Eye Movement Desensitization and Reprocessing (EMDR): The EMDR therapy protocol, hypotheses of its mechanism of action and a systematic review of its efficacy in the treatment of post-traumatic stress disorder. *Revista de Psiquiatría y Salud Mental (English Edition), 11*(2), 101–114. https://doi.org/10.1016/j.rpsm.2015.12.002

O'Shea Brown, G. (2020). Internal Family Systems informed Eye Movement Desensitization and Reprocessing: An integrative technique for treatment of complex posttraumatic stress disorder. *International Body Psychotherapy Journal, 19*(2), 112–122.

Pagani, M., Castelnuovo, G., Daverio, A., La Porta, P., Monaco, L., Ferrentino, F., Chiaravalloti, A., Fernandez, I., & Di Lorenzo, G. (2018). Metabolic and electrophysiological changes associated to clinical improvement in two severely traumatized subjects treated with EMDR—A pilot study. *Frontiers in Psychology, 9,* Article 475. https://doi.org/10.3389/fpsyg.2018.00475

Paulsen, S. (2009). *Looking through the eyes of trauma and dissociation: An illustrated guide for EMDR therapists and client.* Bainbridge Institute for Integrative Psychology.

Porges, S. W. (1995). Orienting in a defensive world: mammalian modifications of our evolutionary heritage—A polyvagal theory. *Psychophysiology, 32*(4), 301–318. https://doi.org/10.1111/j.1469-8986.1995.tb01213.x

Porges, S. W. (2011). *The polyvagal theory: Neurophysiological foundations of emotions, attachment, communication, and self-regulation.* W. W. Norton & Company.

Porges, S. (2017). *The pocket guide to the polyvagal theory: The transformative power of feeling safe.* W. W. Norton & Company.

Robinson, N. S. (2023). Legacy attuned EMDR therapy: Toward a coherent narrative and resilience. In M. Nickerson (Ed.), *Cultural competence and healing culturally based trauma with EMDR therapy: Innovative strategies and protocols* (2nd ed., pp. 383–391). Springer Publishing Company.

Rothman, L. (2023). IFS and polyvagal theory: Healing through compassionate connection. In J. Riemersma (Ed.), *Altogether us* (pp. 51–79). Pivotal Press.

Schwartz, R. C. (2018). *Greater than the sum of our parts: Discovering your true self through Internal Family Systems therapy.* Sounds True.

Schwartz, R. C., & Sweezy, M. (2020). *Internal Family Systems* (2nd ed.). The Guilford Press.

Scott, D. (2017). Self-led grieving. In M. Sweezy & E. L. Ziskind (Eds.), *Innovations and elaborations in Internal Family Systems therapy* (pp. 90–108). Taylor and Francis.

Shadick, N. A., Sowell, N. F., Frits, M. L., Hoffman, S. M., Hartz, S. A., Booth, F. D., Sweezy, M., Rogers, P. R., Dubin, R. L., Atkinson, J. C., Friedman, A. L., Augusto, F., Iannaccone, C. K., Fossel, A. H., Quinn, G., Cui, J., Losina, E., & Schwartz, R. C. (2013). A randomized controlled trial of an Internal Family Systems-based psychotherapeutic intervention on outcomes in rheumatoid arthritis: a proof-of-concept study, *The Journal of Rheumatology 40*(11), 1831–1841. https://doi.org/10.3899/jrheum.121465

Shapiro F. (2014). The role of Eye Movement Desensitization and Reprocessing (EMDR) therapy in medicine: addressing the psychological and physical symptoms stemming from adverse life experiences. *The Permanente Journal, 18*(1), 71–77.

Shapiro, F. (2018). *Eye Movement Desensitization and Reprocessing (EMDR) therapy: Basic principles, protocols and procedures* (3rd ed.). The Guilford Press.

Shapiro, R. (2005). The two-hand interweave. In R. Shapiro (Ed.), *EMDR solutions: Pathways to healing* (pp. 160–166). W. W. Norton & Company.

Siegel, D. J. (2010). *The mindful therapist: A clinician's guide to mindsight and neural integration.* W. W. Norton & Company.

Siegel, D. J. (2012). *The developing mind: How relationships and the brain interact to shape who we are* (2nd ed.). The Guilford Press.

Sinko, A. (2017). Legacy burdens. In M. Sweezy & E. L. Ziskind (Eds.), *IFS: innovations and elaborations in Internal Family Systems therapy* (pp. 164–178). Taylor and Francis.

Sweezy, M. (2011). The teenager's confession: Regulating shame in Internal Family Systems therapy. *American Journal of Psychotherapy, 65*(2), 179–188. https://doi.org/10.1176/appi.psychotherapy.2011.65.2.179

Sykes, C. (2017). An IFS lens on addiction: Compassion for extreme parts. In M. Sweezy & E. L. Ziskind (Eds.), *IFS: innovations and elaborations in Internal Family Systems therapy* (pp. 29–48). Taylor and Francis.

Sykes, C., Sweezy, M., & Schwartz R. C. (2023). *Internal Family Systems therapy for addictions: Trauma-informed, compassion-based interventions for substance use, eating, gambling and more.* PESI Publishing & Media.

Turkus, J. A., & Kahler, J. A. (2006). Therapeutic interventions in the treatment of dissociative disorders. *Psychiatric Clinics of North America, 29*(1), 245–262. https://doi.org/10.1016/j.psc.2005.10.015

Twombly, J. H. (2013). Integrating IFS with phase-oriented treatment of clients with dissociative disordered clients. In M. Sweezy & E. L. Ziskind (Eds.), *Internal Family Systems therapy: New dimensions* (pp. 72–89). https://doi.org/10.1037/e608922012-134

Twombly, J. H. (2022). *Trauma and dissociation informed Internal Family Systems.* Author.

Twombly, J. H., & Schwartz, R. C. (2008). The integration of the Internal Family Systems model and EMDR. In C. Forgash & M. Copeley (Eds.), *Healing the heart of trauma and dissociation with EMDR and ego state therapy* (pp. 295–311). Springer Publishing Company.

van der Hart, O., Groenendijk, M., Gonzalez, A., Mosquera, D., & Solomon, R. M. (2014). Dissociation of the personality and EMDR therapy in complex trauma-related disorders: Applications in phases 2 and 3 treatment. *Journal of EMDR Practice and Research, 8*(1), 33–48. https://doi.org/10.1891/1933-3196.7.2.81

van der Hart, O., Nijenhuis, E. R. S., & Steele, K. (1993). *The haunted Self: Structural dissociation and the treatment of trauma.* W. W. Norton & Company.

van der Kolk, B. A. (2014). *The body keeps the score: Brain, mind and body in the healing of trauma.* Penguin Books.

Venkatraman-Levis, R. (2017). Placing culture at the heart of EMDR therapy. In M. I. Nickerson (Ed.), *Cultural competence and healing culturally based trauma with EMDR therapy: Innovative strategies and protocols* (pp. 97–112). Springer Publishing Company.

Venkatraman-Levis, R., & Siniego, L. B. (2017). An integrative framework for EMDR therapy as an anti-oppression endeavor. In M. I. Nickerson (Ed.), *Cultural competence and healing culturally based trauma with EMDR therapy: Innovative strategies and protocols* (pp. 79–96). Springer Publishing Company.

Wilkins, E. J. (2007). Using an IFS informed intervention to treat African American families surviving sexual abuse. *Journal of Feminist Family Therapy, 19*(3), 37–53. https://doi.org/10.1300/J086v19n03_03

Williams, M., Osman, M., & Hyon, C. (2023). Understanding the psychological impact of oppression using the Trauma Symptoms of Discrimination Scale. *Chronic Stress, 7,* 1–12. https://doi.org/10.1177/24705470221149511

Williams, M. T., Holmes, S., Zare, M. Haeny, A. H., & Faber, S. C. (2023). An evidenced-based approach for treating stress and trauma due to racism. *Cognitive and Behavioral Practice, 30*(4), 565–588. https://doi.org/10.1016/j.cbpra.2022.07.001

Wilson, G., Farrell, D., Barron, I., Hutchins, J., Whybrow, D., & Kiernan, M. D. (2018). The use of Eye-Movement Desensitization Reprocessing (EMDR) therapy in treating post-traumatic stress disorder—A systematic narrative review. *Frontiers in Psychology, 9,* Article 923. https://doi.org/10.3389/fpsyg.2018.00923

World Health Organization. (2020). *International statistical classification of diseases and related health problems* (11th ed.). https://icd.who.int

Yosso, T. J. (2005). Whose culture has capital? A critical race theory discussion of community cultural wealth. *Race, Ethnicity, and Education, 8*(1), 69–91. https://doi.org/10.1080/1361332052000341006

Acknowledgments

I would like to first acknowledge and thank Kate Sample at PESI Publishing for encouraging me to pursue writing this book. To Rona Bernstein, who helped me fully develop this book to strengthen, flesh out, clarify, and simplify the structure and content to help make this book as accessible and clear to readers as it can be. To G. Panzer, thank you for your thorough eye during copyediting.

To Melanie Matkin, who helped keep me disciplined to stay on track and encouraged me to let the words move through me. To Jenna Riemersma, for your belief in me as a writer. To John Davis, for your eye for detail and encouragement. To John Davis, Mary Ann Davis, my family, and close friends, for your continued support and inspiration, always.

To the late Francine Shapiro and to Dick Schwartz for creating life-changing models that help people heal and recover from trauma. The impact of both EMDR and IFS in my personal life has helped me heal, show up, and be myself in the world. Professionally, these models help me be the best therapist I can be.

About the Author

Daphne Fatter, PhD, is a licensed psychologist, international speaker, author, and consultant dedicated to providing education on integrative trauma-informed therapies. She is EMDR certified, is an EMDRIA Approved Consultant, and has 20 years of experience providing EMDR for trauma treatment. She is an expert clinician in Internal Family Systems therapy, having completed over 460 hours of Internal Family Systems training, including training under Dr. Richard Schwartz, the founder of Internal Family Systems therapy, in 2019 and 2023. She is a thought leader in ways to integrate Internal Family Systems therapy with other modalities. As a certified ancestral healing practitioner, she also works with intergenerational and historical trauma.

Dr. Fatter received a master's degree in transpersonal counseling psychology from Naropa University. She was then awarded a doctorate degree in counseling psychology from Pennsylvania State University before completing a postdoctoral fellowship in clinical psychology at The Trauma Center under the direct supervision of Dr. Bessel van der Kolk. She is the former military sexual trauma coordinator at the Fort Worth Veteran Affairs Outpatient Clinic. She has authored works on Internal Family Systems therapy, EMDR, countertransference, mindfulness, and ancestral healing. She provides engaging workshops, webinars, and trainings on trauma treatment, including treating PTSD, complex trauma, and complicated grief. She maintains a private practice in Dallas, Texas.